HAM & PETERSHAM

THROUGH TIME

Paul Howard Lang

AMBERLEY

First published 2018

Amberley Publishing
The Hill, Stroud, Gloucestershire, GL5 4EP
www.amberley-books.com

ISBN 978 1 4456 7330 1 (print)
ISBN 978 1 4456 7331 8 (ebook)

British Library Cataloguing in Publication Data.
A catalogue record for this book is available from the British Library.

Origination by Amberley Publishing.
Printed in Great Britain.

Introduction

During the Second World War artists were employed to paint watercolours of the buildings in and around London thought to be at particular risk from enemy bombing. Thirty watercolours were made of Ham and Petersham, which shows the concentration of buildings of historical importance in the area.

Ham has always had a strong connection with Kingston. Population figures were included with the Kingston parish from the fifteenth century and Ham came under the administrative control of Kingston until 1858, when it became a separate local government district. Ham Urban District was abolished in 1933 when it was decided to split the area between Richmond and Kingston. Richmond gained the greater share, so most of Ham now falls within its borders. The Tudor Estate, which formerly came under Ham, was made part of Kingston. The Hawker Siddeley factory, later British Aerospace, was on the Kingston side of the boundary, but the shops in Ham benefited from the custom of its employees until the factory closed in 1991.

Petersham has less of a connection with Kingston, although historically it was part of the Kingston Hundred and Petersham residents paid their taxes at Kingston; however, it was joined with Richmond in 1892.

Once known as Ham and Hatch, the parish extended as far as the Robin Hood Gate area in Richmond Park. Right up to the Edwardian period and even into the 1930s, Ham and Petersham were far more rural than they are today. The images that particularly reflect this are Manor Farm in Ham Street, Ham Farm in Ham Farm Road, and the scene in The Avenue with the chickens roaming across the grass verge. In the Petersham images the milking sheds of Hornby & Clarke in River Lane, boats at Petersham Vale and the back of the cottages in the Petersham Road all reflect the rural nature of the parish. Although Ham has lost its former farms, both Ham and Petersham have retained vestiges of their rural identities. Ham still has the village pond on the common and Petersham has unspoilt areas such as The Copse as well as Sudbrook and Petersham Parks. Two images, 'Walnut Picking in Petersham' and 'Haymaking in Petersham', also show the agricultural nature of the area

The origin of most of the larger houses in Ham and Petersham lay in the fact that they started as simple farm buildings and gradually evolved into more luxurious residences. Sudbrook Lodge is a good example of this, dating to *c.* 1605. Many locals in both parishes were employed as gardeners for the large houses, as well as in more traditional agricultural-related employment.

There was a very important change in Ham and Petersham in 1949 when the Earl of Dysart sold off a large proportion of his property and land. The Ham and Petersham Estate Sale lasted for two days, the 15th and 16th of November 1949. The properties were sold by auction in lots. In total forty-one houses, many of historical importance, were sold and 350 acres of land was also auctioned. Apart from the more prestigious houses, a farm, four shops, two licensed premises, a rifle range, a gravel and sand works, ninety-nine cottages, plus sundry allotments and plots of land suitable for building, were all included in the auction. Of course, this had a profound effect, redistributing ownership and entirely changing the social structure of the area.

There is a charming passage in Applebee's Original Weekly Journal of 7 October 1721, which describes Petersham as 'reckoned the most beautiful village in England for the number of seats, delicate gardens and green walks, most of which are pleasantly situated near the side of the Thames'. This shows how Petersham was perceived in the eighteenth century and why the nobility were attracted to the area.

The ninety paired images showing old and current views have been ordered into a walking tour of Ham and Petersham. The tour should properly start in Ham Street, this being where the village initially began; however, the image showing the geographical location of Hardwicke House and the surrounding area puts the whole location into such good context that I have started from there. From the northern side of Ham Common the tour continues around the common to explore the southern side then, with a slight detour down Craig Road, it proceeds down Ham Street in the direction of Ham House and the river, and on to Teddington Lock. The walk then continues down Ashburnham Road as far as St Richard's Church, before retracing the route and finally coming out at Petersham Road. Ham Gate Avenue then Upper Ham Road are explored, with a visit to St Andrew's Church along Church Road. The final stop takes us into Richmond Park to view the Pen Ponds, which were once within the parish of Ham.

The walking tour of Petersham starts at St Peter's Church then looks at some of the important houses along the Petersham Road, before continuing down River Lane as far as the River Thames. We then return to the Petersham Road, turning down Sudbrook Lane and going as far as the entrance to the golf club before returning once more to the Petersham Road. We end at the Petersham Hotel on the boundary with Richmond, having passed the former Star and Garter Hotel.

Some images in this book may be familiar to readers, but others I hope less so; for example, the School Houses in Ham Street have not been featured before, nor the photograph of the back of the cottages along the Petersham Road. Both of these images are from original photographs and have not been published before. Of course much more detail could be written about many of these pictures, but I hope this book will stimulate further research.

For further reading I would suggest:

Chave, Leonard (ed.), Ham Amenities Group, *Ham & Petersham at 2000*
Elsden, Gordon, *Remarkable Ham – The Untold Story*
Fison, Vanesa, *A Glimpse of Old Ham and Petersham*
Fison, Vanessa, *The Matchless Vale: The Story of Ham & Petersham & Their People*
Green, J. and S. Greenwood, *Ham & Petersham as It Was*

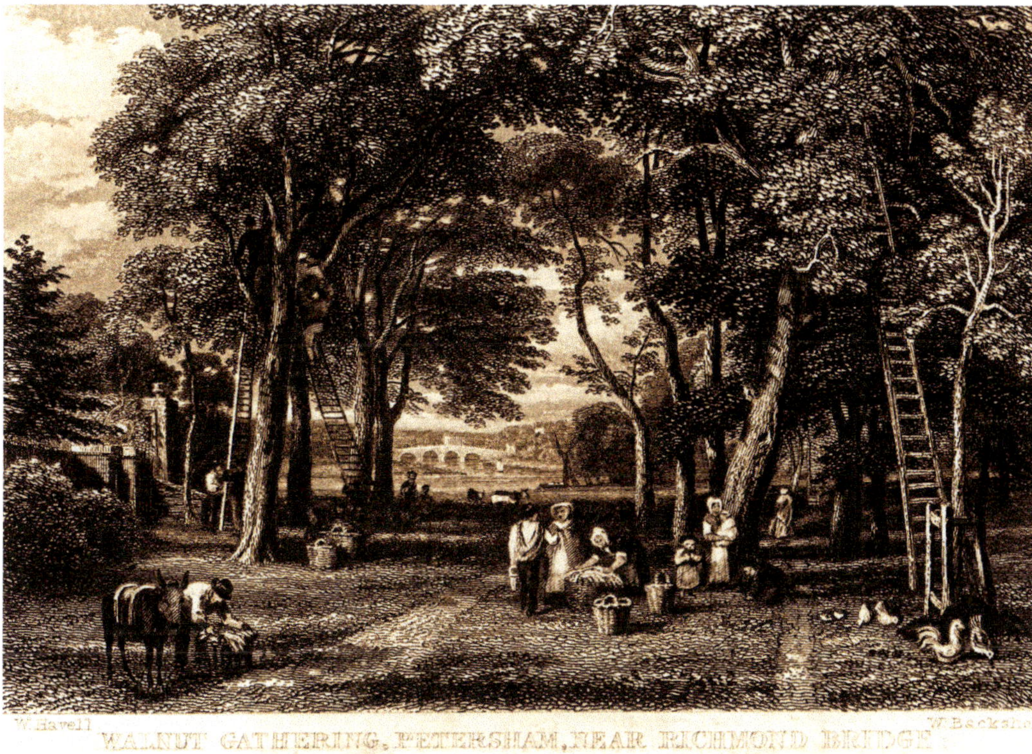

Above: Walnut gathering, Petersham, with Richmond Bridge in the distance.

Below: Haymaking in Petersham, 1890.

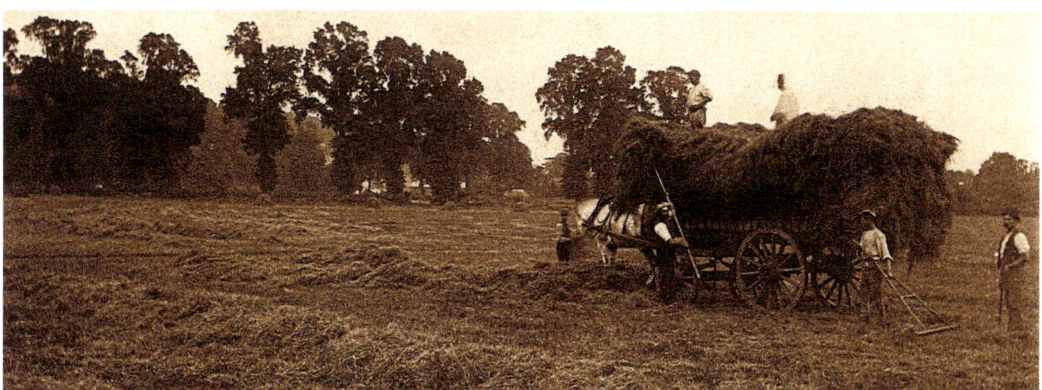

Ham

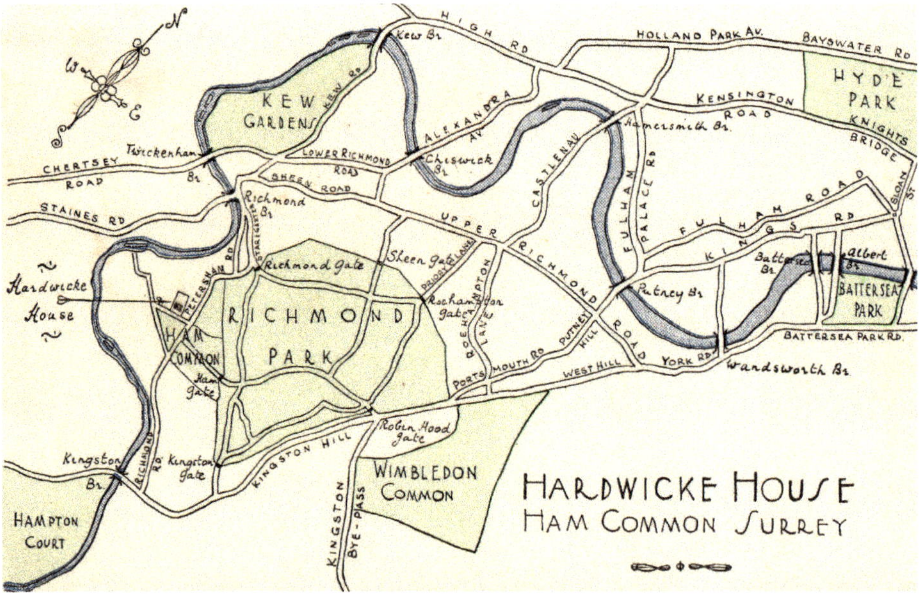

Hardwicke House, Ham Common

It is very rare to find a postcard showing the geographical location of an important house, although it is a pity that no actual representation of the house itself is shown. Thomas Tryon built Hardwicke House in 1688. He was a London hatter who had lived in Barbados and traded in beaver pelts. He sold Hardwicke House to Catherine Bogan in 1693. The house then had a succession of tenants, some of whom were extremely distinguished. In 1868, Sir Lionel Tollemache, Lord Dysart, owned the property. It remained in the ownership of the Tollemaches until 1949. In 1936, the property was let to Edmund Booth, a shipping magnate. In more recent times some of the land attached to the estate has been sold for development.

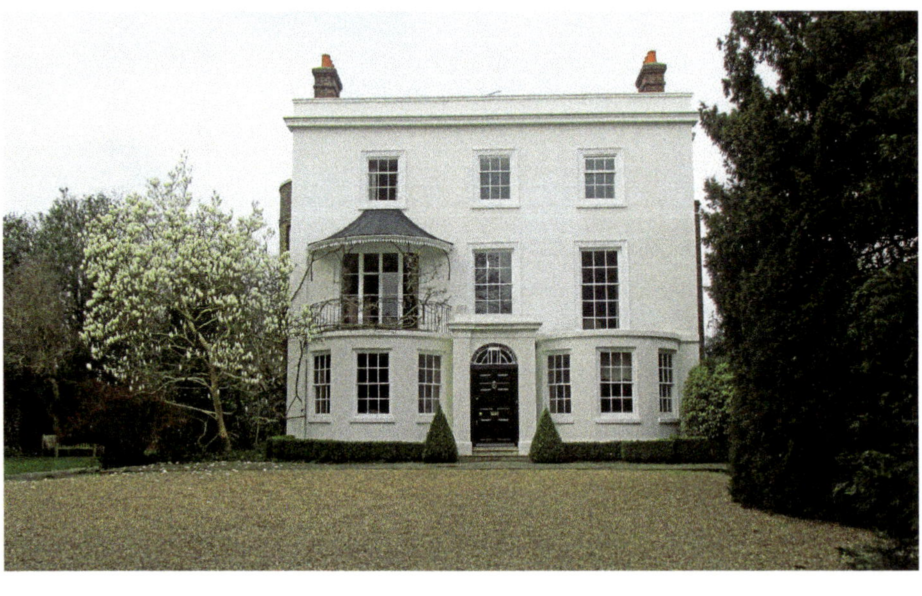

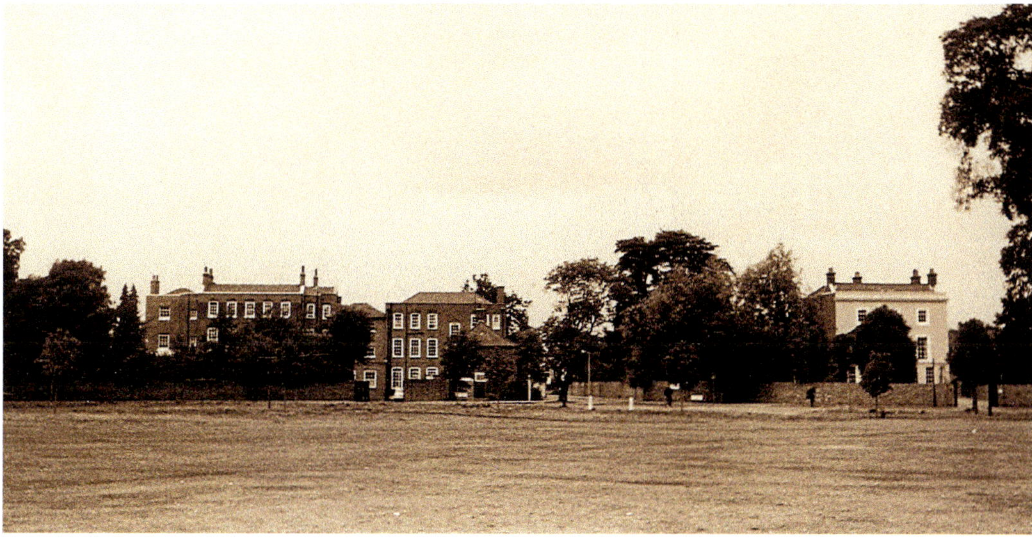

St Michael's Convent and Hardwicke House, Ham Common

The north side of Ham Common can be seen here with St Michael's Convent on the left, Martingales Close in the centre and Hardwicke House on the right. When Martingales Close was created in the late 1960s, the three big houses nearby – Hardwicke House, St Michael's Convent and Avenue Lodge (just out of shot in the picture to the left) – all agreed to split the proceeds of the sale in proportion to the land given up. St Michael's gave up one and a half acres of land. Mr Raffles, who at the time owned Avenue Lodge, sold three quarters of an acre at the bottom of his garden. Hardwicke House supplied the remaining acreage. The older picture dates to 1972.

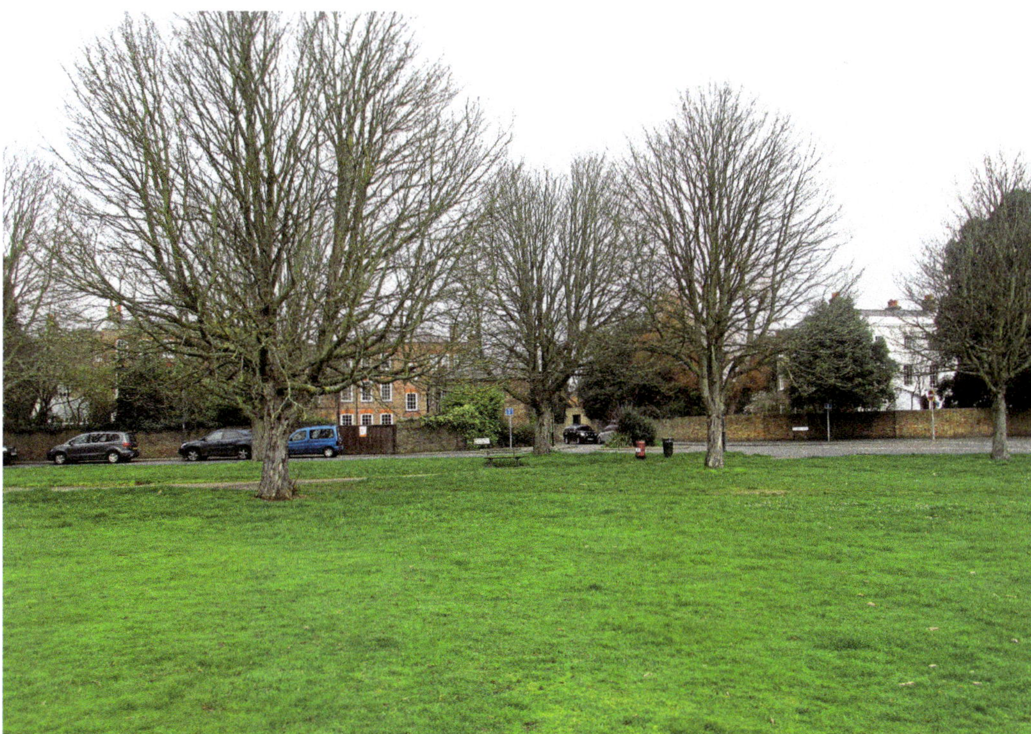

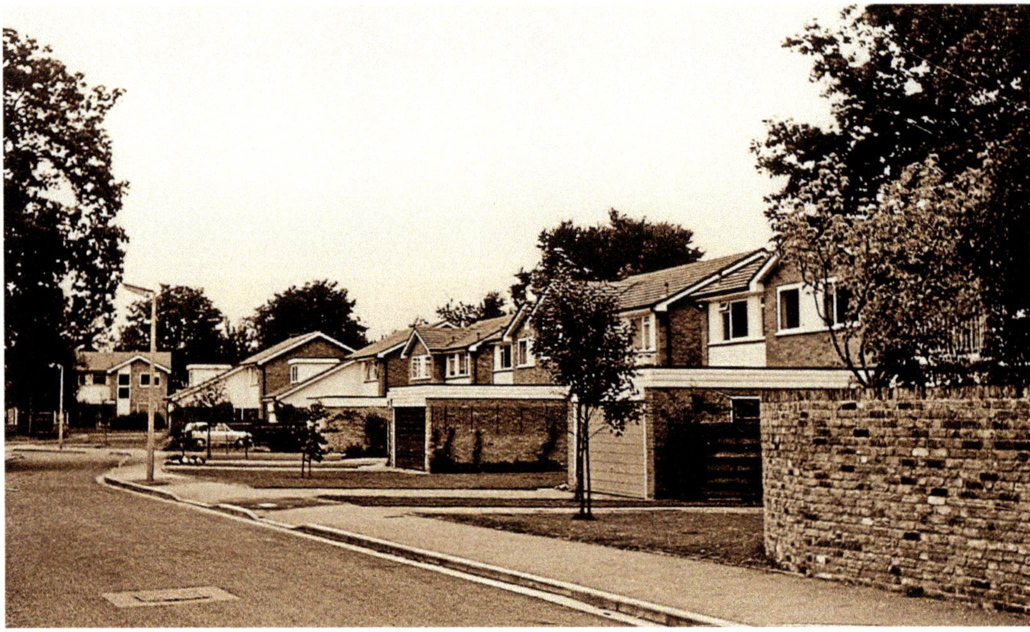

Martingales Close

Named after the part of a harness that prevents the horse from raising its head too high, Martingales Close has other equine associations as there was once a paddock on this site. In the Victorian period General William Eden (1768–1851) had a small house that lay between Hardwicke House and St Michael's Convent. In the late 1950s, pressure was mounting from developers to build more houses in Ham and by 1966 outline planning consent had been granted for building on approximately 4 acres of the grounds of Hardwicke House, St Michael's Convent and Avenue Lodge. In 1969, Martingales Close was cut through on the line of General Eden's former house. The original photo was taken in 1972 shortly after the houses had been built.

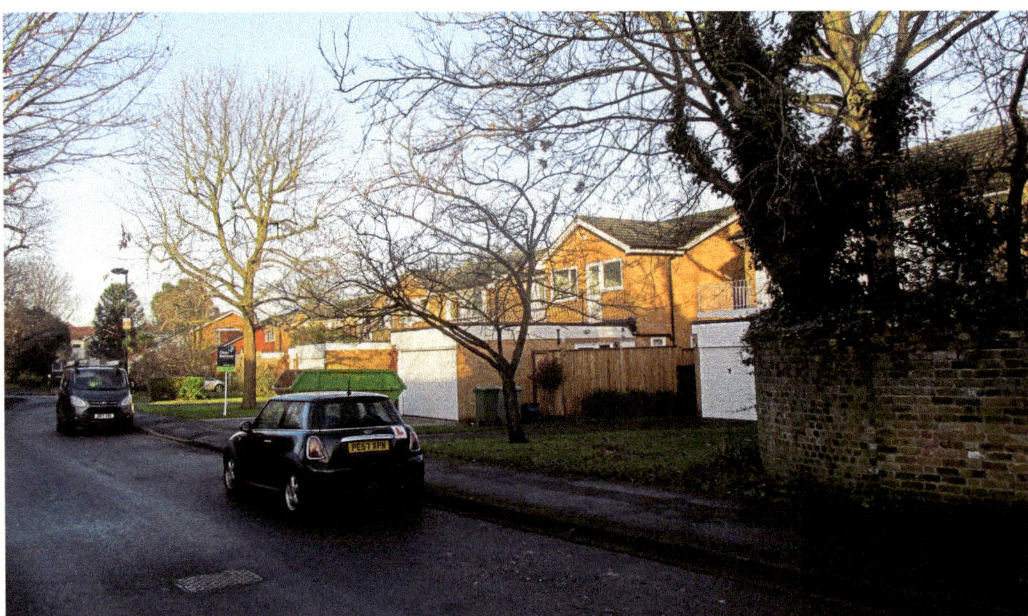

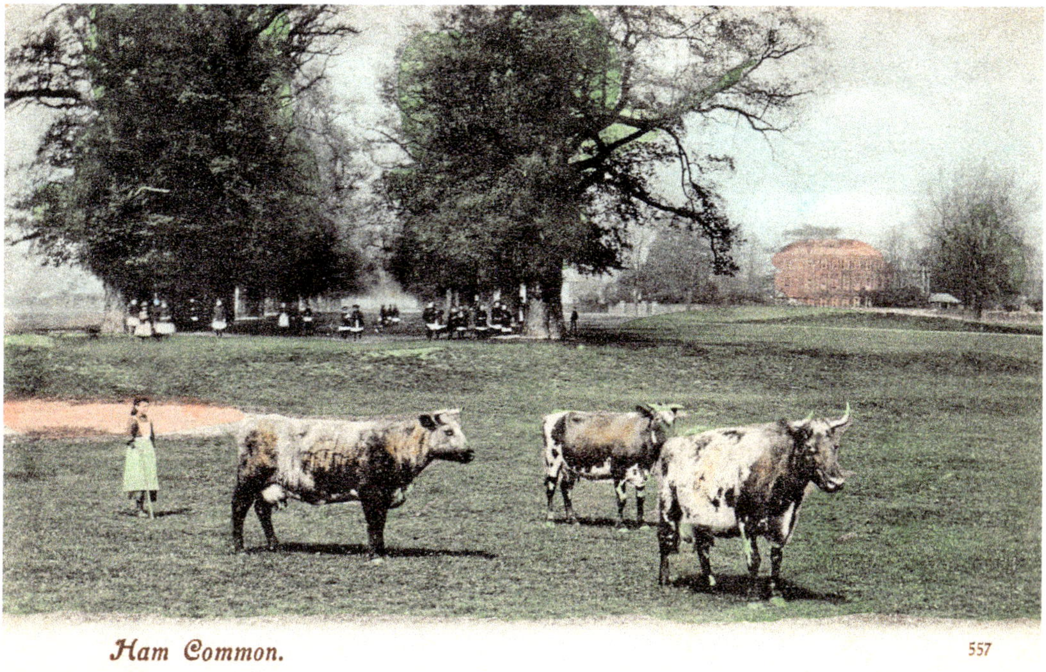

Ham Common with Cattle

Ellen Greenwood can be seen on the left of this image with three of her father's cows. Orford House, later to become St Michael's Convent, can be seen in the background on the right-hand side. The girls lined up are from the nearby National Orphan Home, which was situated just east of Orford House. The card is dated 1912 and marked 'local' and addressed to the Princess Louise Home in Kingston Hill, which was another establishment for young girls, so was probably sent by someone from the National Orphan Home. The current photograph shows that the double line of trees on the common are no more, a victim of Dutch elm disease.

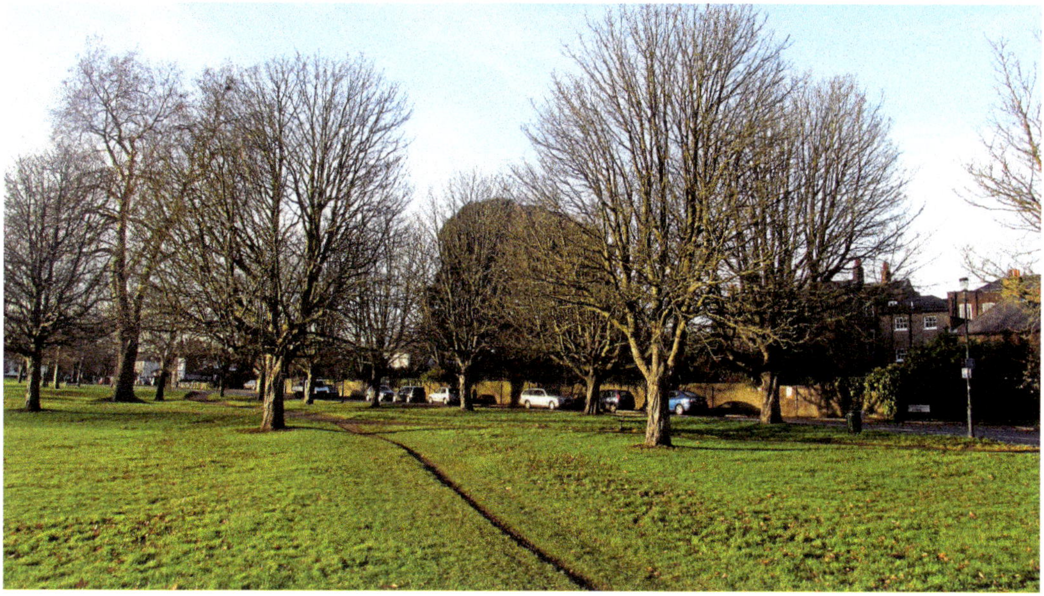

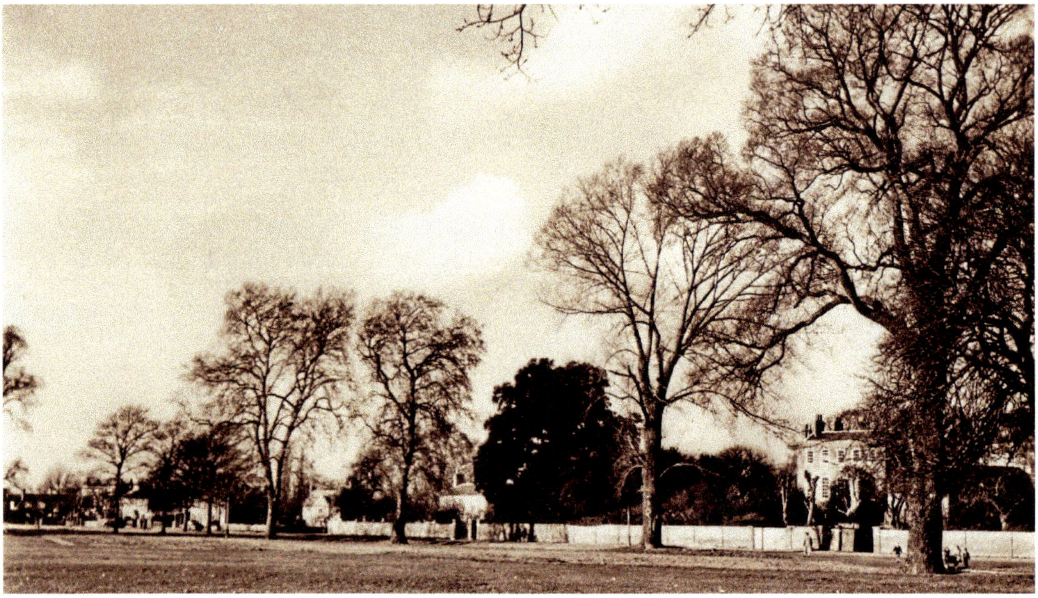

Ham Common

This panoramic view of the north side of Ham Common taken in the 1950s shows the houses from St Michael's Convent on the right to Avenue Lodge and the houses beyond. Note how managed the common appears. This side of Ham Common is very different in character to the land on the other side of the Upper Ham Road, which is covered in quite dense woods. When the animals were allowed to graze on the common, which continued right up to the 1930s, this part of the common would have been far more like open scrubland in its appearance than it is today.

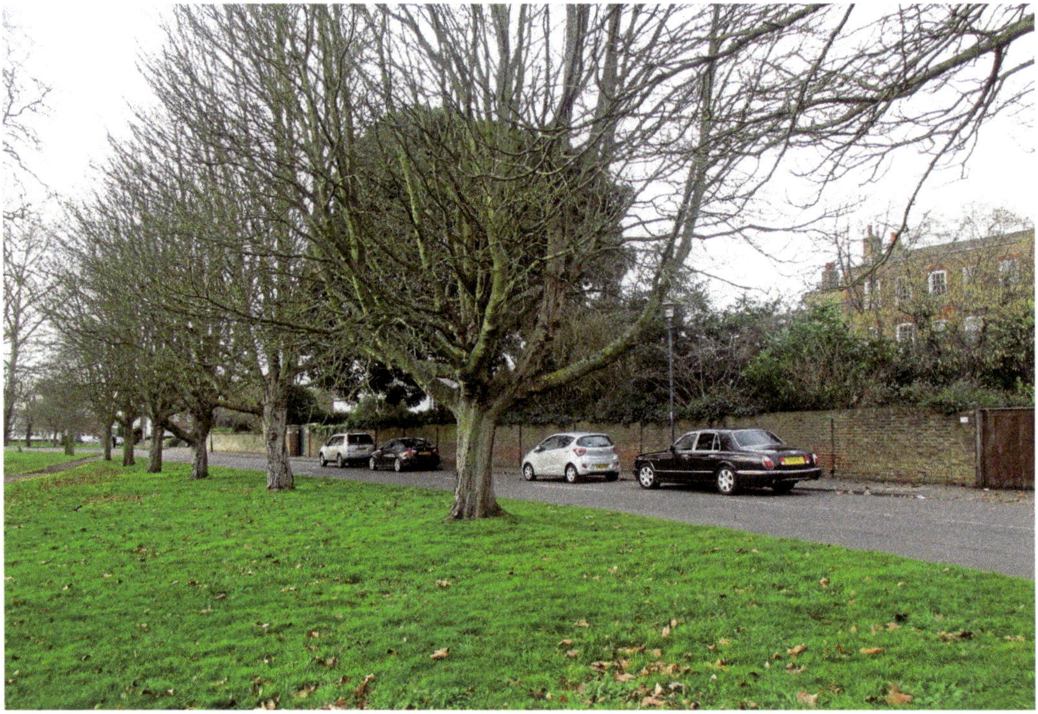

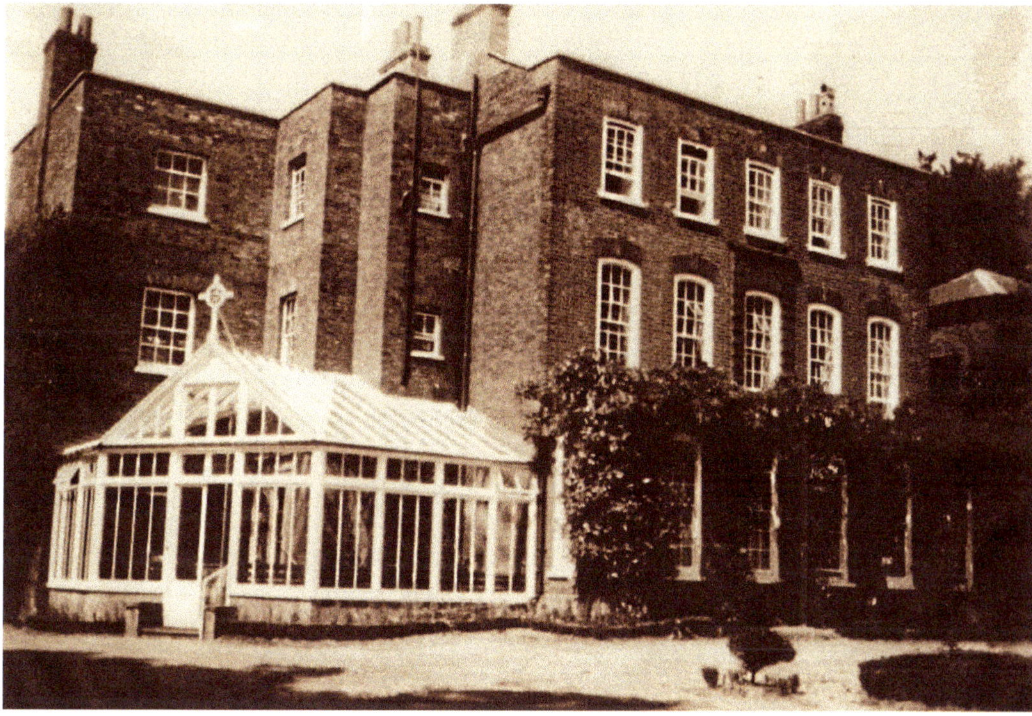

St Michael's Convent

William Genew was the person initially responsible for building a cottage on the site, which eventually became the convent. He died in 1730 and his son, also named William, had the cottage demolished and a far more prestigious house built in 1734. Distinguished residents of the house included Vice Admiral Sir John Sutton, KCB, and Col Spencer Pratt. The house was originally called Oxford House, but by the 1901 census is named Orford House. In the 1950s, two wings and a chapel were added to the main body of the house and it was renamed St Michael's Convent. The Sisters have recently vacated the premises, having moved to Gerrards Cross, and the house is currently awaiting new owners.

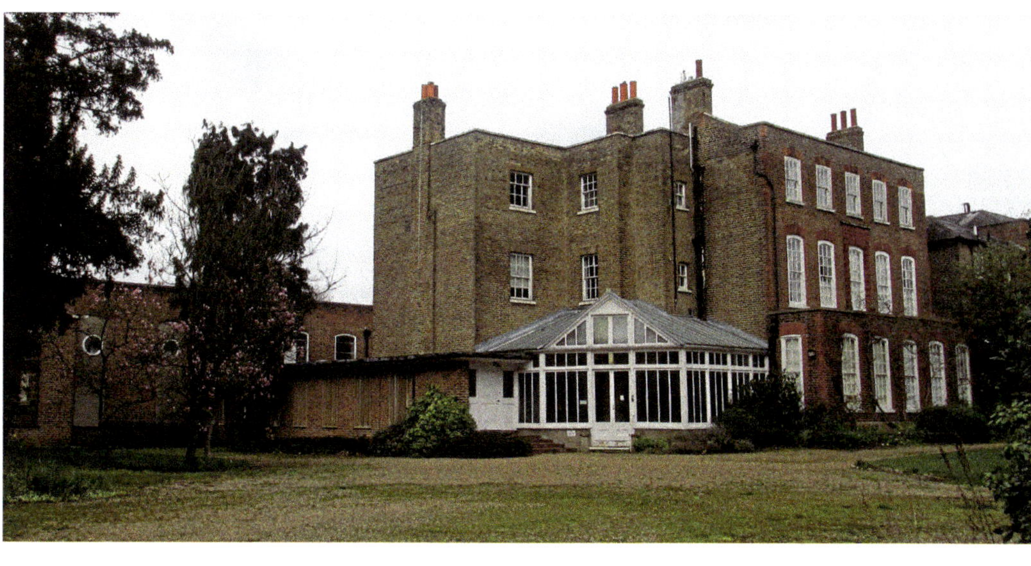

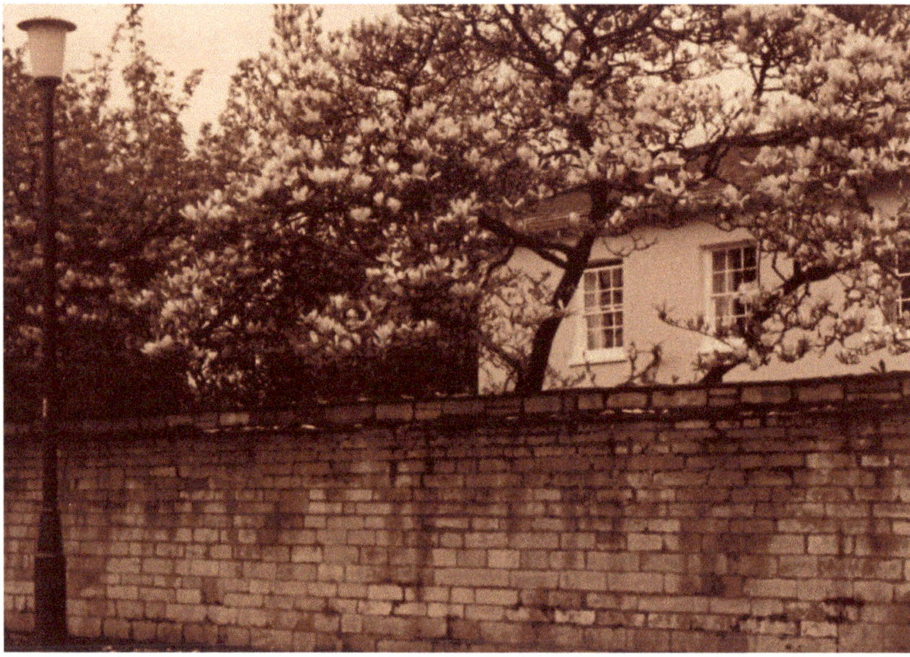

Avenue Lodge, Ham Common

The Dysart Estate Sale of 1949 included many of the major houses in Ham. Among them was Avenue Lodge, which was described at the time as 'Georgian, with 7 bedrooms, 4 staff bedrooms, 4 reception rooms, kitchen and staff quarters, with a summer house and sun loggia and included Avenue Cottage in the sale'. The house was built between 1731 and 1734, and the owner was William Genew, who unfortunately overstretched himself financially and ended up in the Fleet prison for debt. Towards the end of the nineteenth century Avenue Lodge was purchased by the Earl of Dysart, who let the property to William Parnell Feiling of the Admiralty. The house was requisitioned by the army during the Second World War.

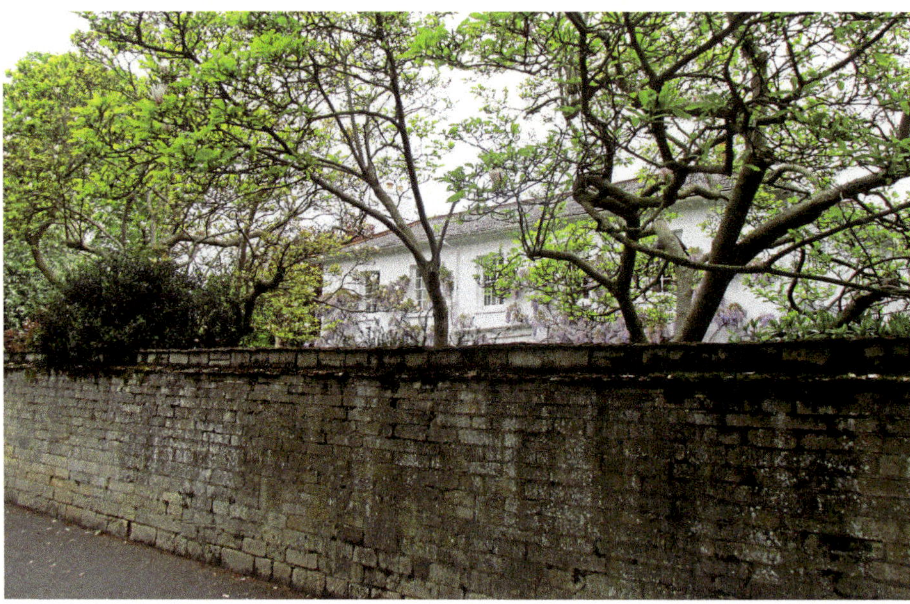

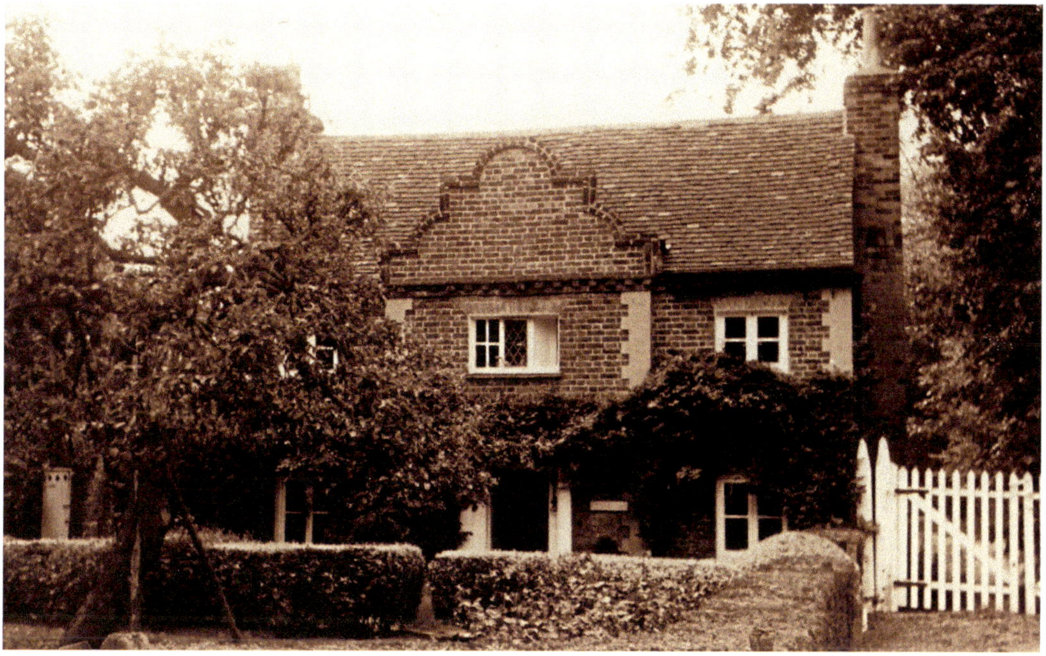

Avenue Lodge Cottage, Ham Common

These two elegant cottages, with their fine Dutch gables, stand either side of the Avenue and date to the seventeenth century. They are reminiscent of the Farm and Avenue Lodge buildings in Petersham. In earlier times the Ham Lodge gates to Ham House stood on this site. The lodge featured here was extended in the 1950s; the lodge on the other side does not stand out to the same extent. The beautiful wisteria adds to the attractiveness of the building in the current photograph.

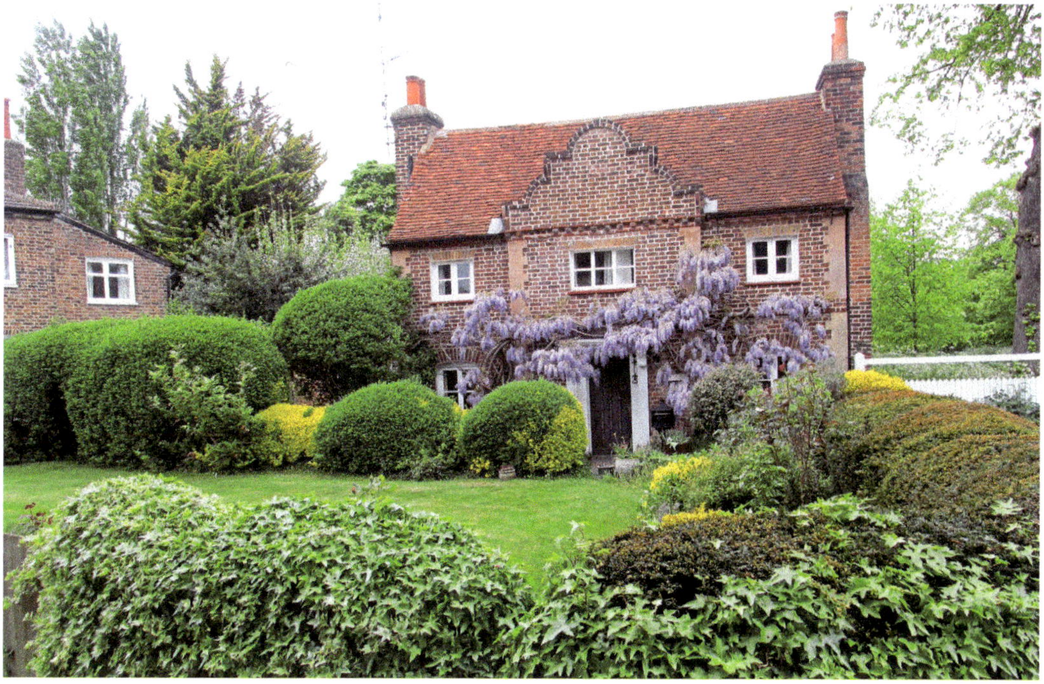

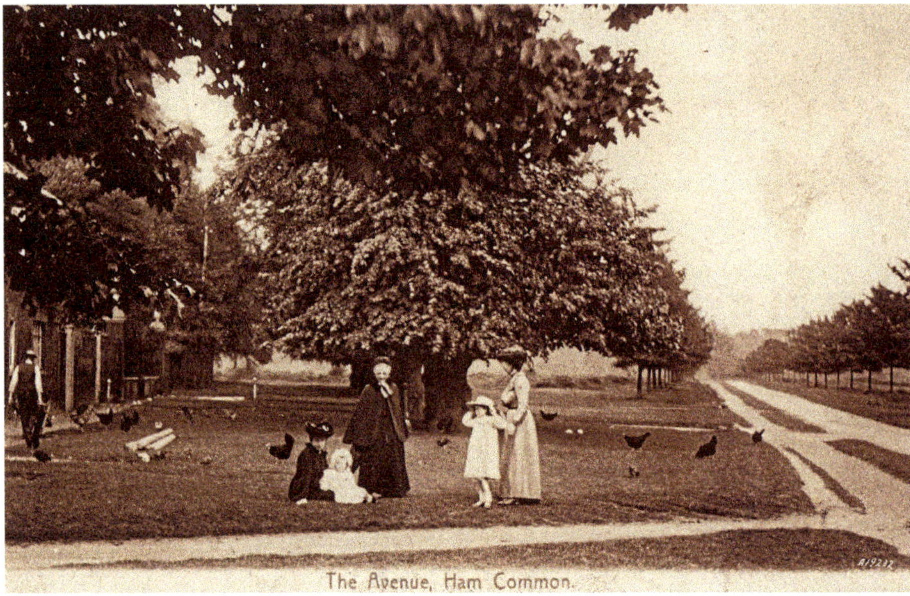

The Avenue, Ham Common

The avenues leading to Ham House are clearly marked in a plan of the grounds dating to 1671, although frustratingly they only depict the parts of the avenues nearest to the house itself. The north-south avenue to Ham Common seen in this image was completed by around 1680. It is shown in John Rocque's map of 1746, being two thirds of a mile in length and leading across Sandy Lane to terminate at the common. However, in the seventeenth century the Avenue continued across Ham Common – a double line of trees still marks its former route. The charming Edwardian view shows how open the area was in comparison with today. The outbuildings behind Avenue Lodge can be seen on the left-hand side near the man with the wheelbarrow.

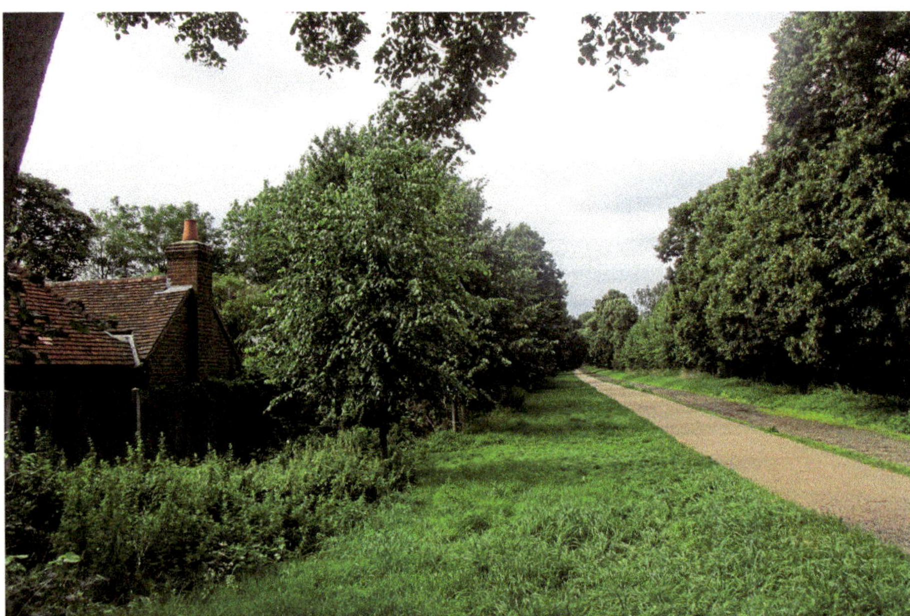

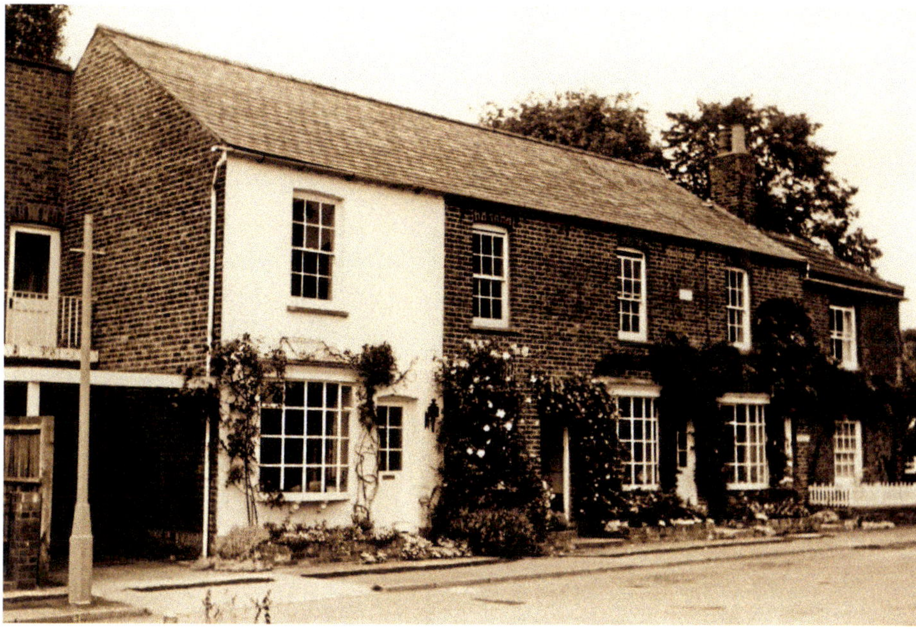

Boxall Cottages, Ham Common

John Fitzwater was the first occupier of this property, described as an ancient messuage divided into two parts, and each constituent part being further divided into two, making a total of four cottages. John Fitzwater died in 1722 and his three sons then became the new copyholders. At this time it is mentioned in a document that there was a barn and other outbuildings attached to the end cottage. Copyhold owners included Robert Watts, in 1757, Elizabeth Stanley, in 1773, and Richard Bolton, in 1774. In the early nineteenth century James Boxall became the new owner, and he passed it to his sons in 1835. A new upstairs extension has been added in the modern photograph.

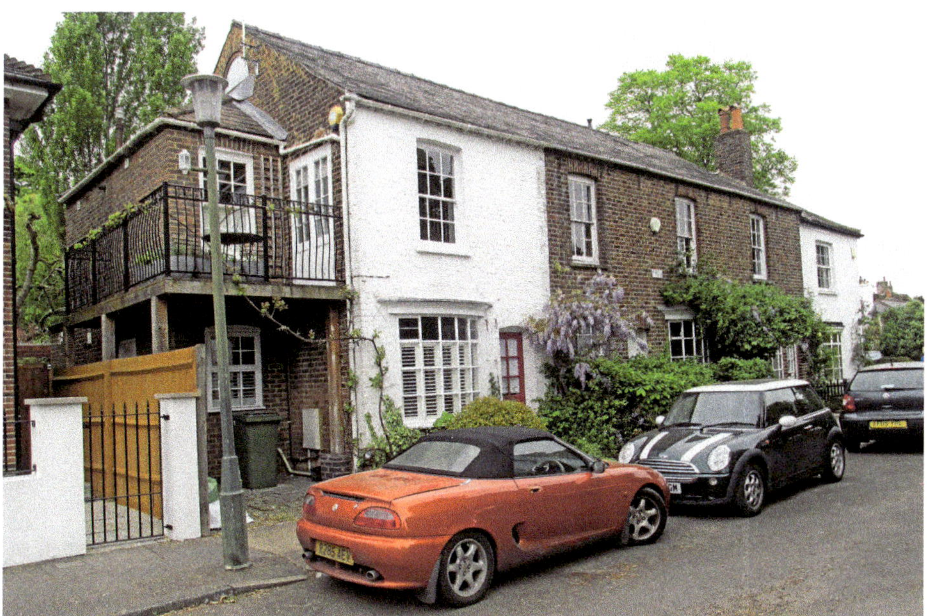

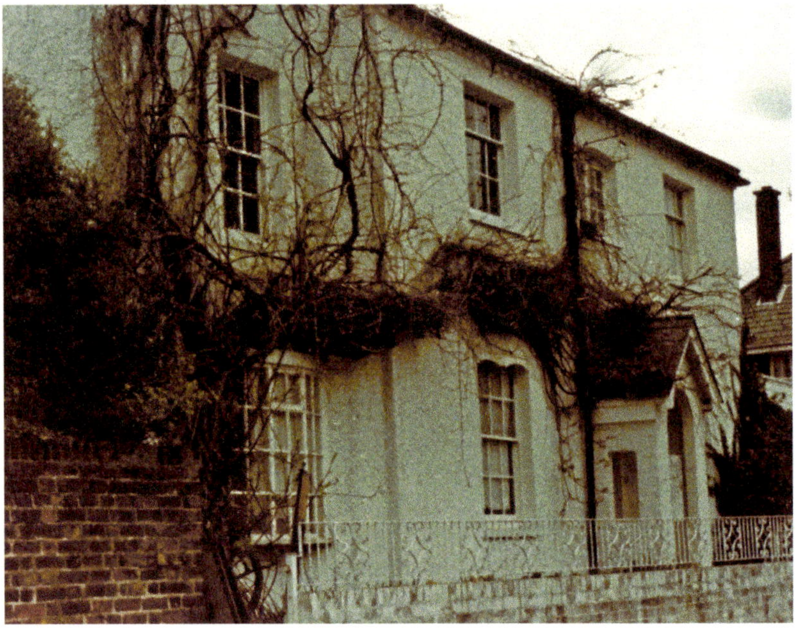

Vine Cottage, Ham Common

Mr John Neville, one of my wife's distant relatives, resided at Vine Cottage certainly from 1841 and possibly before this date. He lived there with three of his daughters and a servant. By 1851 his daughter Mary Benbow had taken over the ownership and was still there in 1861. It is not until the 1901 census that Vine Cottage is actually mentioned by name, then owned by Charles Sims, a master builder. Vine Cottage is a distinctive Georgian property, originally two separate residencies but now combined and modernised. In 1924, Mr A. H. Etherington, manager of Barclays Bank, opened a sub-branch of the bank in these premises. In the 1930s, the Headmaster of St Andrew's School resided here and kept beehives in the back garden.

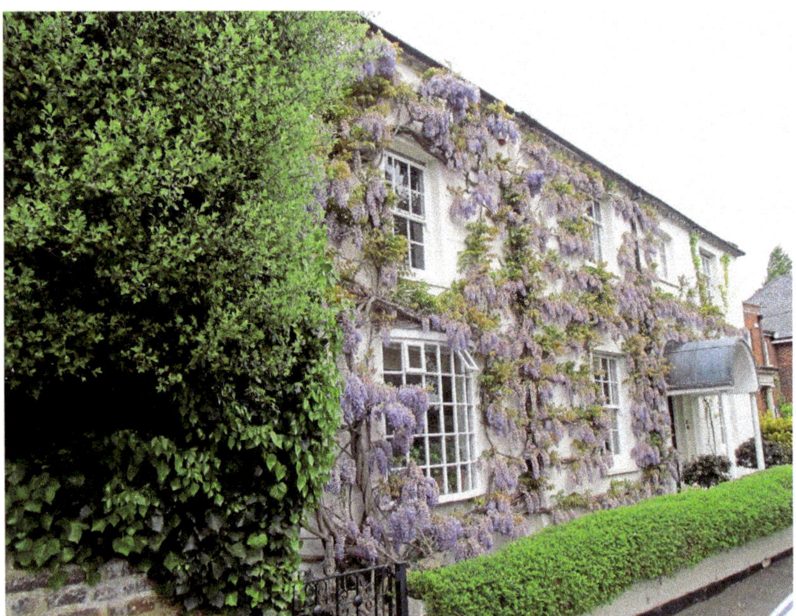

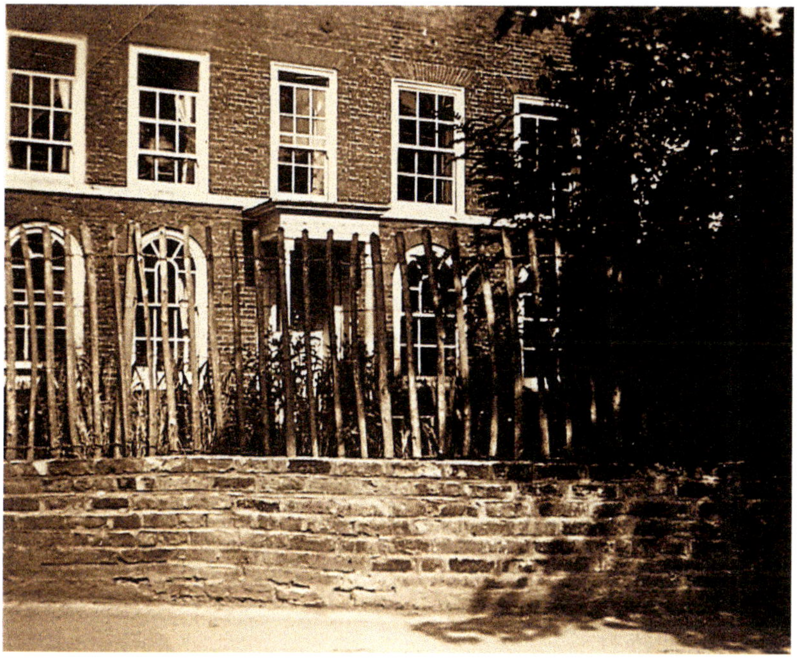

Selby House, Ham Common

George Henry Benbow, another distant relative of my wife's, lived at Selby House in the 1860s. He resided there with his wife, two children and three servants. Benbow was a perfumer by trade, his business premises being in Westminster. Selby House dates to the late seventeenth century. The land was called Three Elm Square Piece and is mentioned in the 1649 Survey of Ham Manor. By 1695 a farmhouse occupied the site, the area being known as Brimsweech Close. A grander house was constructed later; it was not until the nineteenth century that the name was changed to Selby House. The original image is severely cropped, but the current view of the house portrays it in its entirety.

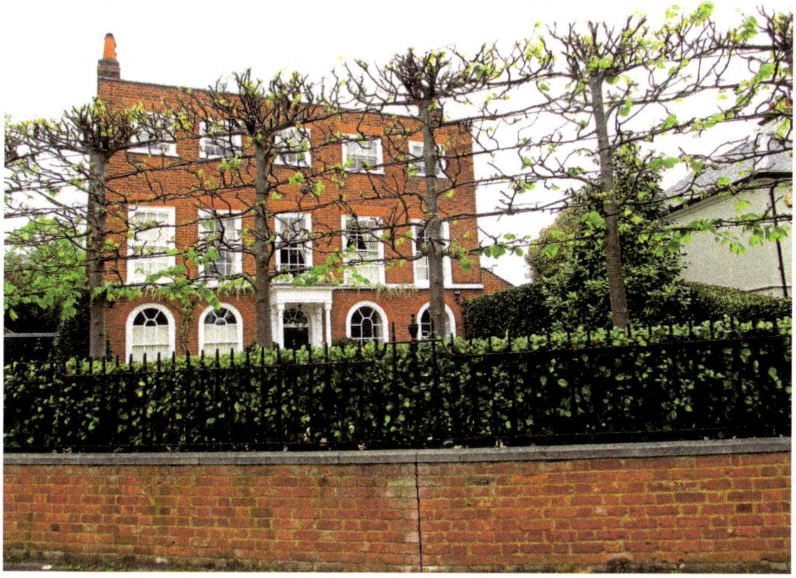

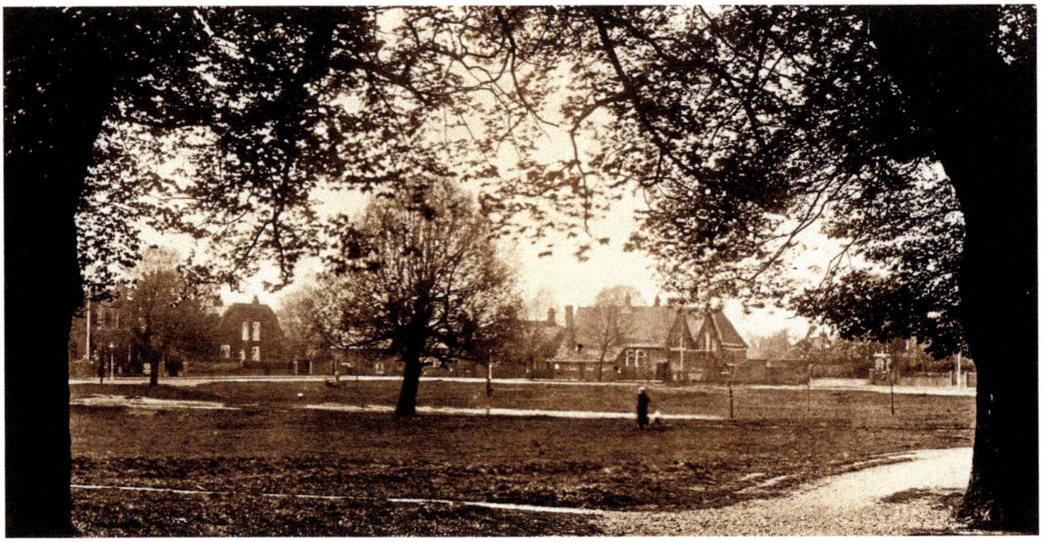

Ham Common, Close to the Pond

Ensleigh Lodge, which dates to *c.* 1800, can be seen on the left in this view of Ham Common taken near to the pond. The house has an unusual semi-mansard roof and looks quite striking in its design. A decorative shell design can be seen on the windows, similar in style to designs on the Cassel Hospital – the lodge and hospital may possibly be of the same age and architect. Ensleigh was for many years the home of Miss Baxter, a well-known and kindly lady in the village. The large building just off-centre in the view shows St Andrew's School, now St Thomas Aquinas Church. The current photograph demonstrates how the trees have considerably grown since the earlier picture was taken in the 1930s.

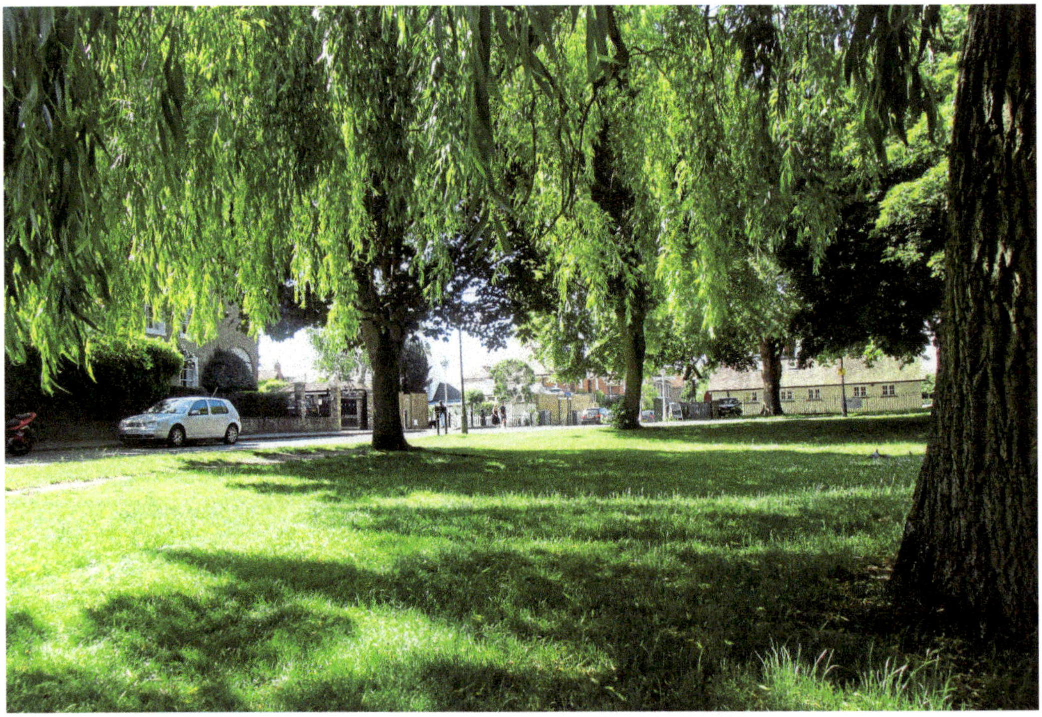

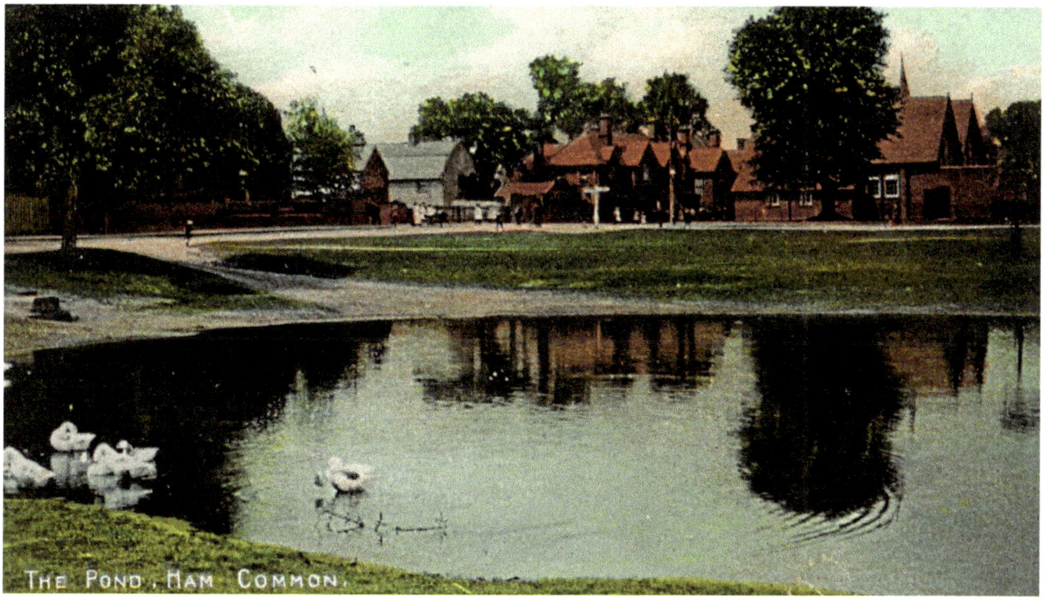

The Pond, Ham Common

The tithe map of 1842 shows another pond on the common opposite Ham school, called Neville's Pond. That pond, which was named after a distant relative, was unfortunately filled in around 1858. The pond shown here lies on the western corner of the common and adds a picturesque aspect to the area. The original image clearly shows the school and schoolchildren, as well as the houses in Ham Street and the rebuilt malt house in Lock Road. However, in the current photo the trees have grown to such an extent that you can only see a part of the building. The small island helps keep the waterfowl safe from prowling nocturnal foxes.

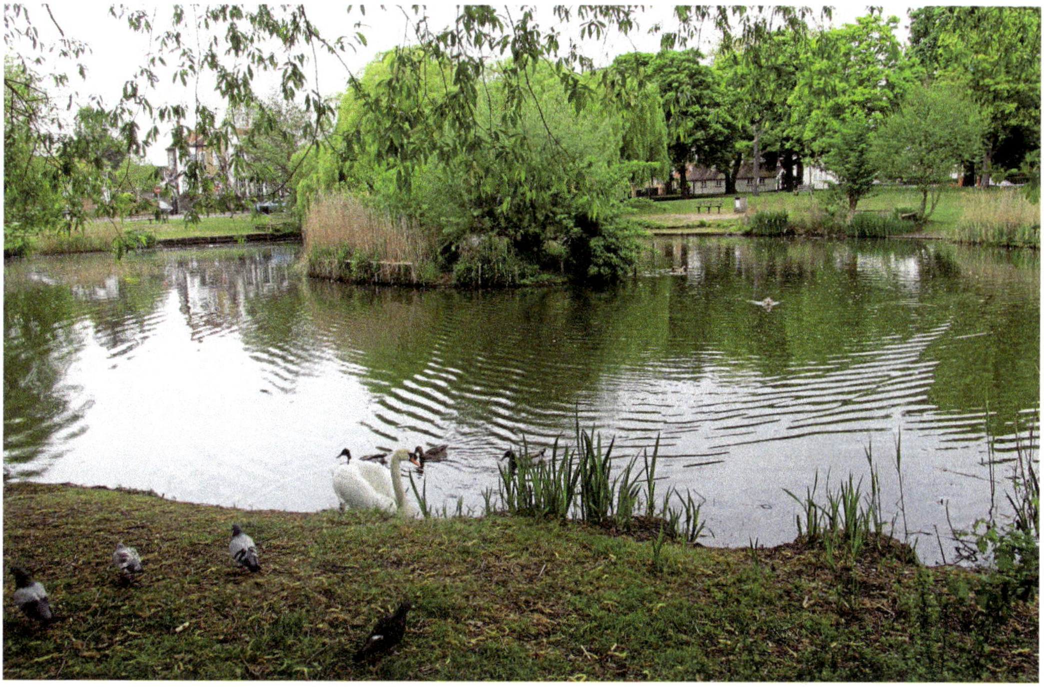

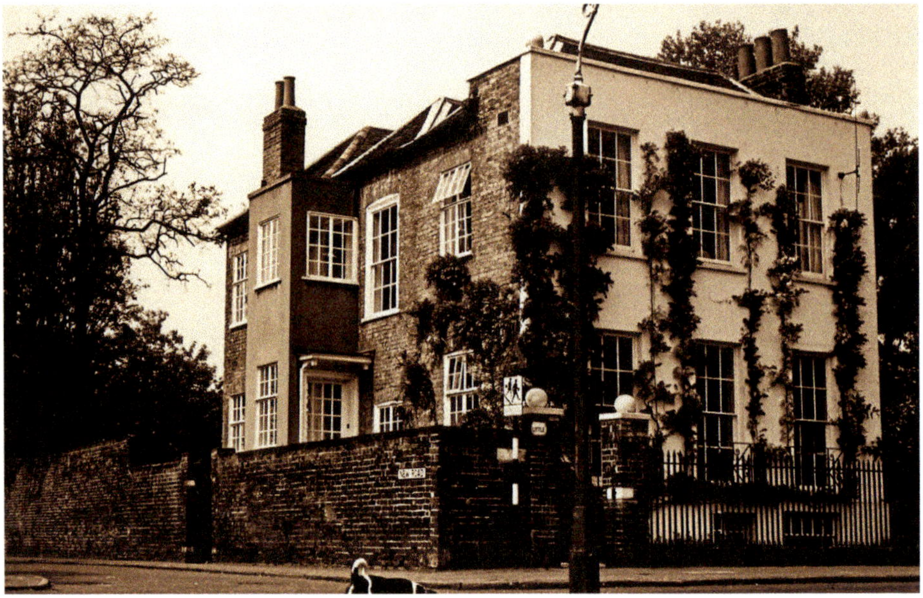

The Little House, Ham Common

Writer Miss Hesba Stretton lived with her sister Elizabeth at Ivycroft, now renamed The Little House, from 1891 until her death in October 1911. The house is on the corner of New Road not far from the pond. Miss Stretton, whose real name was Sarah Smith, contributed stories to Dickens' *Household Words* and to *All the Year Round*, and wrote many novels. The house was initially called Laurel Cottage in the 1840s then changed its name to Ivycroft in the 1890s and finally to The Little House. A baptismal font, which had been kept in the garden at Ivycroft, was placed on the sisters' grave in Ham churchyard. They had purchased the font from a mason's yard in Wellington, Shropshire; it was highly significant to the sisters as they had been baptised in the parish church in Wellington and had spent their childhood in the area.

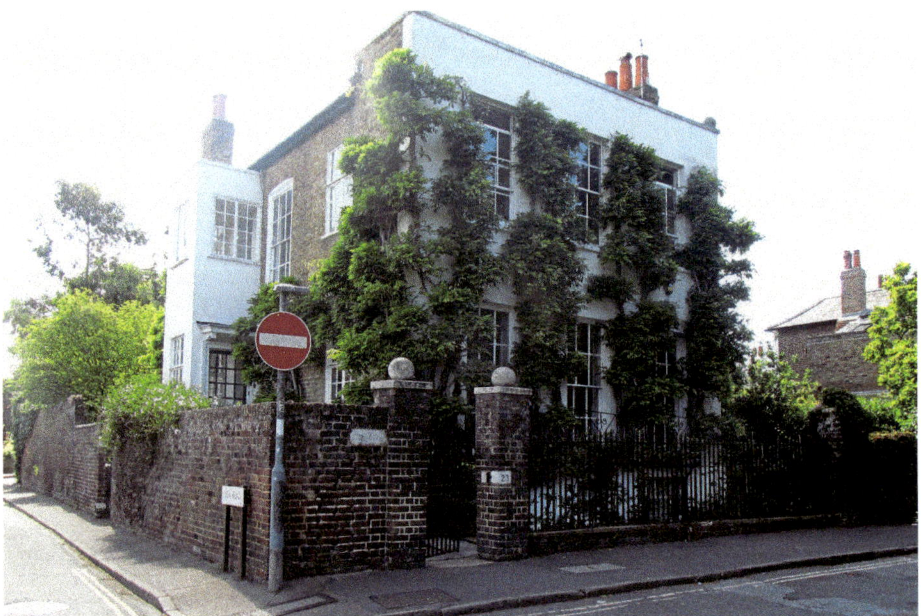

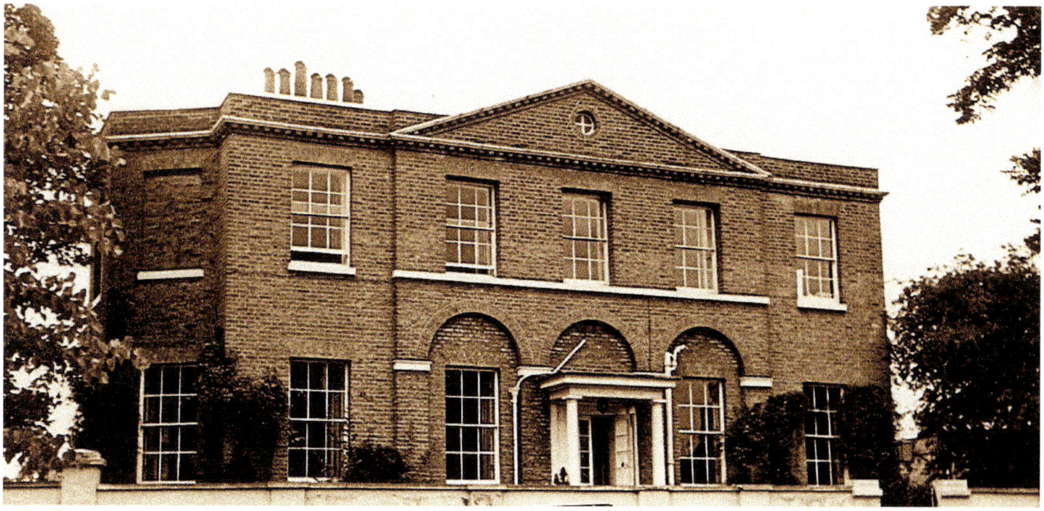

Gordon House, Ham Common

Major Gordon Forbes, who had a long and distinguished military career, lived at Gordon House from 1783; he had previously resided at Richmond. Although Gordon House appears to be Georgian, it dates to the period of Charles II. The house was briefly a boys' school from 1841 to 1845, when William May was the schoolmaster. In the 1860s it remained unoccupied for some time, until Mr Sharpe, a solicitor, took up residency in the 1870s. During the First World War, Major Milner lived here, followed by another distinguished military gentleman, Major Alan Bott, in 1929. The Dowager Marchioness Linlithgow lived here from 1954, vastly improving the gardens; she died after a car accident in 1965. Later in the 1960s part of the garden was sold when Mornington Walk was built.

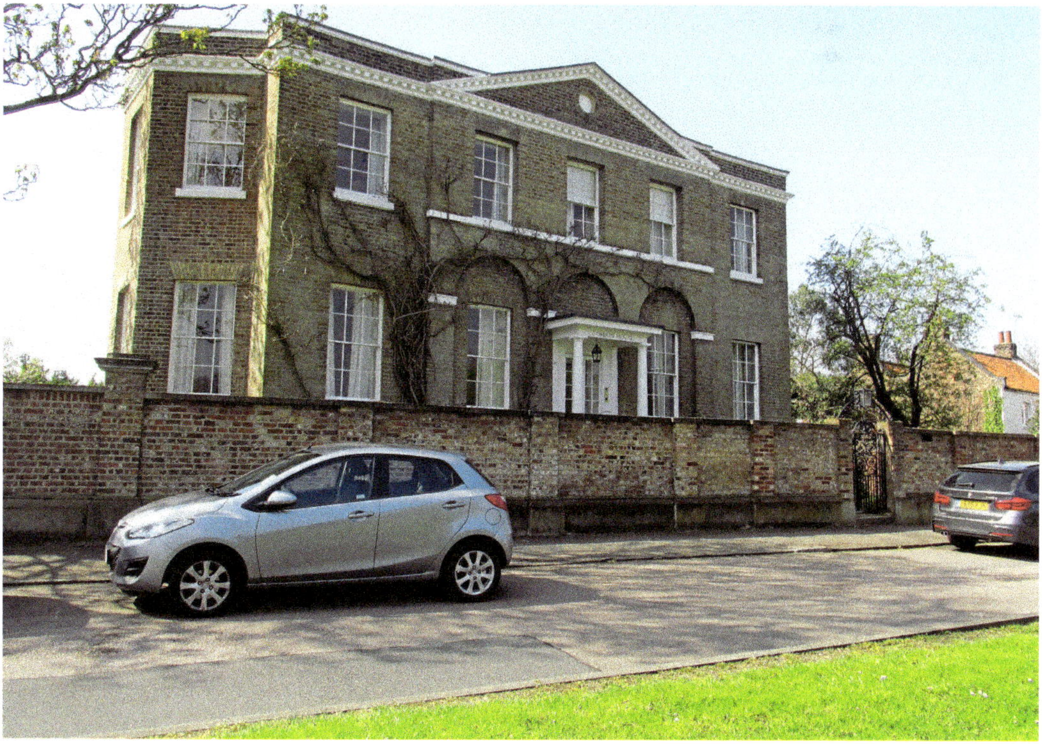

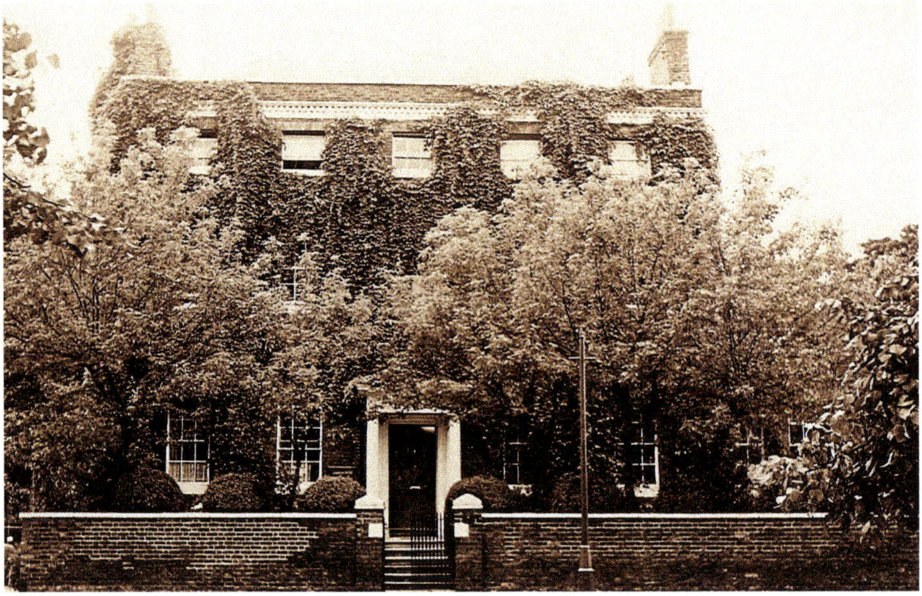

Langham House, Ham Common

The house was constructed around 1709 with three storeys and a fine Tuscan porch. From 1780 until 1790 the Marquis of Tweedsdale occupied the premises. Another notable owner of this residence was Charles Sneyd Edgeworth, who bought the property in 1851. He was a member of the management committee of the National Orphans Home, also situated on the common. Charles Edgeworth died in 1864 and in September that year there was a large sale of all the contents of the house. Admiral Lord Fisher took up residence in 1913. He was First Sea Lord from 1904–10 and again in 1914–15; he resigned in protest over the continuance of the Dardanelles campaign. In 1949, the Tollemache family moved to Langham House while Ham House was being transferred to the National Trust. In more recent times the house was converted into flats, but the external appearance remains the same.

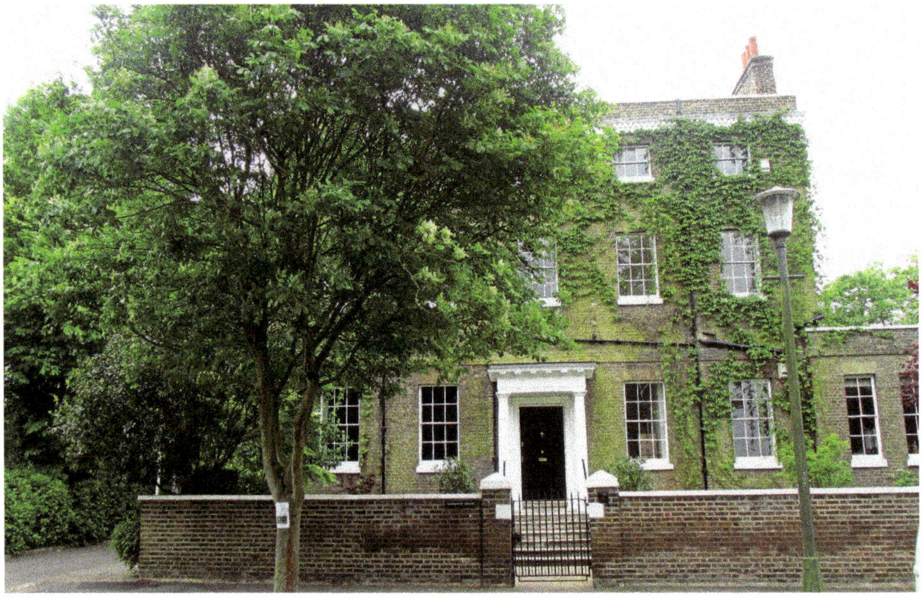

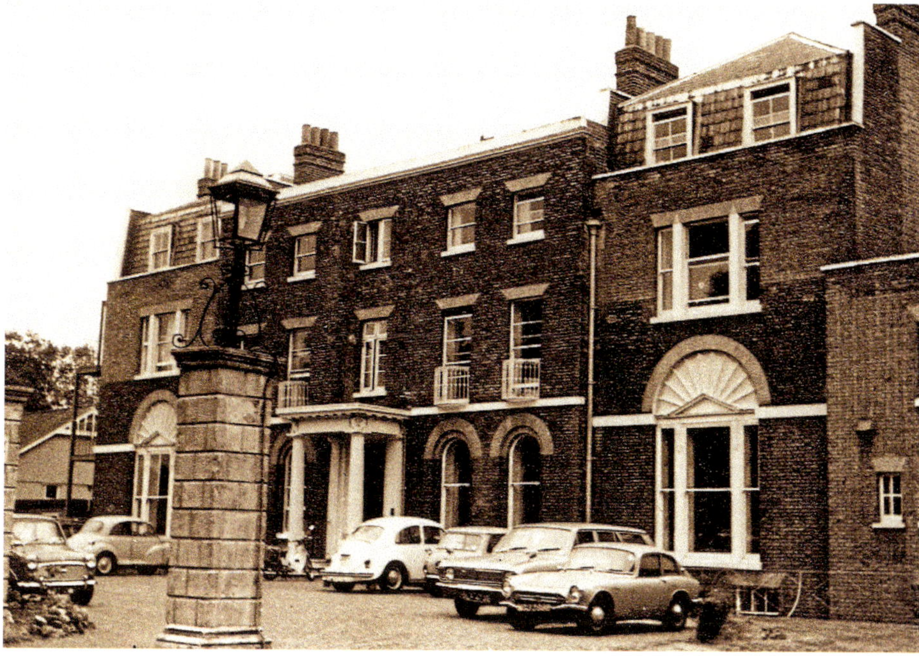

The Cassel Hospital, Ham Common

Sir Ernest Cassel founded the Cassel Hospital in 1919 as a hospital specialising in nervous disorders. It was a pioneering centre experimenting in the psychotherapy of neuroses. The hospital became part of the National Health Service in 1948. The site itself can be dated back to 1683 when Thomas Jenner resided here. There was also another house owned by the Bishop family and in 1763 Elliot Bishop further extended the property by purchasing a further 4 acres, making the land 8 acres in total. In the Edwardian period a first-class hotel called the Lawrence Hall Hotel occupied this historic country mansion.

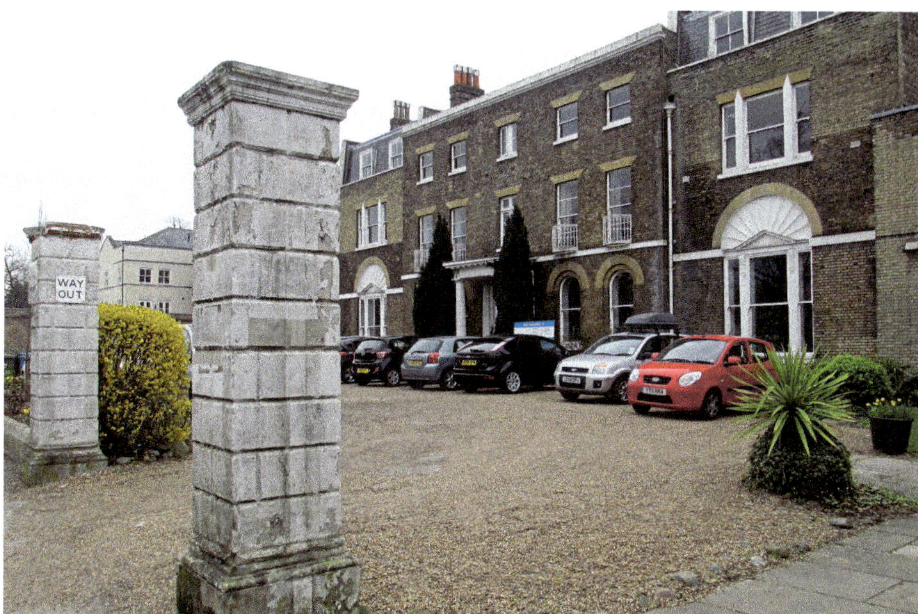

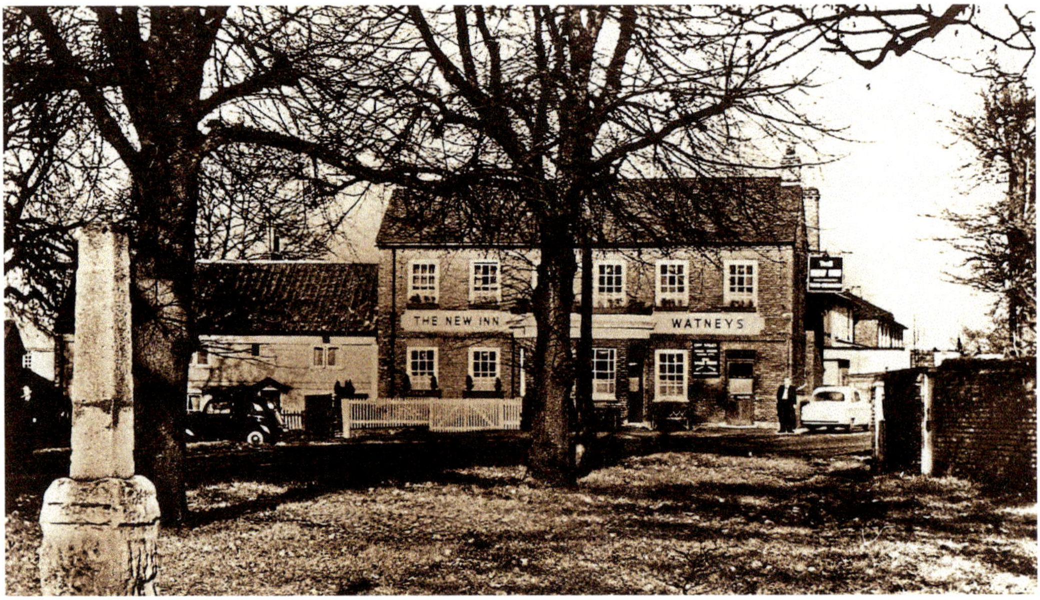

The New Inn and the Ham Obelisk

Originally known as the White Hart, the inn can be dated back to the 1670s. After being known as the 'New Inn', the name changed to the Hobart Arms, most likely named after the Hon. George Hobart (1731–1804) who resided in a house called Sans Sourci in Ham in the 1780s. The inn reverted to its title of the New Inn again in 1822 and has remained so to this day. The Ham Common obelisk can be seen near the inn, but today has been relocated to the other side of the Upper Ham Road. The obelisk stone is very weathered and bears no inscription. However, the best clue as to its origin was furnished by one of Ham's oldest residents, a Mr Warner, who recalls it as a lamp standard outside Ormley Lodge on the common.

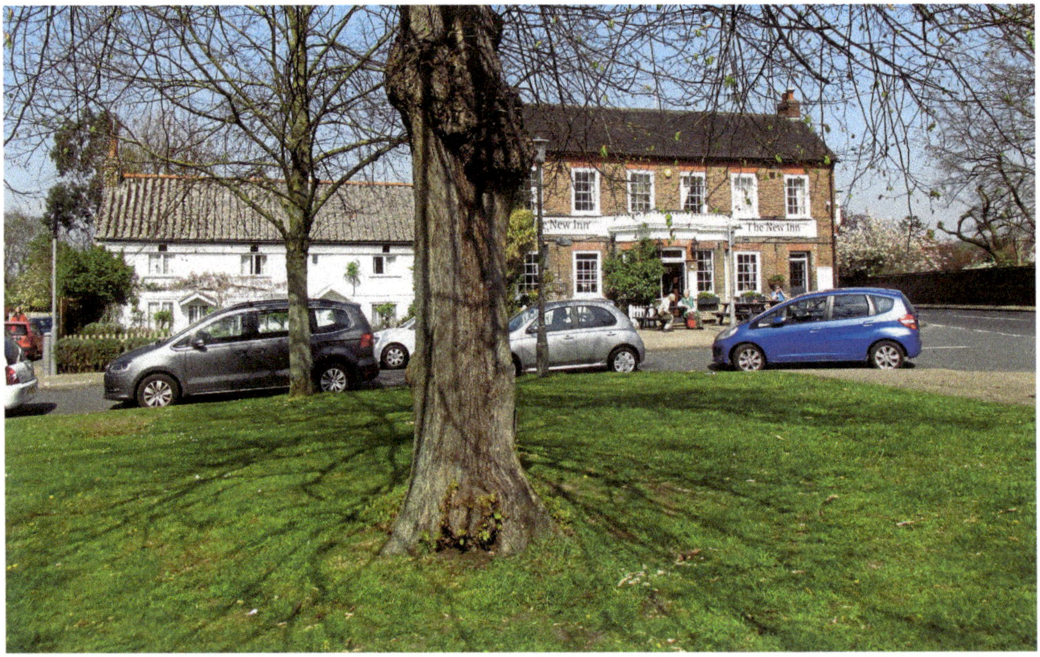

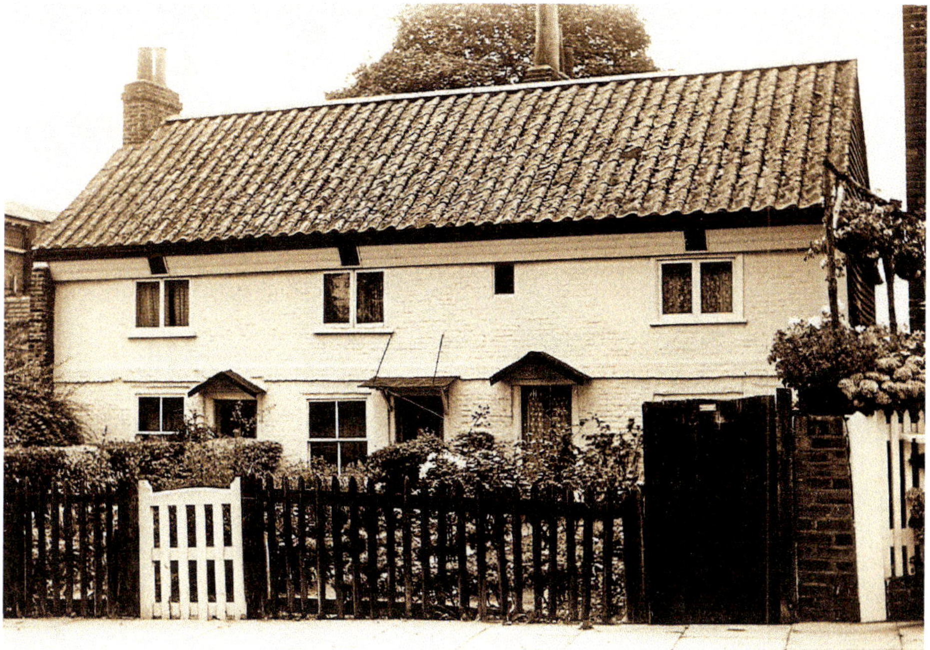

Stafford Cottages, Ham Common

The cottages are believed to date to an early part of the seventeenth century and may possibly be even earlier. They are the earliest buildings on the whole of Ham Common. William Stafford bought the cottages around 1845 and that is when they were first named Stafford Cottages. Unfortunately, it is not known what the cottages were named before this date. The building was not subdivided into three separate dwellings until the very end of the eighteenth century. They have now reverted to a single residency. The garden always looks extremely picturesque and well kept. The cottages stand next to the New Inn on the corner of the common.

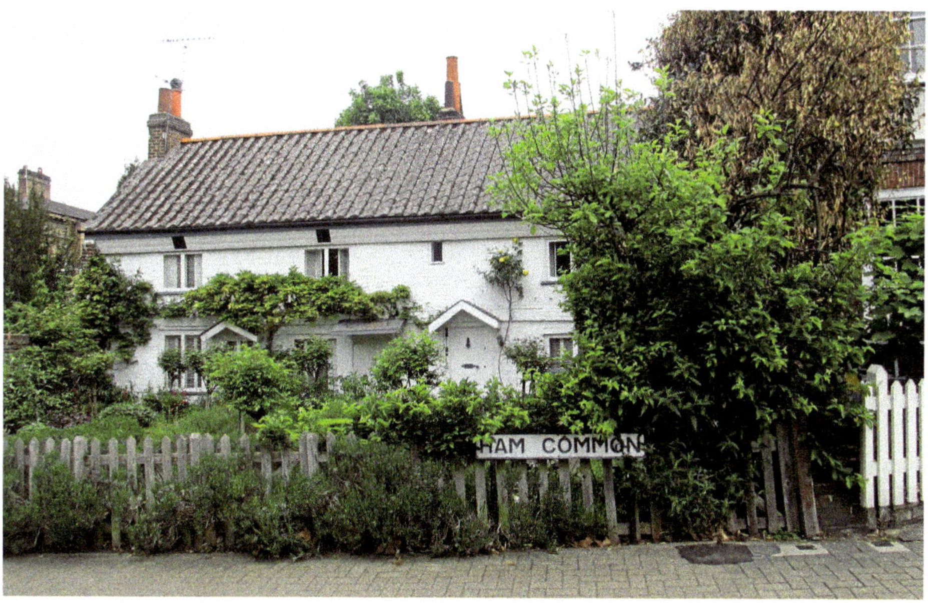

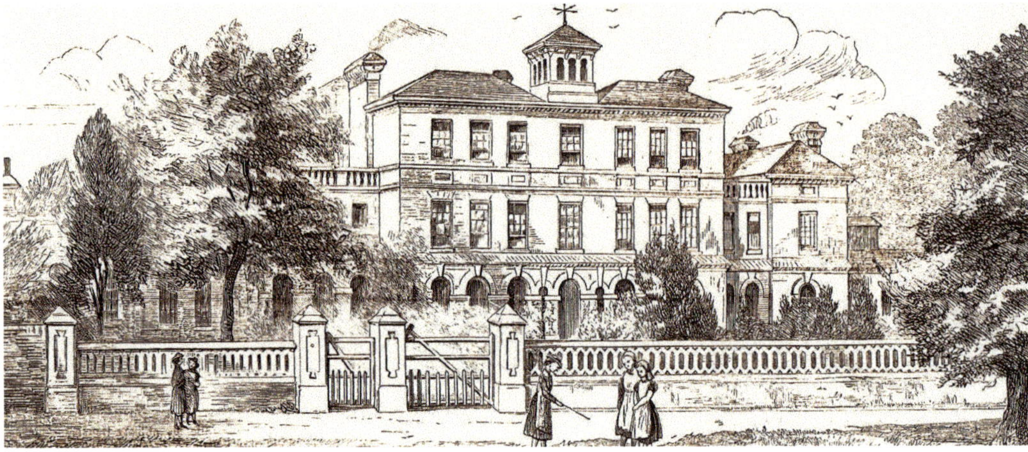

National Orphan Home, Ham Common

John Minter Morgan (1782–1854) and the Revd J. Brown founded the National Orphan Home, originally called the Cholera Orphan Home, on Ham Common in 1849. The reason for this was that there had been a huge outbreak of cholera in that year and many children had been left orphaned. The foundation stone for the new building was laid in 1856 by the Marquis of Clanricarde. The home was exclusively for girls (only one boy was admitted very early on) and could accommodate up to 120, although numbers fluctuated over the period of its existence. By 1922 numbers had dwindled to forty-three occupants and the home was finally closed. Prior to the Orphan Home there had been a hydropathy establishment on this site called the Concordium. In the 1840s it became fashionable to take water cures, and there was also a similar establishment at Sudbrook Park in Petersham. The orphanage at Ham became known as South Lodge and was converted into flats after the Second World War.

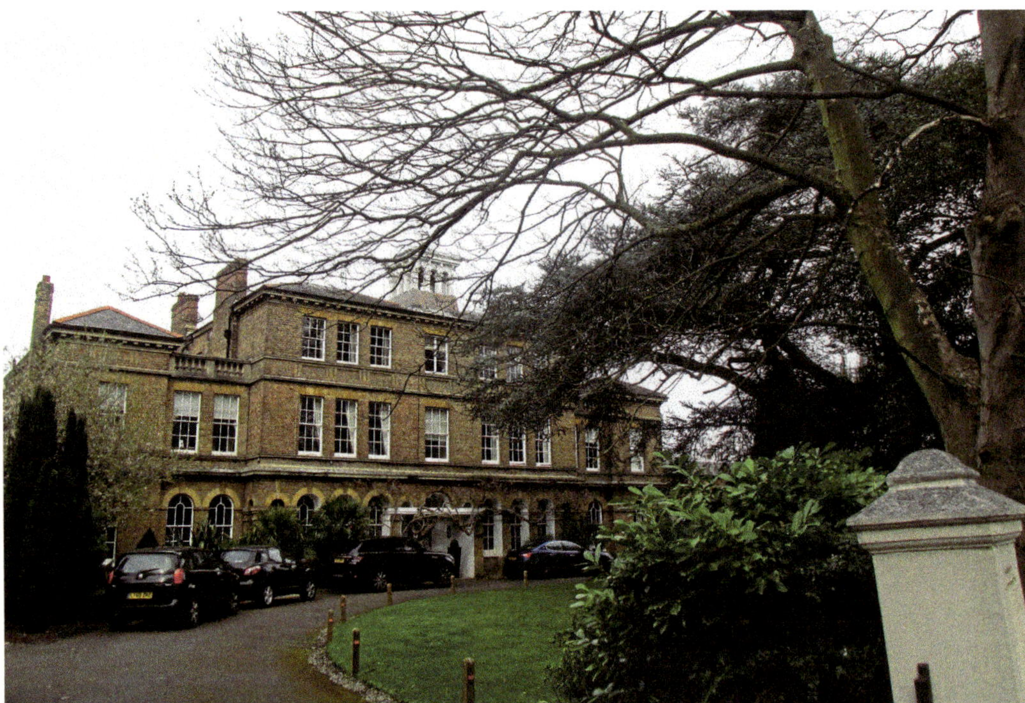

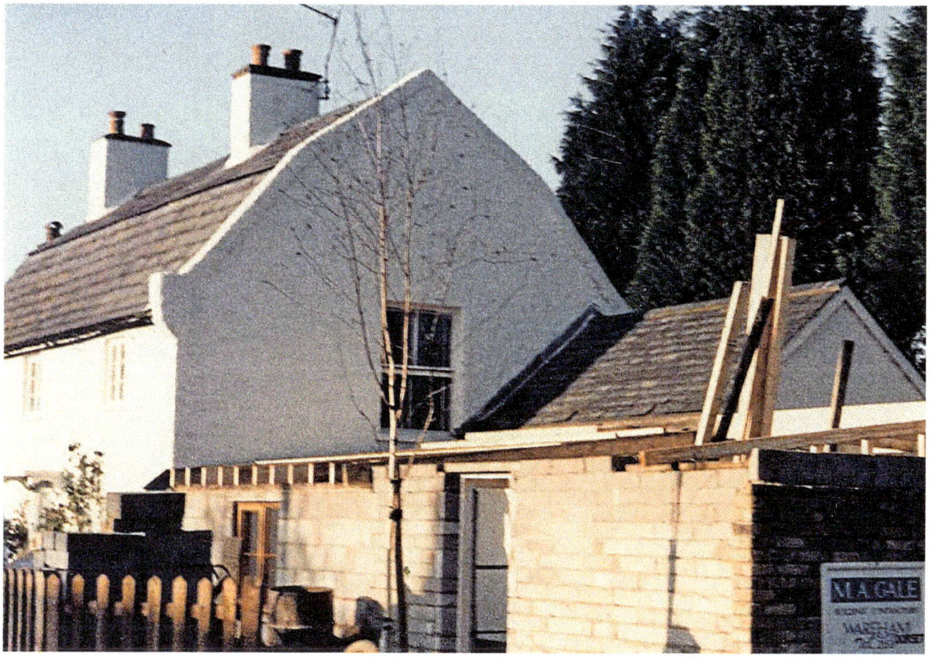

The Malt House

A prominent feature of the original old Malt House was the large louvered ventilator that perched on top of the red roof. The building itself was an oak-framed structure owned by Mr Daniel Light, as maltster of Ham, a supplier to local breweries. In the early Victorian period brewers would source their malt from maltsters. Mr Light sold his produce as far afield as Guildford. Many amateur artists painted the picturesque-looking Malt House from the common until Lock Road was widened and the old building knocked down in 1906. The current house still has an individuality about it that makes it stand out from the other buildings.

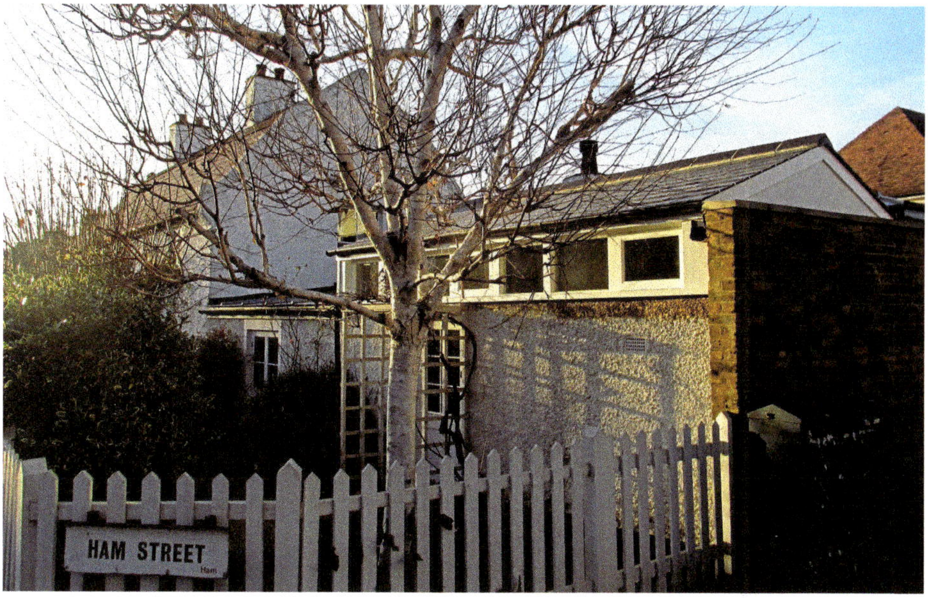

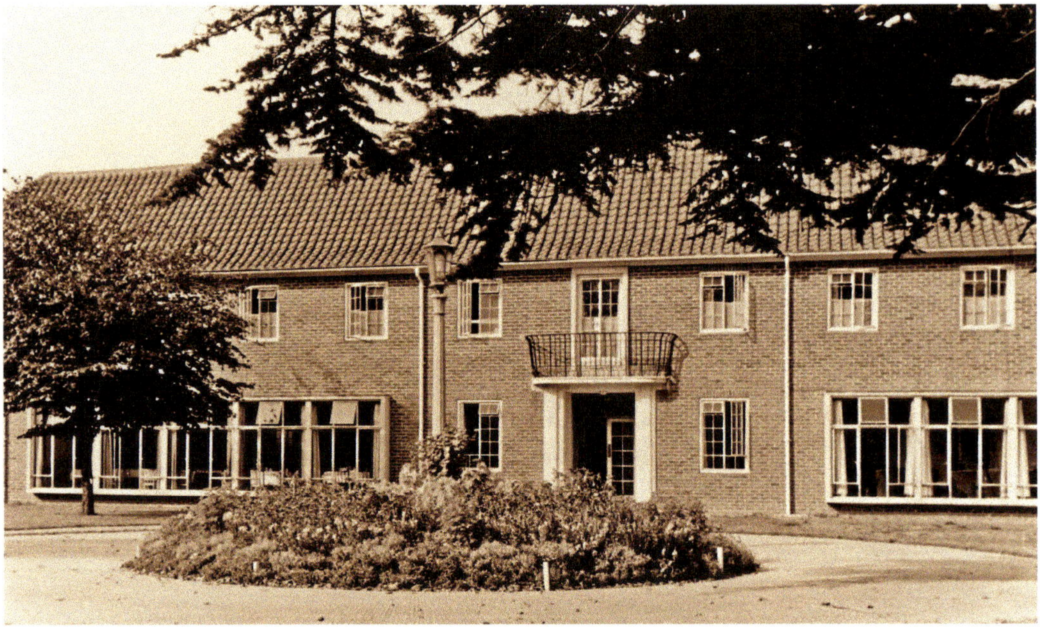

Craig House, Craig Road

Lady Dorothy MacMillan, wife of the then Prime Minister, opened Craig House in June 1958. Craig House was a home for elderly people situated in Craig Road, on the corner of Butler Farm Close. The home had accommodation for fifty-one senior persons and, for that period, the building was very up to date. After the opening ceremony Lady Dorothy cut an iced cake made to represent Craig House and Forbes House. Lady Dorothy then went on a tour of inspection of the house with the matron, Miss Weatherby. The current photograph shows the building that replaced Craig House in February 2007, consisting of thirty-four flats and five three-bedroom houses.

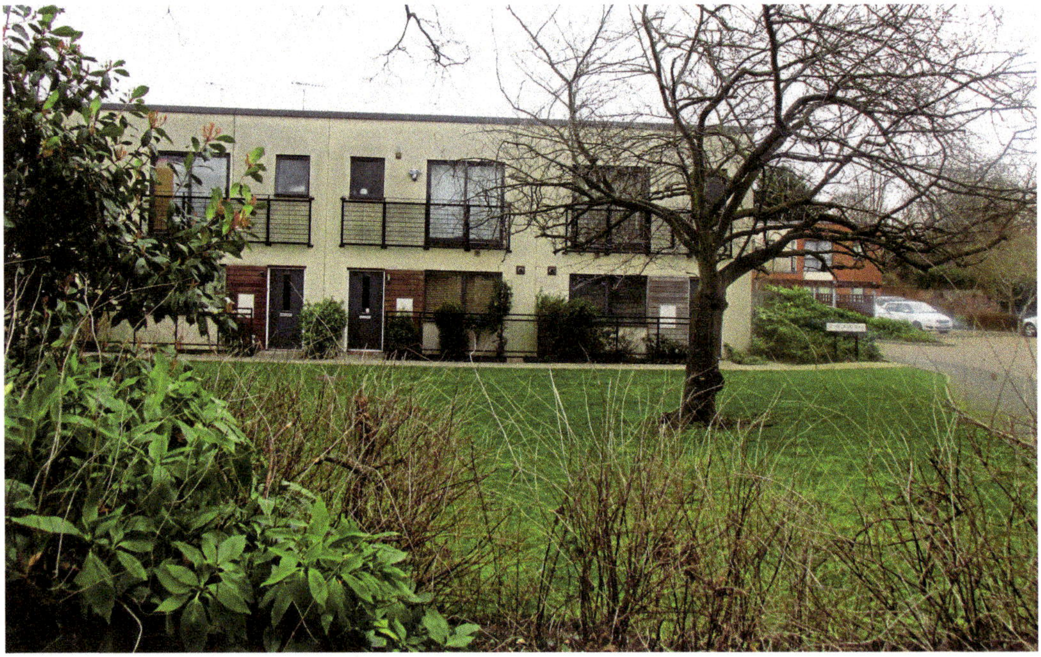

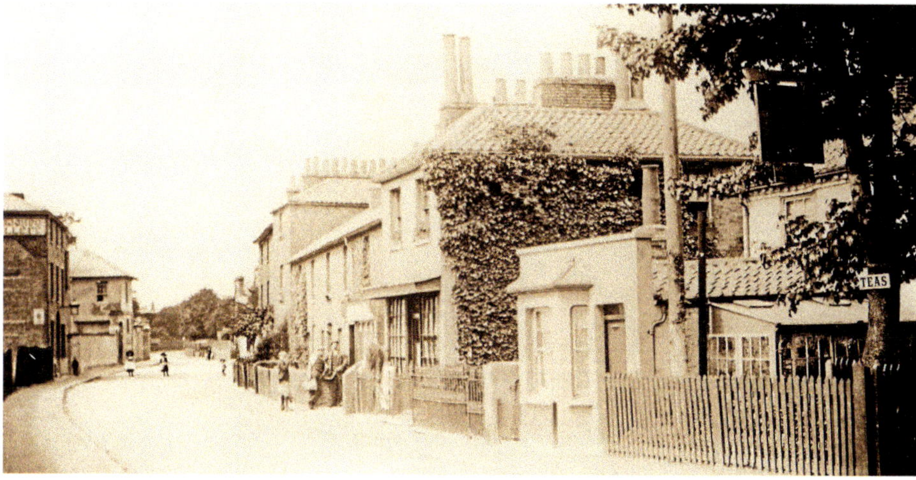

The Crooked Billet, Ham Street

Mr Patrick Johnson owned The Crooked Billet in December 1775 and his heirs surrendered it to Elizabeth Rowells of Kingston. In 1861 the publican was Mr Daniel Trollope and, in 1891, Mr William Wood. The photograph seen here dates to 1907 and shows the pub on the left-hand side. In 1935 a new public house building further back was erected in a semicircular pattern, which lasted up to the 1990s. When British Aerospace closed there was a decline in customers and the building was eventually demolished. The Ham General Stores now occupies the former older public house building. The Ham Brewery Tap on the other side of the road dominates the view in the current photograph.

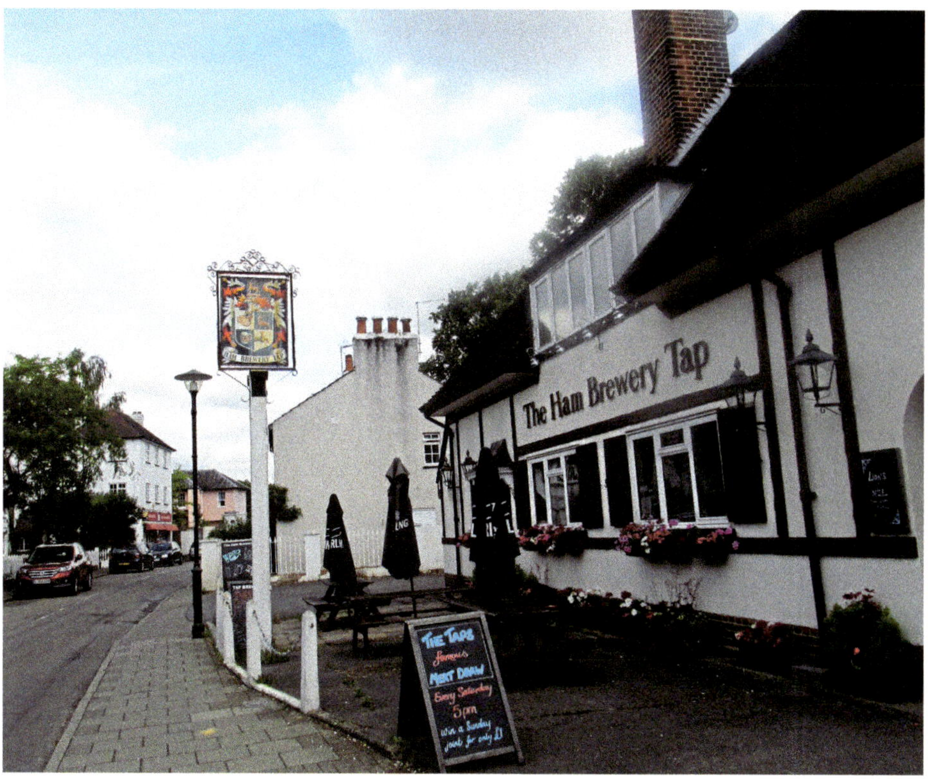

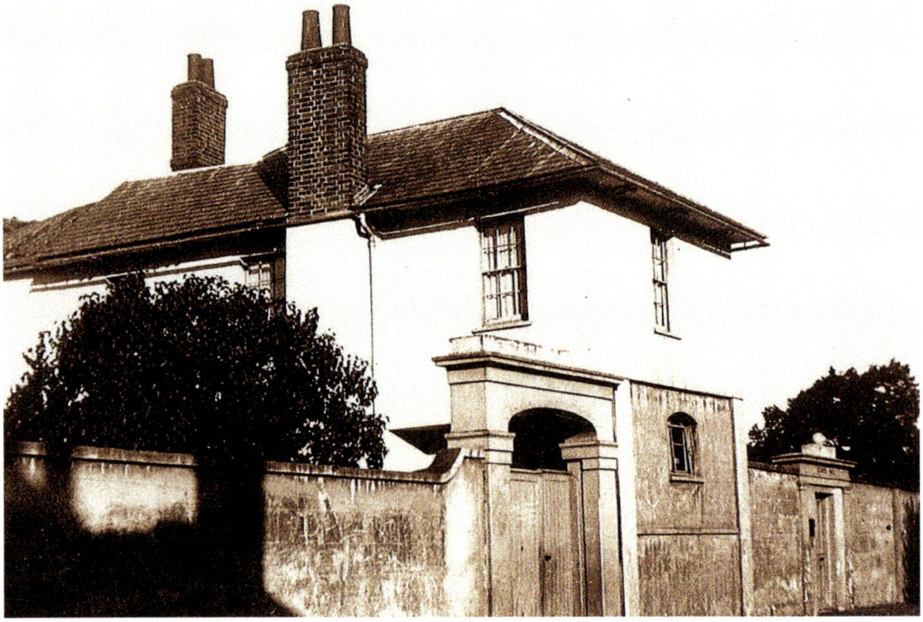

Bench House, Ham Street

Originally called Stokes Hall, the property has now been divided into two separate houses, Stokes House and Bench House. Documents referring to this property describe it as the 'Kings Bench', but it changed to the 'Queens Bench' when Victoria came to the throne. When it was still Stokes Hall in 1853 it briefly became a ladies school run by three sisters, Ann, Charlotte and Sarah Barker; however, the school was not a great success. The barrister, actor and co-founder of the Oxford Dramatic Society, Samuel Brandram (1824-1892), lived here in 1865. Another distinguished resident in the 1920s was Lady Frederick Cavendish. It will be noticed from the current photograph that the original entrance to the house has been bricked up.

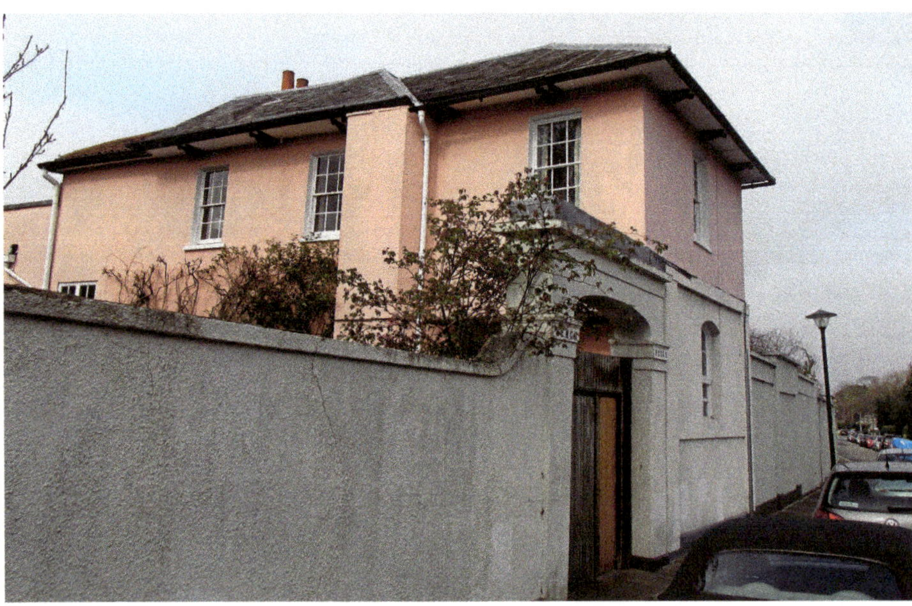

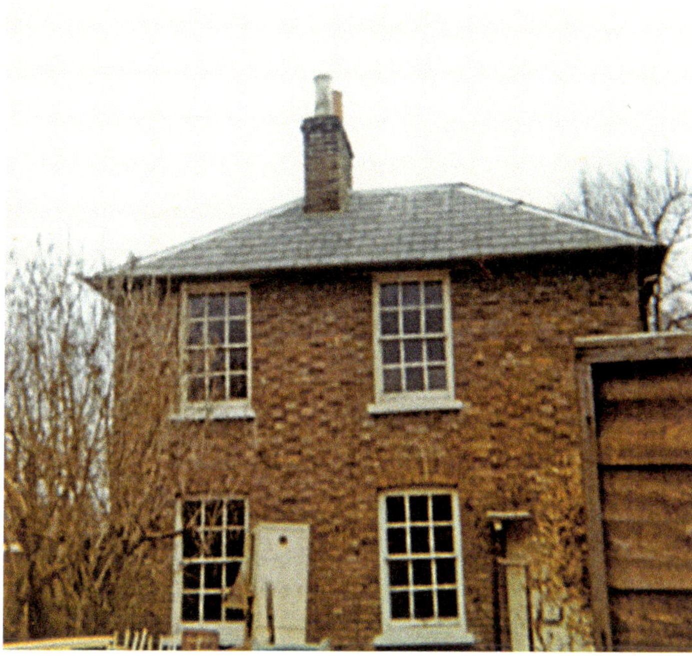

Schoolhouses, Nos 36 and 38 Ham Street

In the 1840s, the Revd Thomas Hore left money for the poor and for schools. Three houses were built for the schoolteachers in Ham Street opposite Stokes Hall. At the time, the girls were on the common and the boys at St Andrew's Church. One house (now No. 36) was divided as two separate residences and in 1851, Mary Bridger (1805–1867), the infant schoolmistress, lived in one of them. At the same time, Mr William Charles Johnson, a schoolmaster, was living next door in School House (now No. 38) with his children. In 1891 Louisa De-Pury, the schoolmistress, lived there and another schoolmistress, Ada Clarke, resided next door. In the late 1800s, a new St Andrew's School and new schoolhouses were built. Nevertheless, in 1911 Archie Francis Barnes, head teacher, resided in School House with his wife Emma, who was an assistant teacher. In 1966, St Andrew's School moved to the St Richard's School site and was known by both names for many years, but now the St Andrew's has been dropped. The original photo of No. 38 Ham Street shows how the original building would have looked before the extension was added in the 1970s.

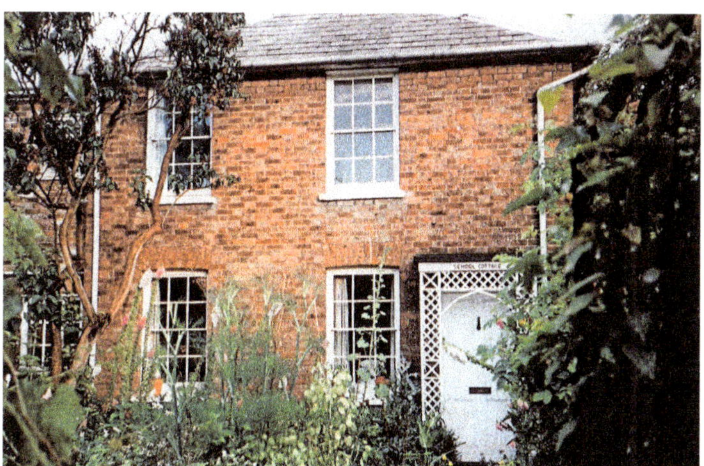

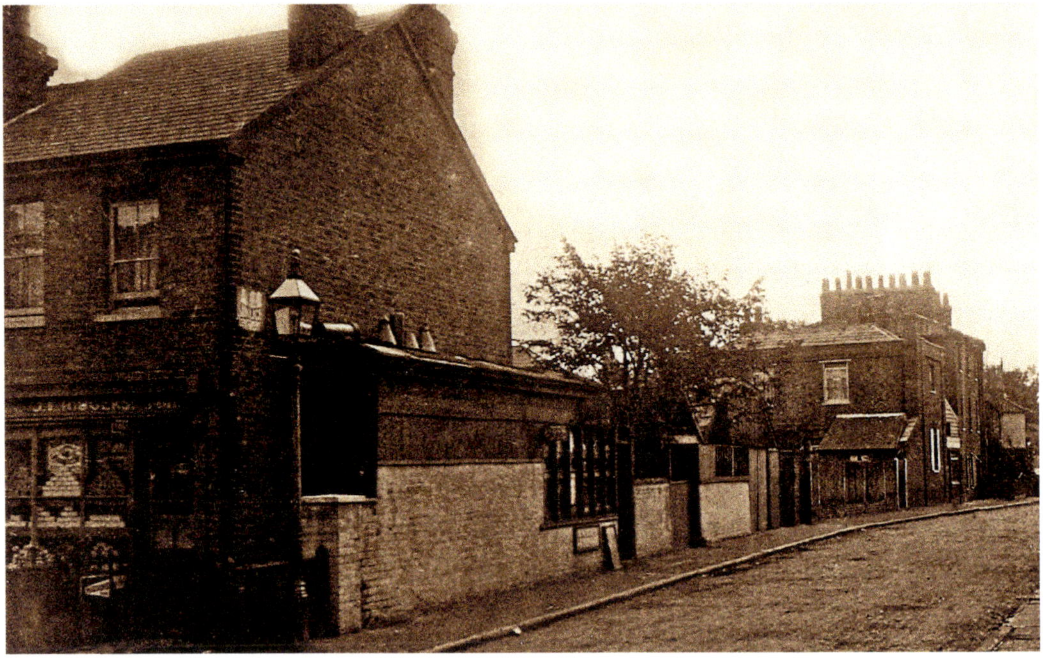

Ridgers Grocery Store, Evelyn Road

It comes as something of a surprise to find there was a grocery store in Evelyn Road. John Robert Ridgers owned the shop, although he was a carpenter by trade. His second wife Frances, known as Fanny, actually ran the store at No. 10 Evelyn Road. Ridgers started trading in 1901 and continued up until 1911, so the photograph has to have been taken between these years. John Ridgers died in 1917. The former shop is now a private residence as seen in the modern photograph.

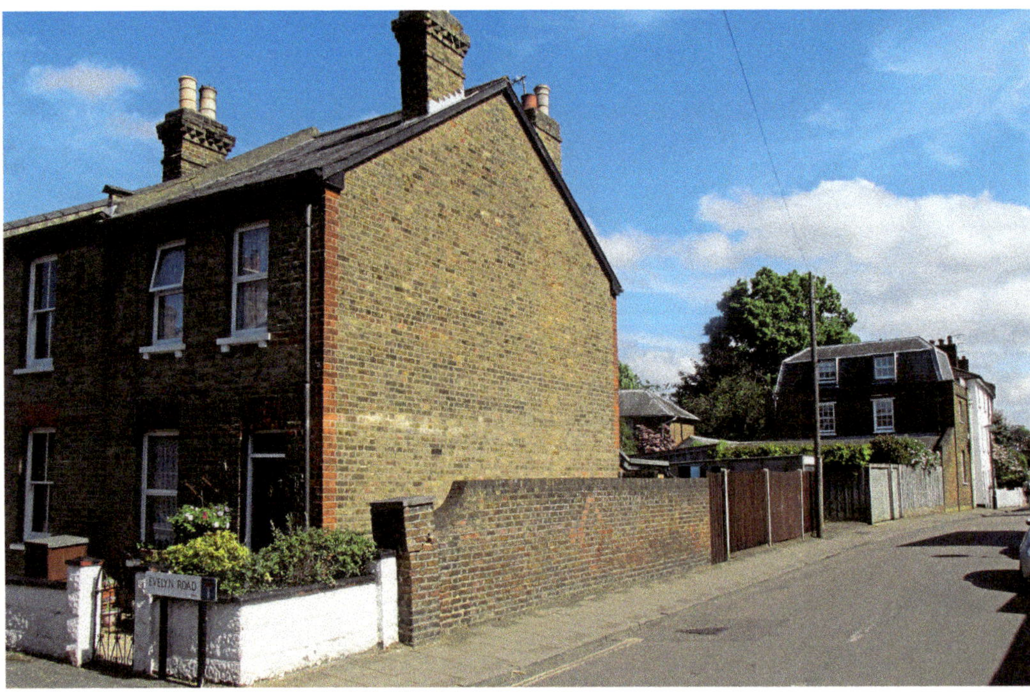

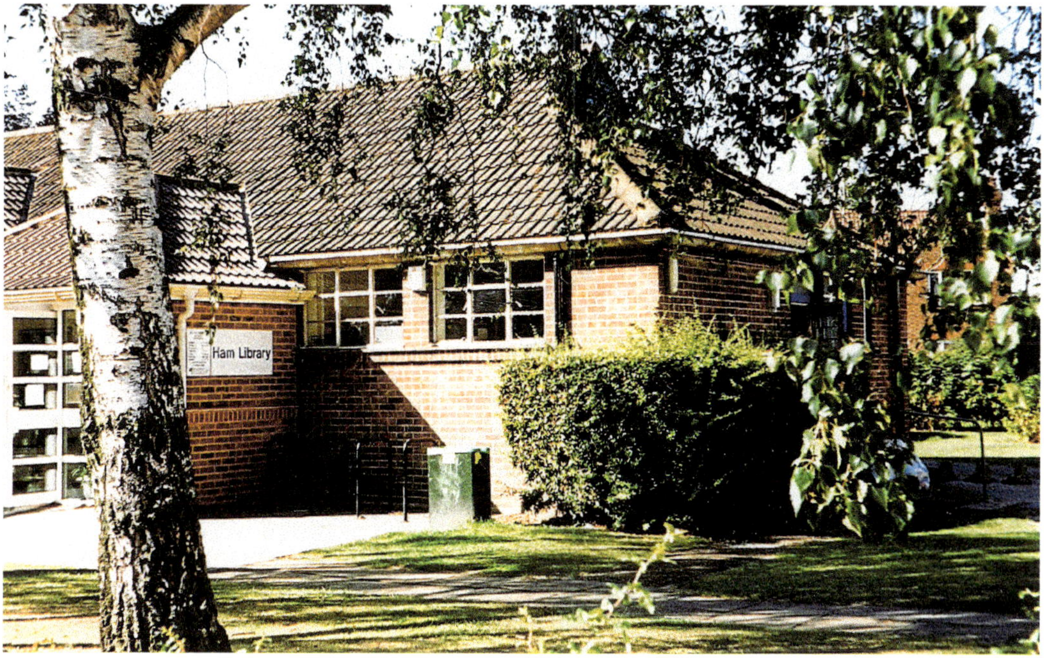

Ham Library, Ham Street

Sir Compton Mackenzie (1883–1972), the famous writer, opened Ham Branch Library on the 6 September 1952. Ham Library's claim to fame is that it was the first permanent library to have been built in Surrey since the end of the Second World War. It took ten months to build and cost £5,000. It was designed by Mr G. S. Weedle, the Borough Engineer. The building is pleasantly positioned with lawns and shrubs surrounding it. The library often hosts interesting local history talks and is a good focal point for the community.

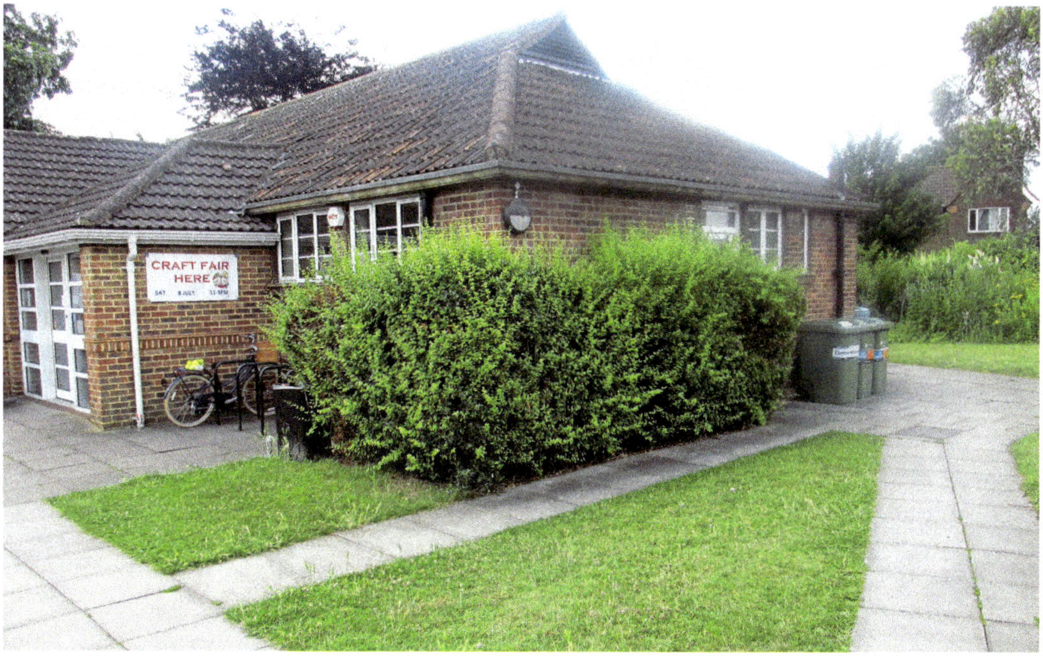

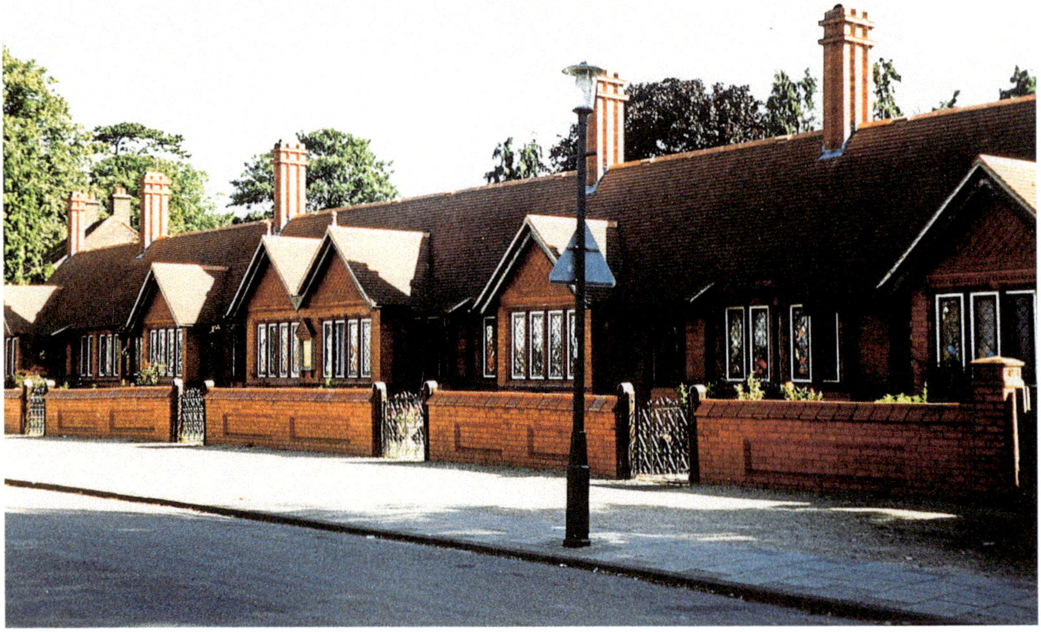

Tollemache Almshouses, Ham Street

The Hon. Mrs Algernon Tollemache had these fine almshouses built in 1892 to honour the memory of her husband, The Hon. Algernon Gray Tollemache. They were conveyed to trustees by an indenture dated 16 November 1892 for use in perpetuity as six almshouses for the benefit of the inhabitants of the parish of Ham. The almshouses are still in use and provide accommodation for nine persons, three of them being designed for married couples and three for single persons. Also in Ham Street, not far from the Tollemache Almshouses, were the Hore and Colyear Dawkins Almshouses that stood from 1845 until 1948 when they were converted to a bungalow called Hatch End.

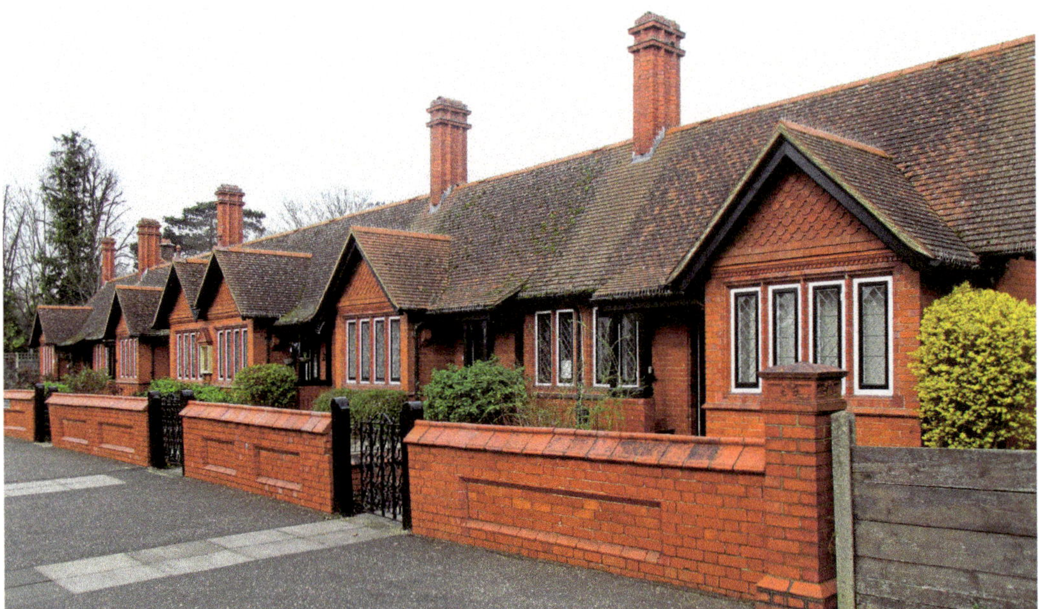

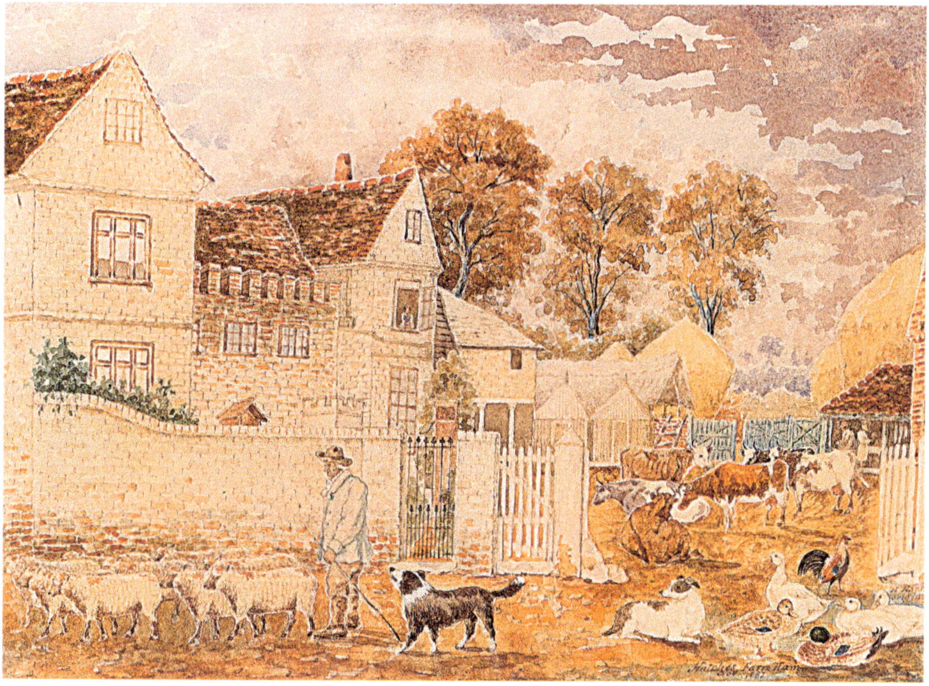

Ham Manor Farm

William Hatch was the tenant farmer and in 1851 he had 220 acres and employed seventeen labourers. By 1861 the acreage had increased to 306 and by 1871 it was 416. Mr Hatch remained for such a long time that it was known locally as Hatch's Farm. The farm was actually owned by the Earl of Dysart and can be traced in the land tax records back to 1780. The 1841 census lists Mr John Sawyer as the tenant farmer. The current photograph shows that a block of shops near to Ashburnham Road now occupies the former site.

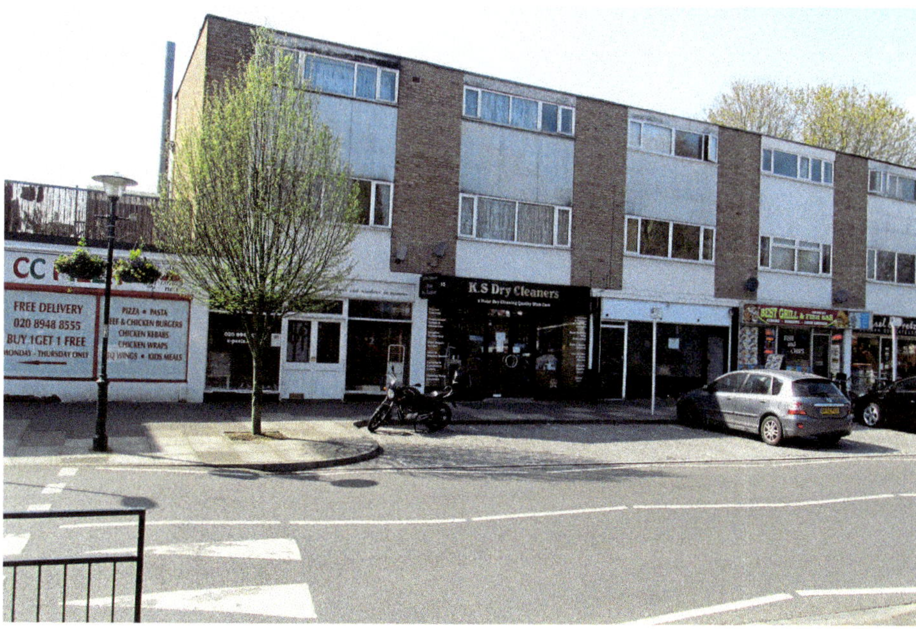

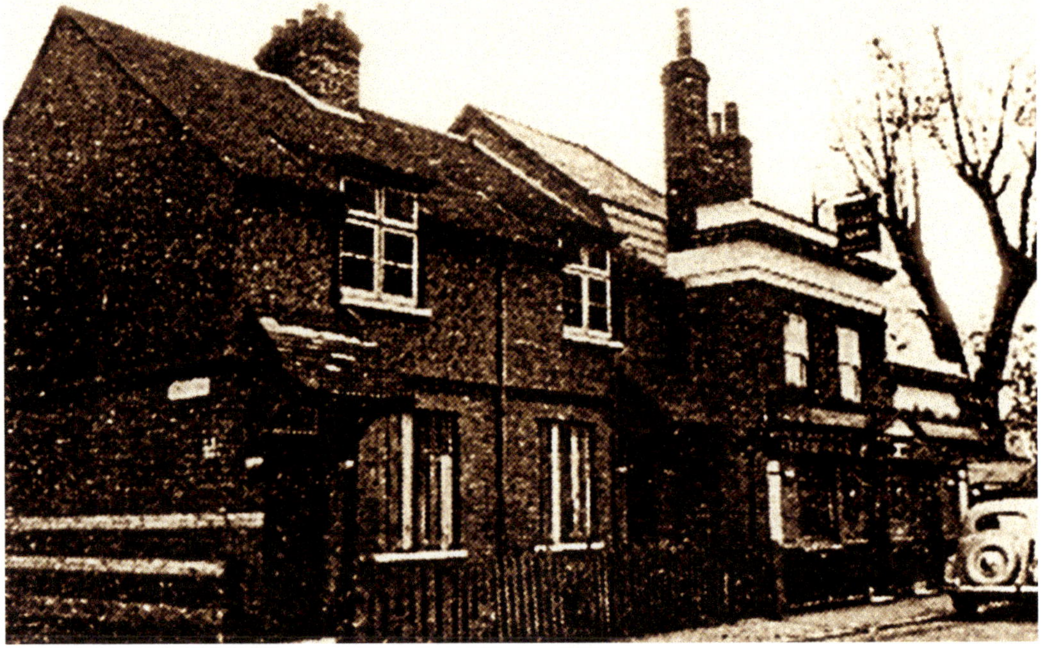

The Royal Oak Public House, Ham Street

The cottages next to the Royal Oak on the corner of Ham Street and Sandy Lane were demolished in the early 1960s for the purpose of road widening. As to the Royal Oak itself, a licence was granted in an indenture dating to 23 December 1828, although its origins go back to the 1700s. Farnell's, an Isleworth Brewery, owned this establishment in the Victorian era; in more recent times Watney's took over the ownership. The modern photo shows that the pub is now closed and has been since 2011. The Ham Institute, which used to be located in New Road, has now become the Ham Village Centre and has recently moved to the Royal Oak, giving new purpose to the building.

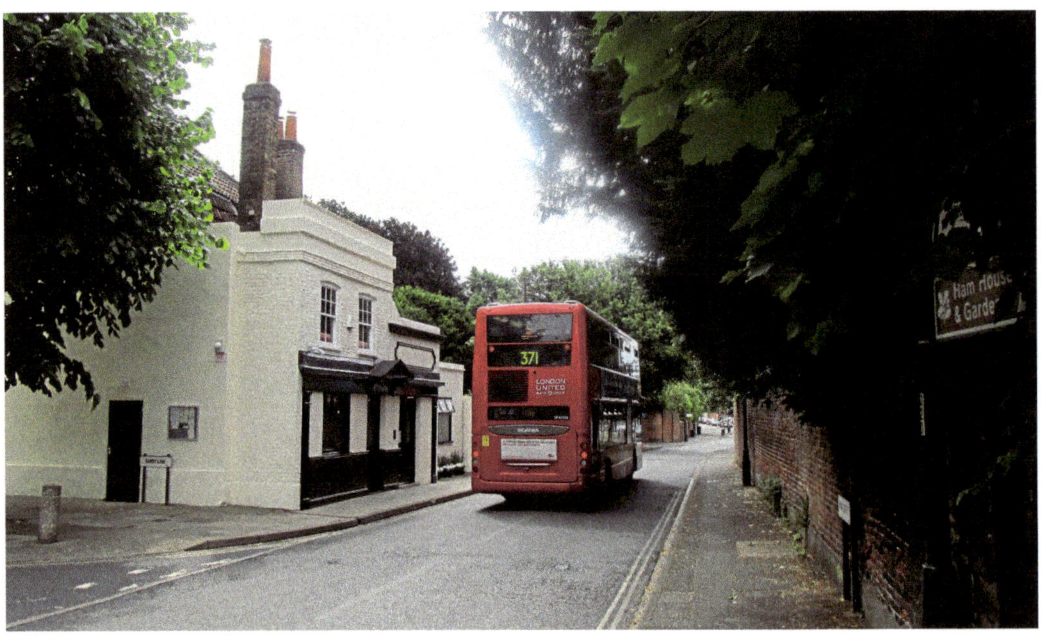

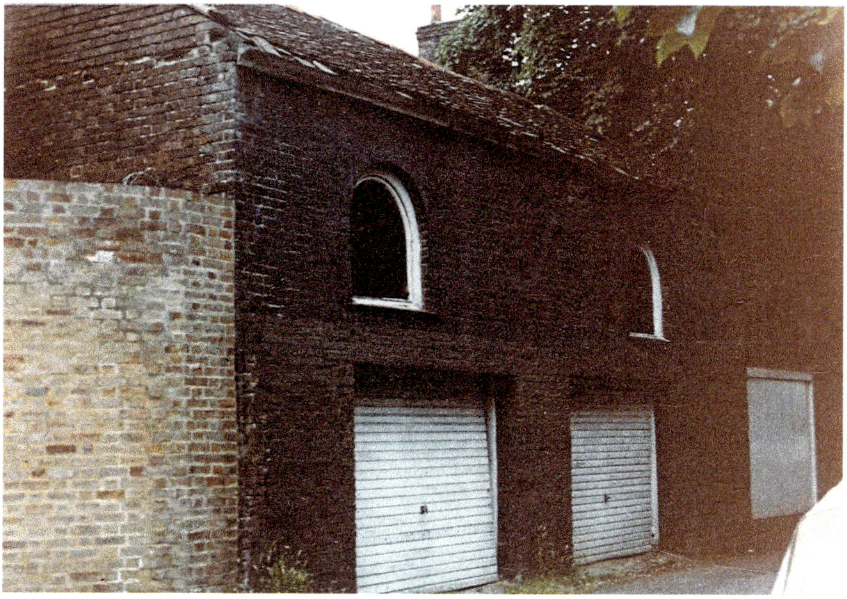

Beaufort House Chapel, Wiggins Lane

A chapel, built in 1822, stood on the site of what are now garages in Wiggins Lane, then called Back Lane. Joseph France was the chaplain for thirty-two years. This chapel was the only place of worship in Ham until St Andrew's Church was built in 1831. Lord and Lady Dysart worshipped at this chapel, having two special high-backed chairs placed either side of the altar. The building itself could seat forty persons, but could accommodate a further eighty standing. Joseph France, the chaplain, was buried in St Andrew's churchyard in 1854. In the church there is a tablet to him, in the form of a shield, which was subscribed for by the inhabitants of Ham. Sadly, no images of the original chapel could be found. The earlier photo shows the garages date to the 1980s.

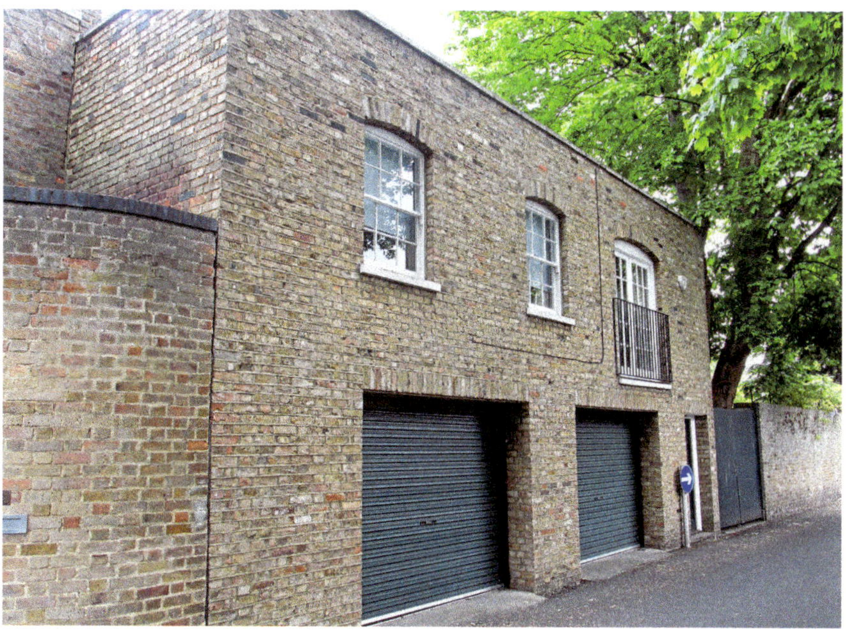

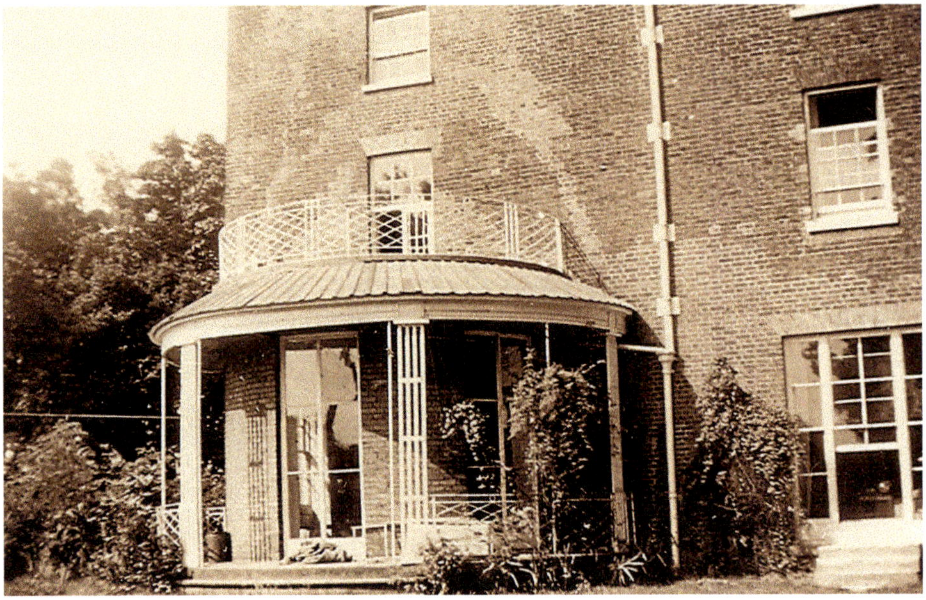

Beaufort House, Ham Street

Lord and Lady Dysart's doctor, Dr Claudius Fonnereau, was the first owner of Beaufort House in 1801. The Borrodaile family lived at Beaufort House from 1864–65. Their son Edward went out to explore the Northern Territories of Australia but was never heard from again, presumably expiring in the harsh environment. After the Borrodailes the Revd J. C. Holdstock, a Catholic priest, lived here. Two other ministers followed: Revd George Carnac in 1880 and the Revd Arthur Atherlay in 1883. In the 1950s, Countess Lewenhaupt, the English wife of a Swedish ambassador, lived at Beaufort; she was reputed to have been the friend of the Nicholas ll, Czar of Russia. The countess had the rooms hung with rich silk panels during her occupancy. The original photograph shows a side view of the house taken from the garden, but in the current photograph the whole frontage has been depicted, giving a better overall view.

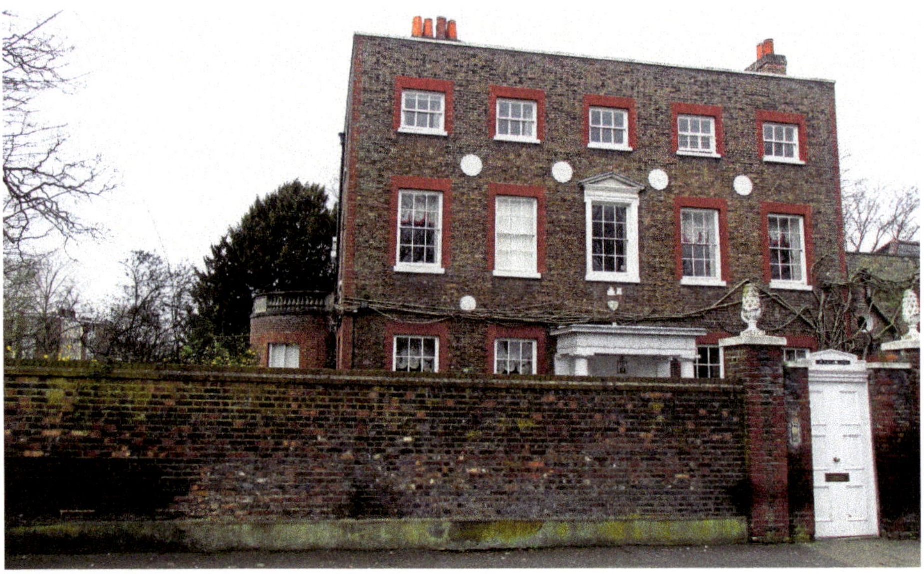

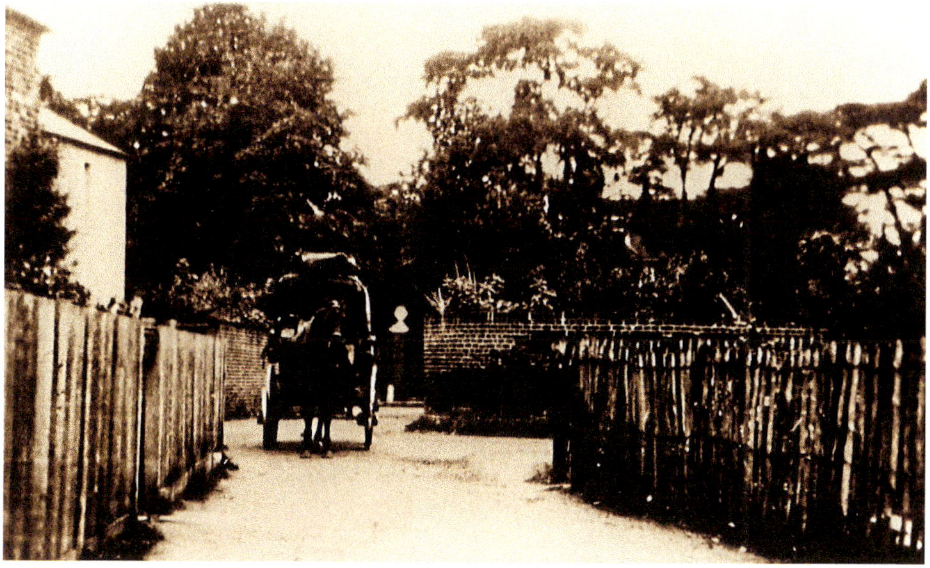

Wiggins Lane

Mr Walters, the oilman, can be seen here driving his horse and cart down Wiggins Lane just off Ham Street – the horse was later killed in a collision with a bus. In the background the gate pier of the Manor House, which stands in Ham Street, can be seen. Wiggins Lane was named after William Wiggins, who had a grocery shop in this area in the 1850s. Wiggins Cottages were built in what was then Back Lane, where his shop was located. Part of one of these cottages can be seen on the left-hand side. Just out of view further down the lane are the equally charming Pointers Cottages. It will be seen that the old wooden fencing has gone in the current photograph; however, Wiggins Lane still retains a semi-rural aspect to this day.

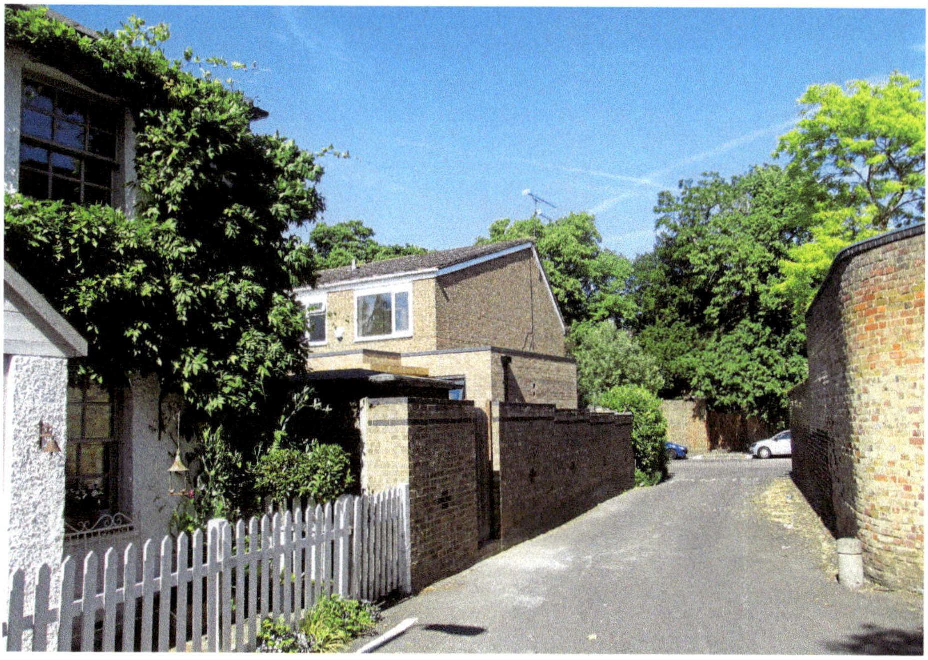

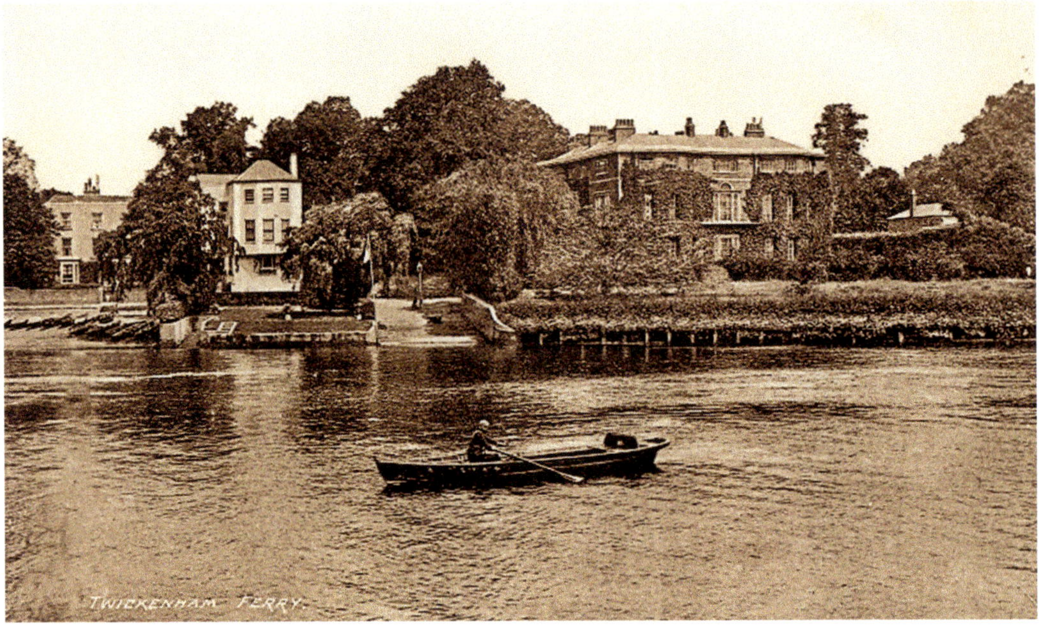

Ferry to Twickenham

This view shows the original ferry crossing looking across to the Twickenham side; the boat-launching ramp can be seen by the building with the projecting bay. The ferry crossing gave access to the nearby Ham House and had existed at this spot from the late seventeenth century. However, Walter Hammerton initiated a new ferry service in 1908 and a legal battle ensued in which he eventually triumphed and was allowed to continue his service. The modern view shows that Ferry House, the building with the projecting bay, is still standing. The house to the right of Ferry House was called Mount Lebanon, but has now been replaced by other buildings.

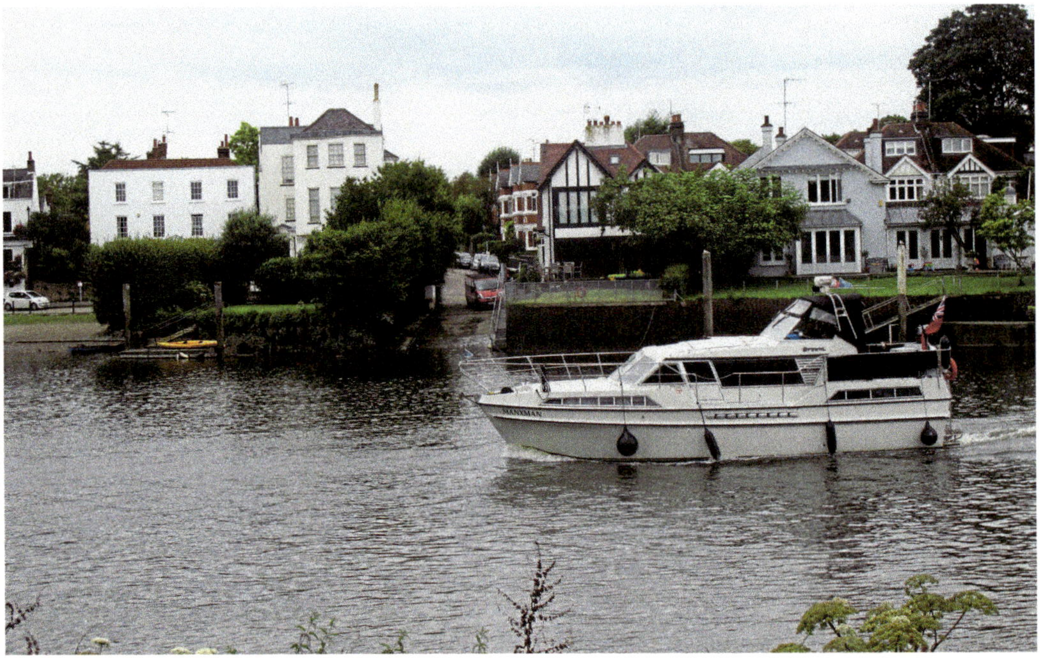

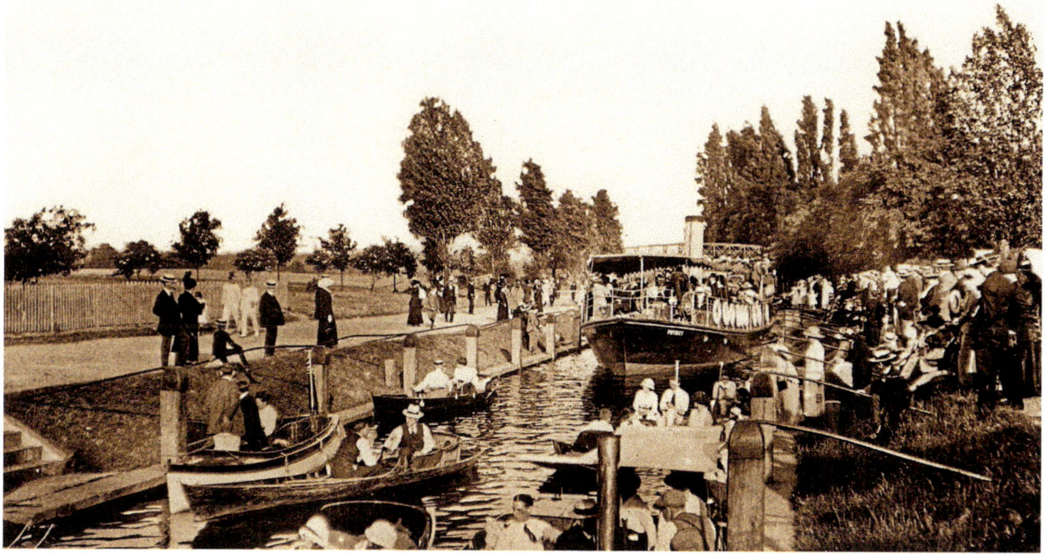

Teddington Lock

Remarkably few images show the Ham Lands, but they can be seen in this lively scene on the left-hand side of the picture. Archaeological finds from the Bronze Age have been found in this area. Although named Teddington Locks, they are positioned closer to the Ham bankside than that of Teddington. The original locks were constructed in 1811 but larger locks had to be built owing to the expanding number of rivercraft. The last phase of redevelopment of the locks was in 1904. Note the footbridge that can be seen in the distance. The current photo shows rivercraft are still popular.

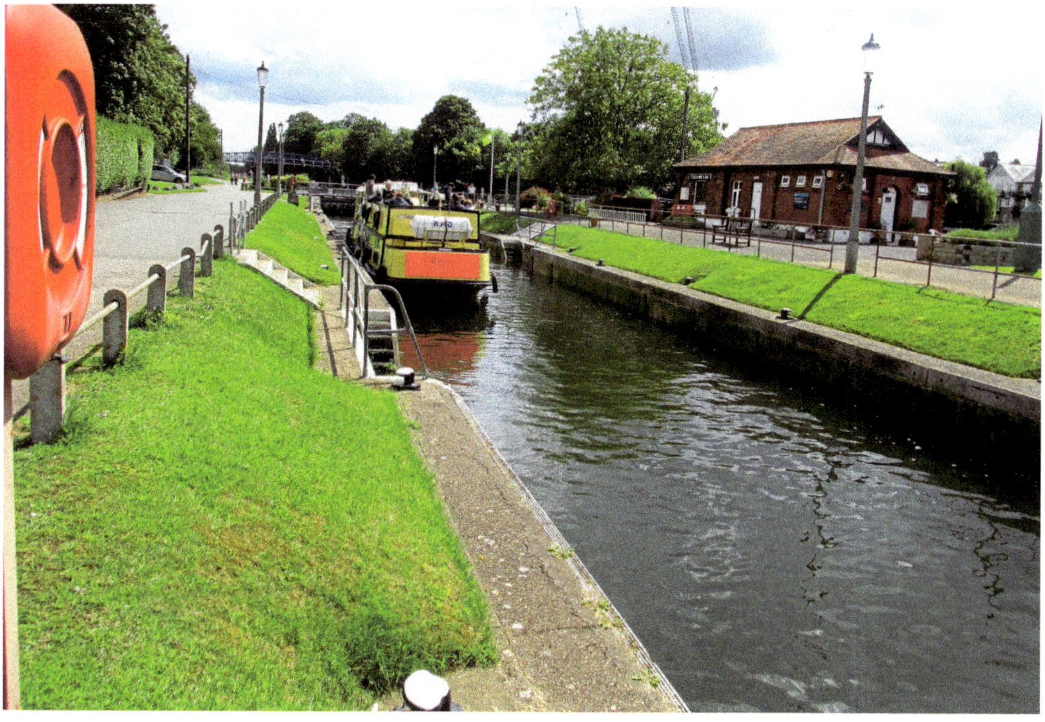

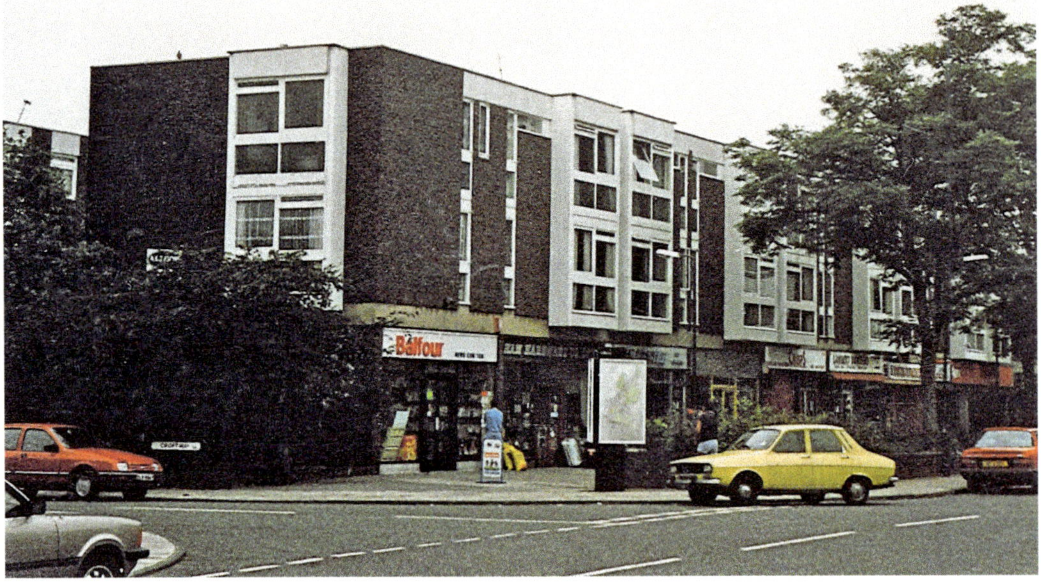

Wates Estate, Ham

Constructed on an area of former gravel pits, the Wates Estate covers around 60 acres and was developed from 1963 to 1968. Approximately 700 houses were built along with St Richard's Church, a school and the block of shops featured in this image. Although the estate laid out by Wates Built Homes Ltd is modern in design, it has good transport links as the bus connects local residents with Kingston and Richmond. Another benefit is that the beautifully unspoilt Ham Lands are close by, giving access to riverside and wildlife walks. Beautiful specimen trees can be found dotted around the estate, and open green spaces give the whole area character and shows how well it was planned.

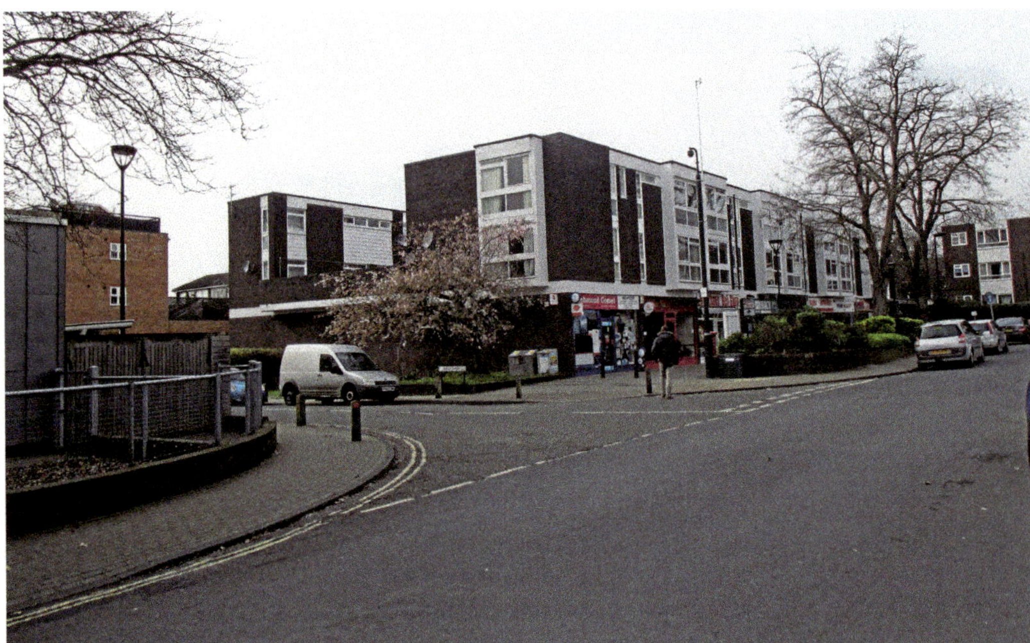

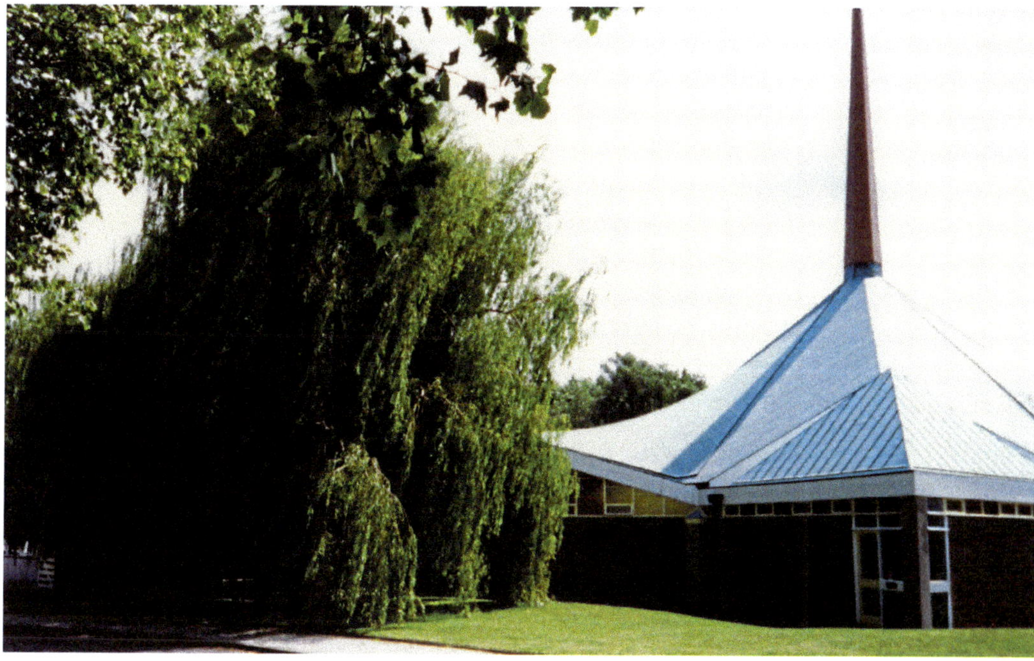

St Richard's Church, Wates Estate, Ham

Looking strikingly modern even by today's standards, St Richard's Church stands in the centre of the Wates Estate. Its remarkable geometric design represents the Star of David. At first, local residents were quite shocked by its ultra-modernism, but most now see it as a bold architectural statement. It was consecrated in 1966 by the Archbishop of Kingston. Covell, Matthews & Partners were the architects and the initial cost was £22,000. The current photograph shows that the weeping willow tree has now gone but the architecture still surprises.

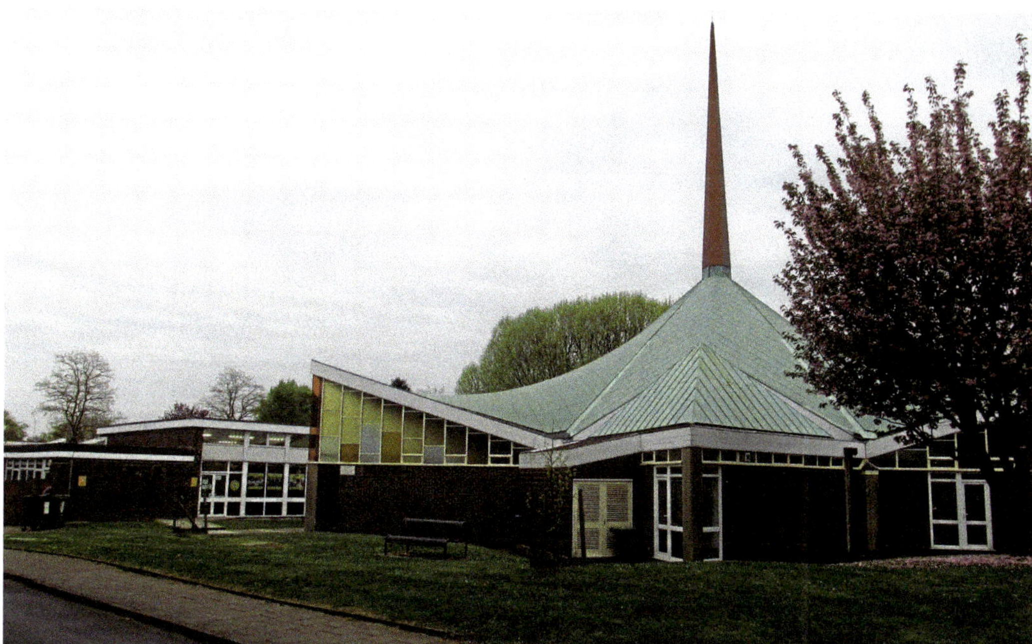

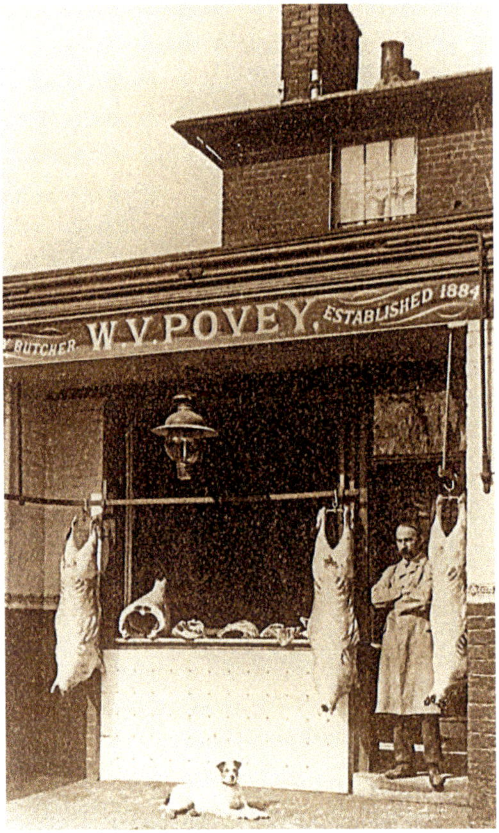

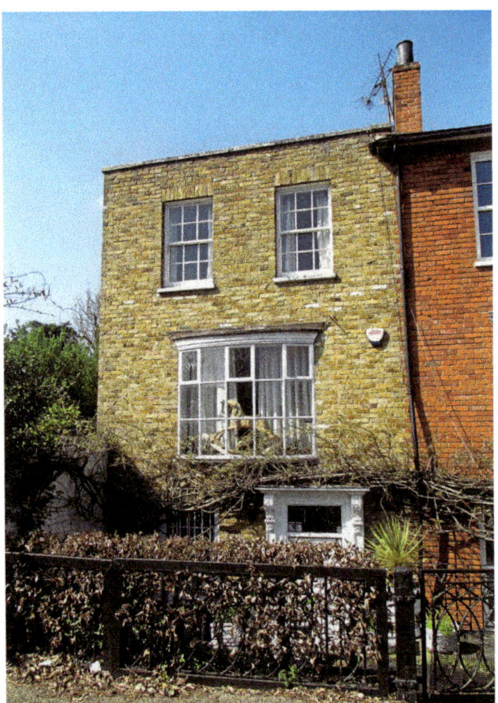

W. V. Povey, Petersham Road, Ham

Before the retail outlets in the Upper Ham Road were established, Ham did not have many shops in the village, apart from Mr Sibley, a cobbler in Ham Street. The only row of useful shops were the ones roughly opposite Sudbrook Gardens. These consisted of Mr Povey, a family butcher (featured here); a shoe repairer; a grocer; post office; and a baker. The original photo shows Mr Povey and his dog Toby around 1900. Note the sign above the shop saying that it was established in 1884. Povey is listed in the 1930 Kelly's Directory at No. 343 Petersham Road. As can be seen in the current photograph, the former butcher's shop is now a private residence.

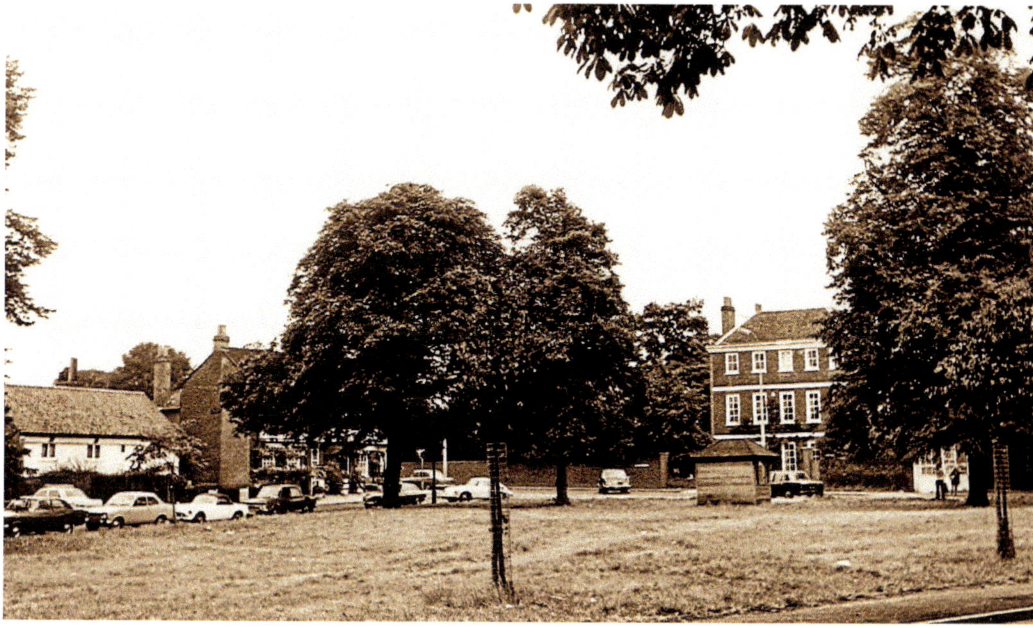

Sudbrook Lodge, Petersham Road

When Sudbrook Lodge was built in the early seventeenth century the current road from Richmond to Kingston did not exist. The old road, which ran along Sudbrook Lane before curving on towards Kingston, was the main thoroughfare right up until the 1730s. Therefore the house was far more secluded than it appears today. The lodge is shown on the right-hand side of the image, with the New Inn shown on the left. The earliest resident that can be traced was Mr Thomas Hunt, a timber merchant who died in 1625 leaving the house to his daughter Elizabeth. Richard Wigington, a wealthy merchant, owned the property until his death in 1650 when his wife Elizabeth acquired it. The Countess of Catherlough lived here from 1764 to 1767. During the Second World War author Sir Compton Mackenzie lived here.

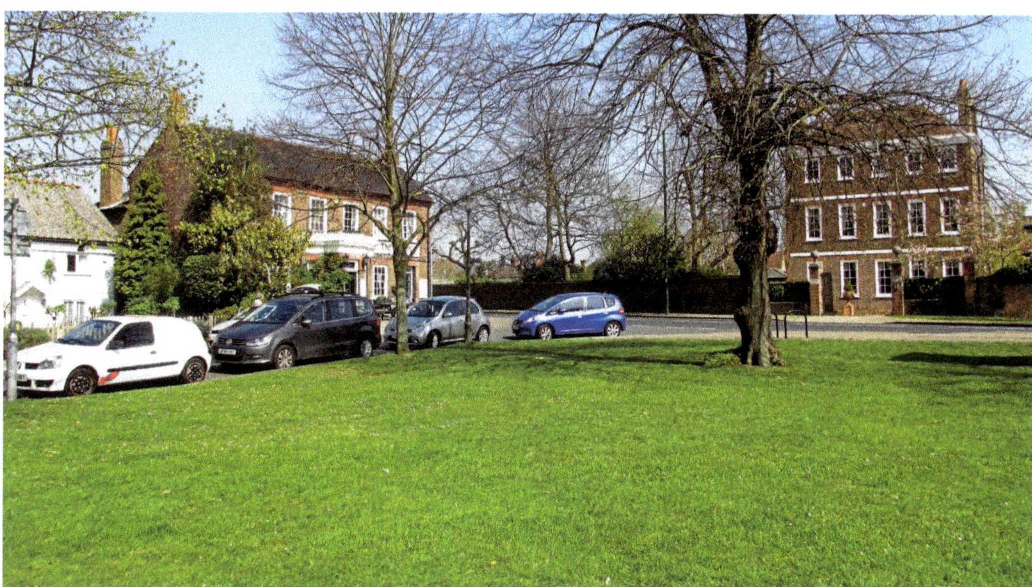

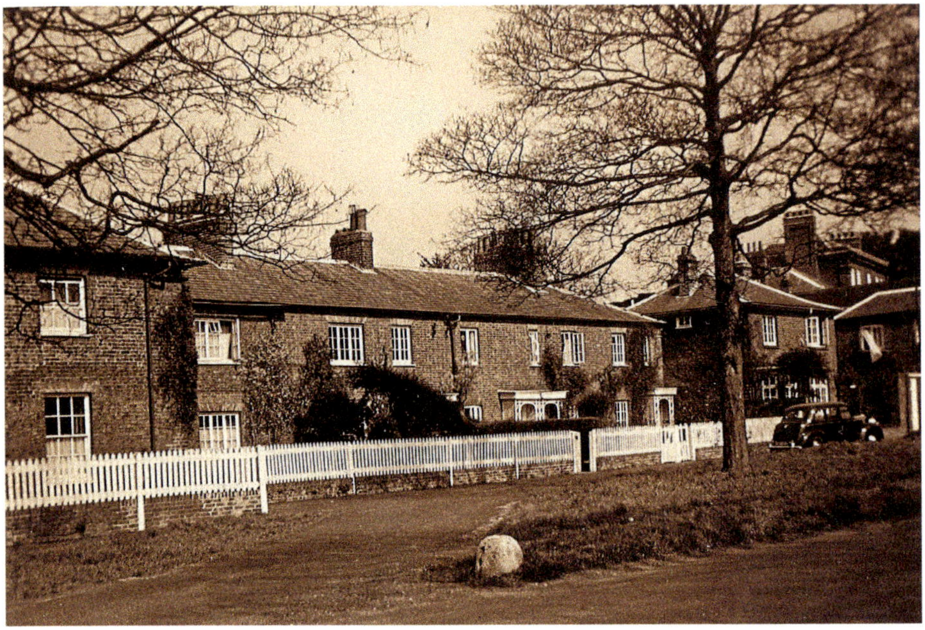

Sudbrook Cottages, Ham Gate Avenue

The Earl of Dalkeith purchased the land on which the Sudbrook Cottages were subsequently erected in 1749. The old 'Farm House' was demolished and the cottages constructed – initially for the gardeners tending the kitchen garden of Sudbrook Park. The sale particulars of 1819, when Sudbrook Park was auctioned, describe the properties as 'a gardener's house and five tenements brick built, pleasantly situated upon Ham Common'. In more recent times, Beverley Nichols (1898–1983), famous author, created a magnificent garden in the rear of Sudbrook Cottage.

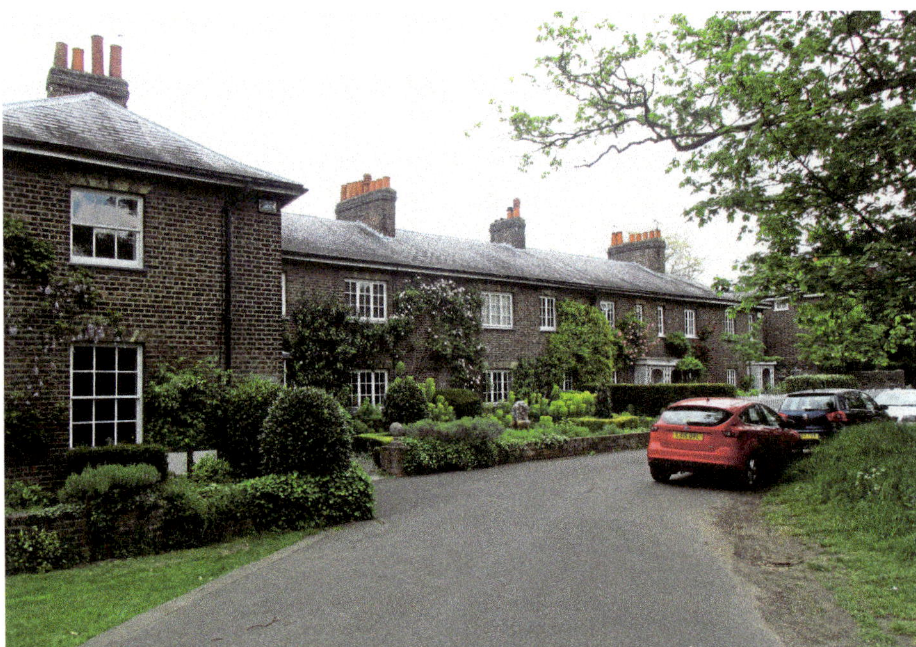

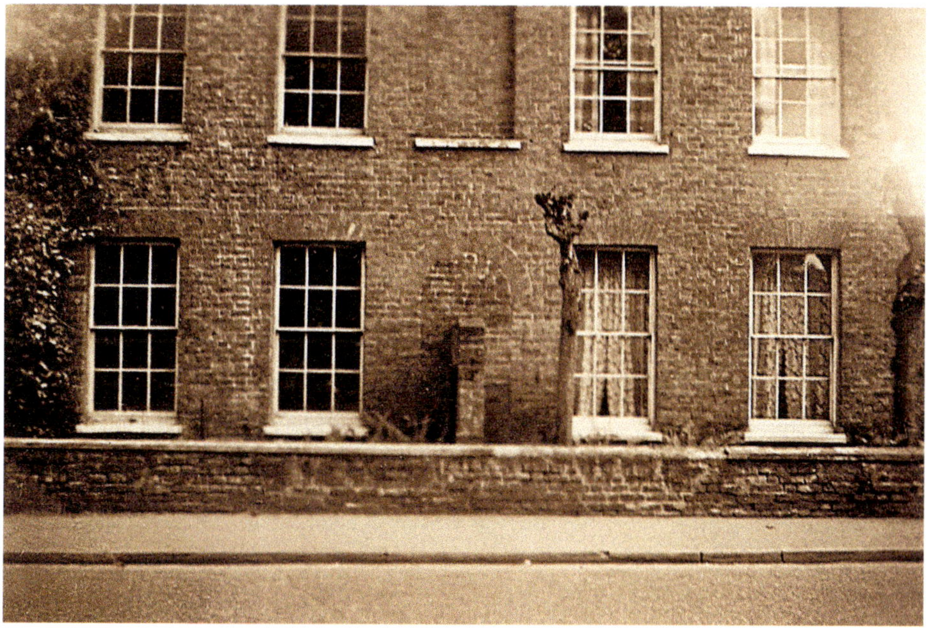

Ivy House, Upper Ham Road

There are actually three parts to this fine Georgian property situated in the Upper Ham Road. The main part of the house has been divided, the left-hand section being Ivy House, and the right-hand section being Ivy Cottage. Adjacent to this main block is Ivy House Cottage. All three are Grade ll listed. It will be seen that the original photo has been severely cropped so that only the two lower storeys are visible; however, in the modern photograph the whole building is depicted to give a better overall picture. Just discernible in the brickwork of the older photograph is a semicircular feature, below the bricked-up window.

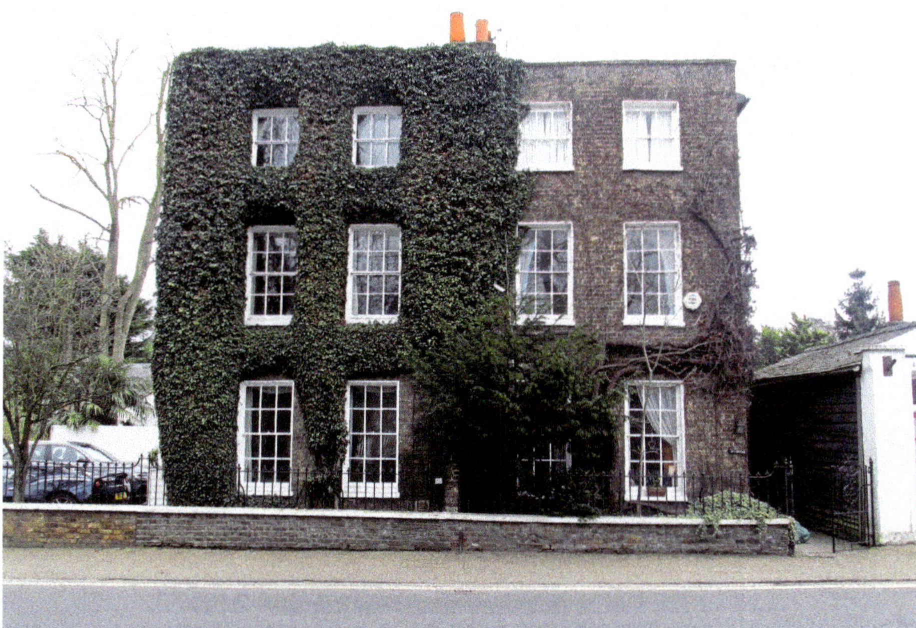

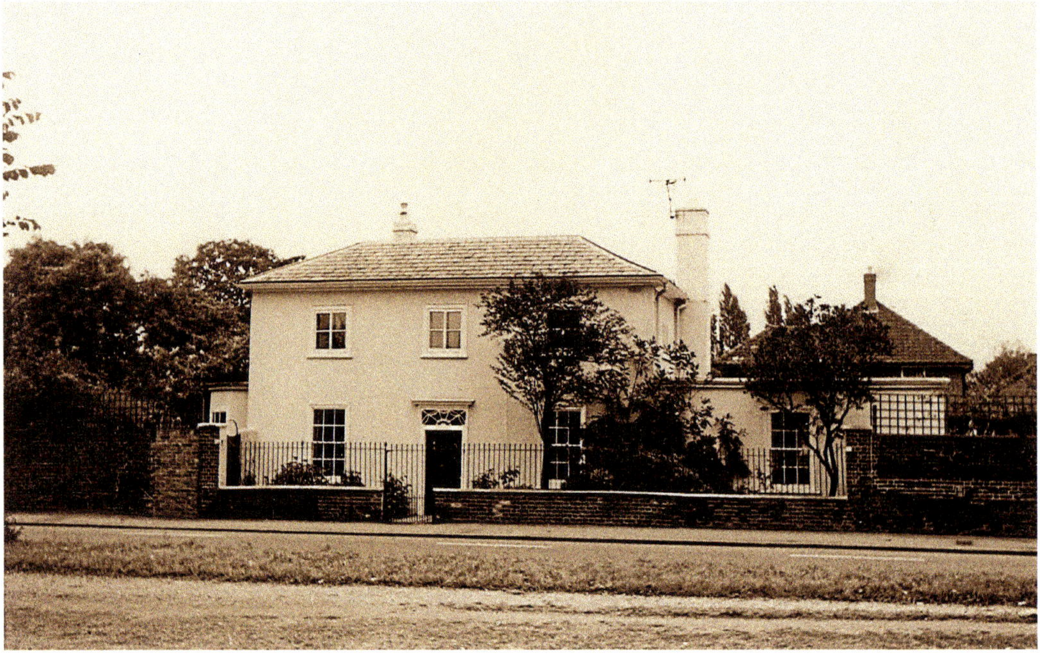

The Rosary, Upper Ham Road

John Denton, a carpenter, built Chestnut Cottage, later called The Rosary and now Fox House, in *c.* 1776. The Marchioness of Tweedale was an early occupant of the house, in 1778. Mrs Jordan (1761–1816), famous actress and mistress of the Duke of Clarence, is said to have stayed here. Other residents included a surgeon, Mr David, in 1824; Dr John Valentine Bridgeman, who lived here from 1829–46; Charles Edward Withall, from 1846–79; and Lord Chichester, in 1871. The house was renamed Fox House as Charles Fox once lived here. The house is well located, being on the main road between Kingston and Richmond.

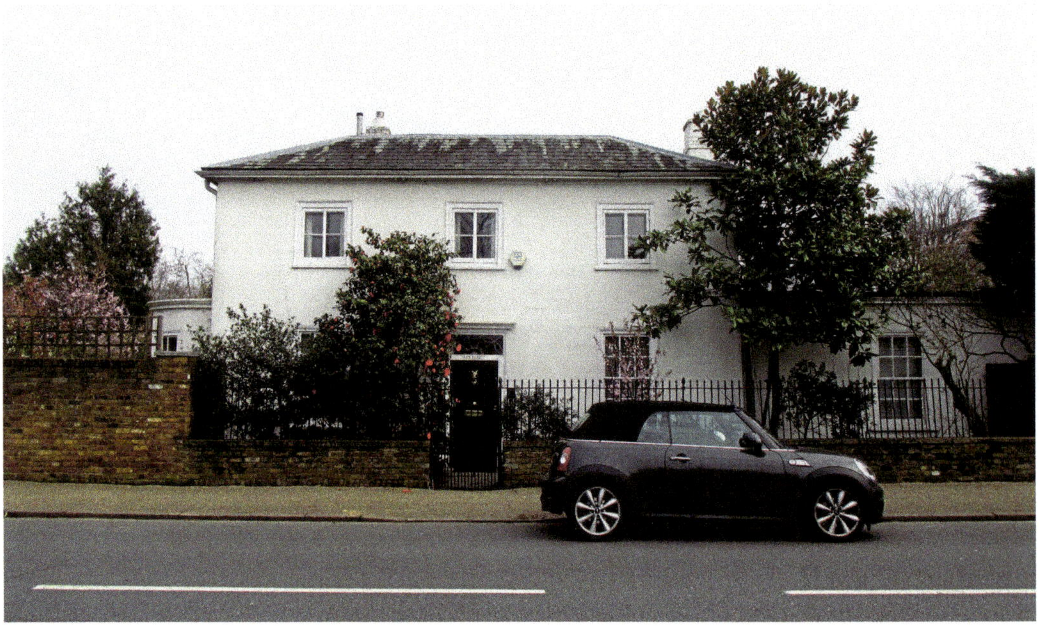

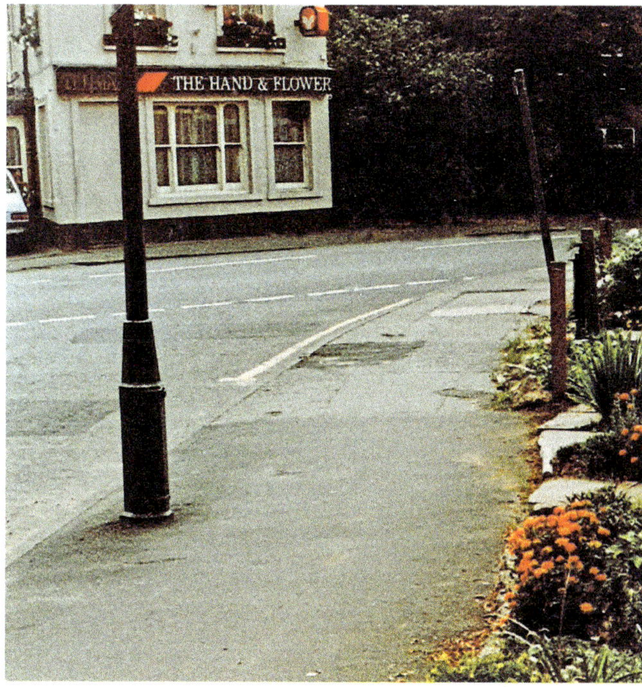

Hand & Flower Public House, Upper Ham Road

In 1861, Henry Barnett was the victualler of the Hand & Flower, this being when the property was first licensed. Before that it had been a beerhouse, although consensus varies as to the exact date of its origin. In 1871, George Timms was the publican with his wife Ellen; he was still there in 1881, but by 1891 his wife Ellen, then a widow, had taken over – she hired a potman, Edward Parrott, to help clear the tables. In 1911, Ernest Lord was the licensed victualler. The building is described as having four rooms. One of the two 'modern licensed premises' mentioned in the Ham and Petersham Estate Sale of 1949 was the Hand & Flower, the other being the Fox & Duck. This was because the Tollemache family, the Earls of Dysart, had owned these establishments. Note the Ham Amenities Group Garden on the other side of the road. The original photo was taken in 1982. In recent years the pub has included a dining room, which currently serves Thai food.

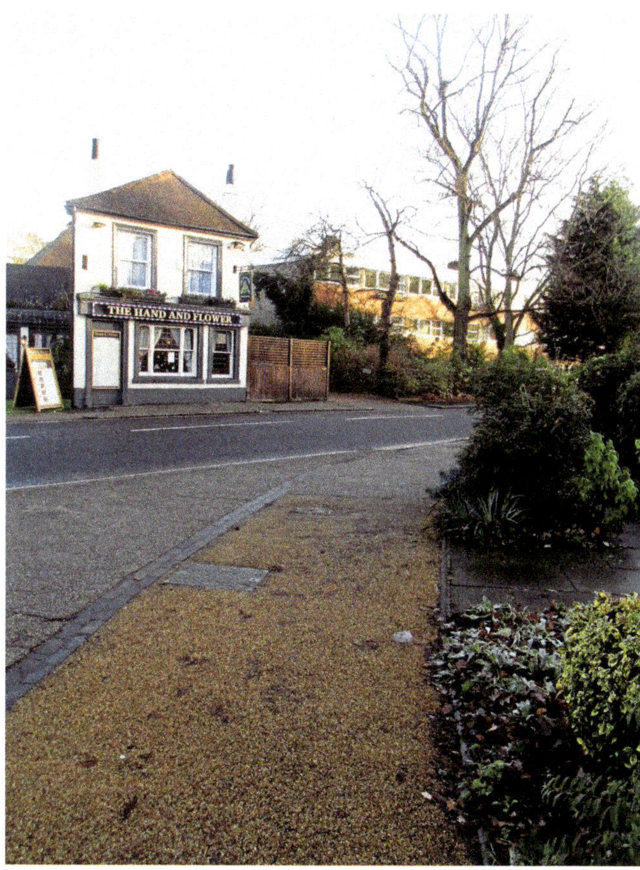

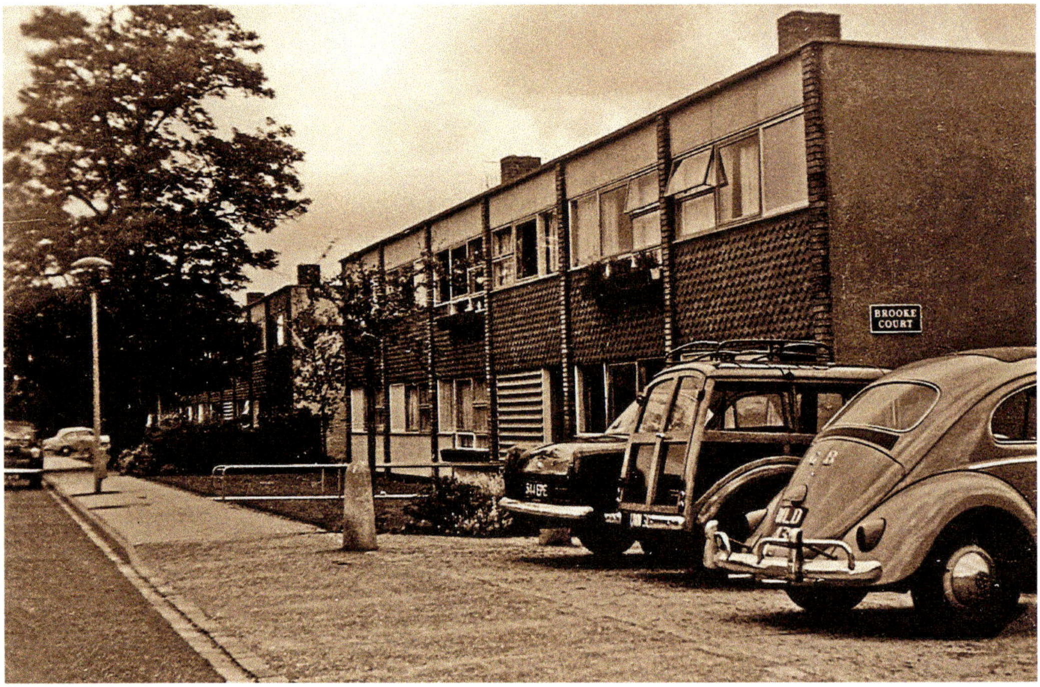

Parkleys, Upper Ham Road

Sir Eric Lyons designed the Parkleys Estate, the houses of which were constructed in 1954–56. It was praised by Nikolaus Pevsner, who described it as 'the most refreshing housing of the 1950s in Surrey'. It is now Grade ll* listed. All the courts are named after specific poets – twelve in total. It was built on the grounds of a former fruit farm and a large house called The Elms. Local historian Evelyn Pritchard lived at Parkleys. She wrote about early Victorian Ham and the street names of Ham and Petersham.

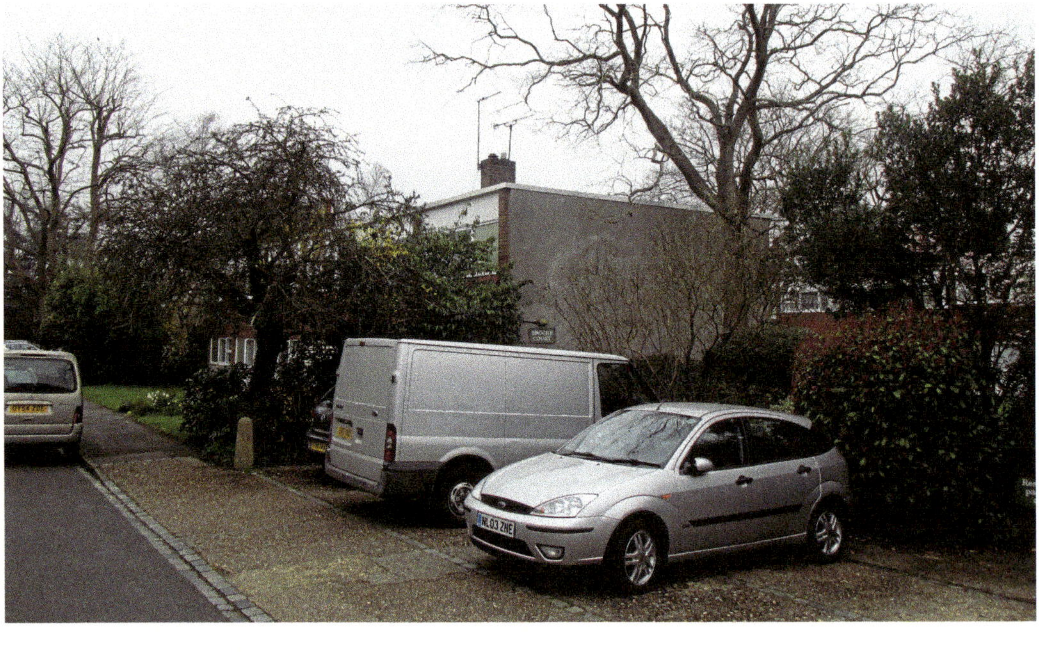

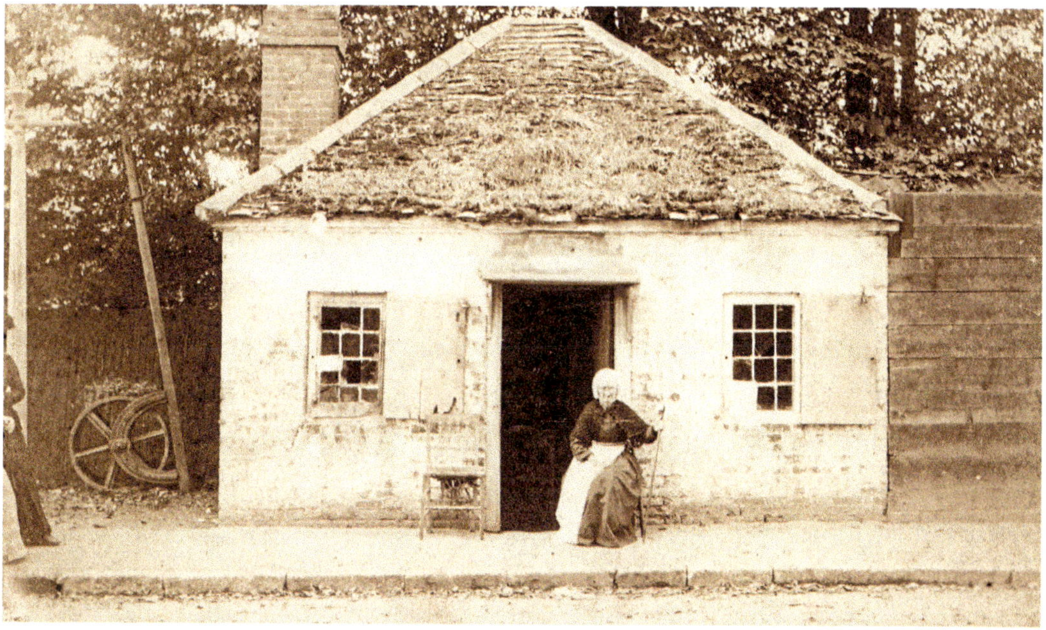

Gate House, Upper Ham Road

Sarah Morffew, known as Granny Morffew, lived in this gatehouse for forty years. She was reputed to have lived to the age of 104. She died in March 1892 and was buried in Ham churchyard. The Gate House was originally meant to be one of four small almshouses, one to be built at or near each of the gates on the common. Insufficient funds meant that only two were constructed – the companion gatehouse was on the east side of the Petersham Road, almost opposite to the New Inn but was later demolished. The vestry wanted to remove the Gate House in Kingston Road (now Upper Ham Road), but Mrs Algernon Tollemache financed the restoration of this house. The work was undertaken by Mr William Warner, a local builder. Several inscriptions can still be seen on the exterior of this building, which is now a 'Physio-extra'.

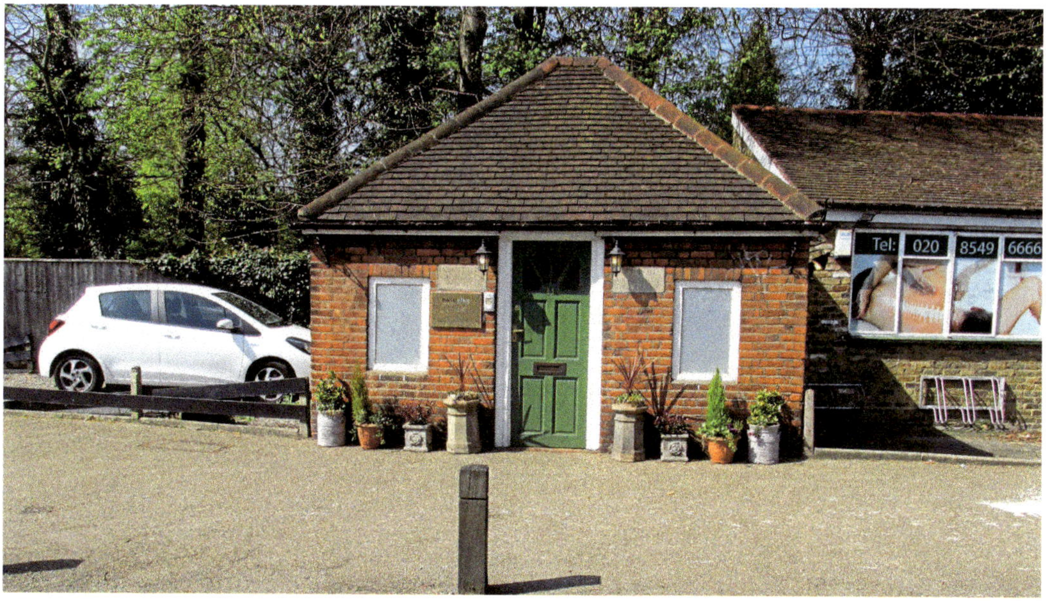

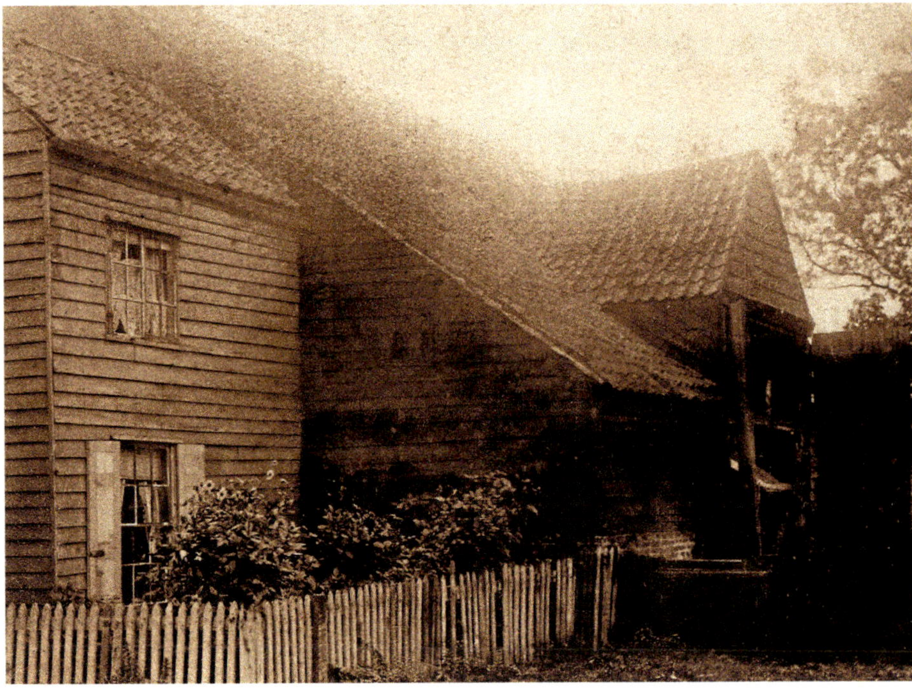

Ham Farm, Ham Farm Road

Ham Farm Road now stands as a reminder of the farm that once dominated this whole area. Just a short way along this road (which did not exist at the time) from Upper Ham Road stood the farmstead buildings. In the 1820s and 1830s, James Davis was the tenant, the land itself belonging to Lord Dysart. The farm later became known as Church Farm, as St Andrew's Church is situated not far away. The farm, mainly arable, covered 134 acres and extended eastwards beyond Latchmere Lane. To the west the fields abutted the Richmond Road. The farm has now gone and secluded residential houses now line Ham Farm Road.

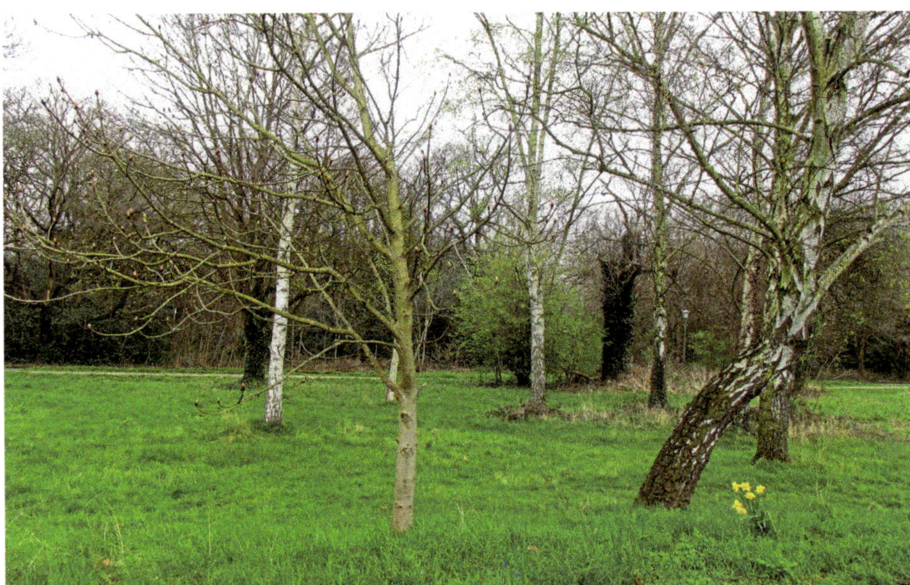

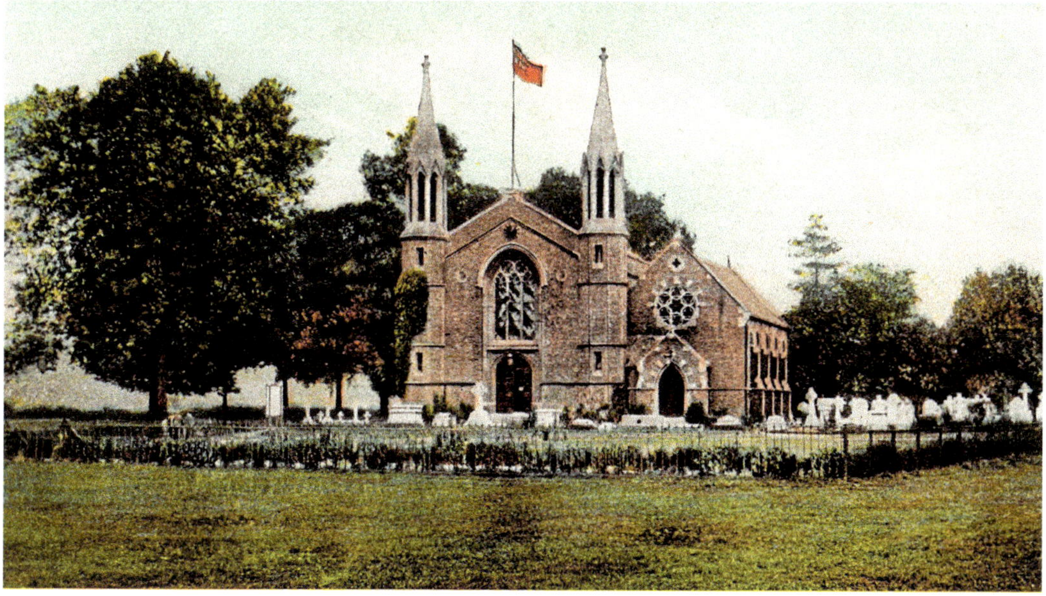

St Andrew's Church, Ham

Louisa, Countess of Dysart, gave permission for the church to be built on Ham Common, as she was herself one of the Common Commissioners. St Andrew's was constructed in a neo-Gothic style in 1831–32 by the architect Edward Lapidge. The church has two very fine eighteenth-century funeral hatchments, one to Sir Lionel Tollemache, 4th Earl of Dysart, dating to 1770 on the north wall, and one to Lady Grace Carteret, dating to 1755 on the south wall. The church also has eleven superb stained-glass windows and some fine wooden carvings. A beautifully painted ceiling in red and gold and designed by Bodley can also be admired.

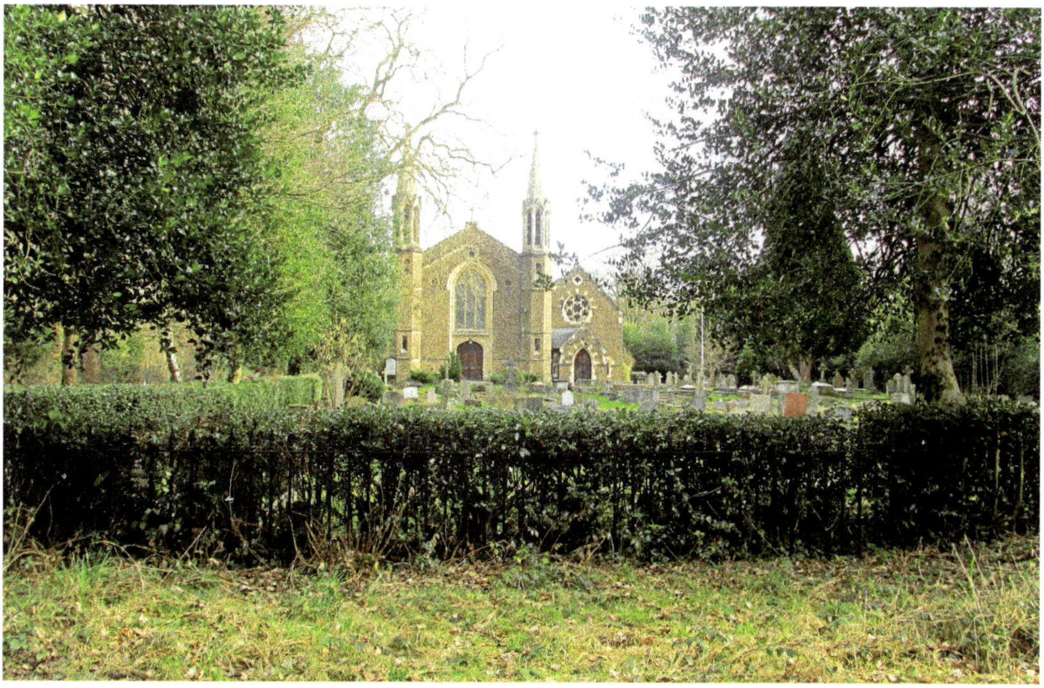

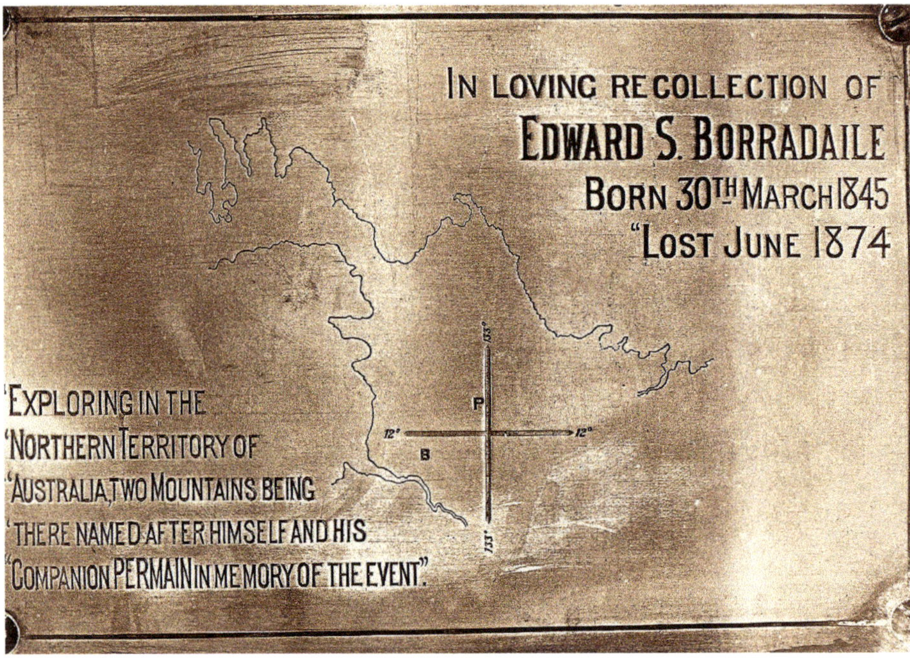

Edward Borradaile Plaque, St Andrew's Church

The most extraordinary brass plaque inside St Andrew's Church commemorates Australian explorer Edward Borradaile (1845–74), with family connections to Beaufort House in Ham Street. Borradaile and his companion Permain set off with Timor ponies from Port Darwin in the Northern Territories of Australia to explore the area around Port Essington. They were never heard of again and presumably died of starvation or thirst in the outback. Mr John Lewis searched for them but found nothing. However, even though their expedition was ill fated, both Borradaile and Permain have mountains named after them, so will never be forgotten.

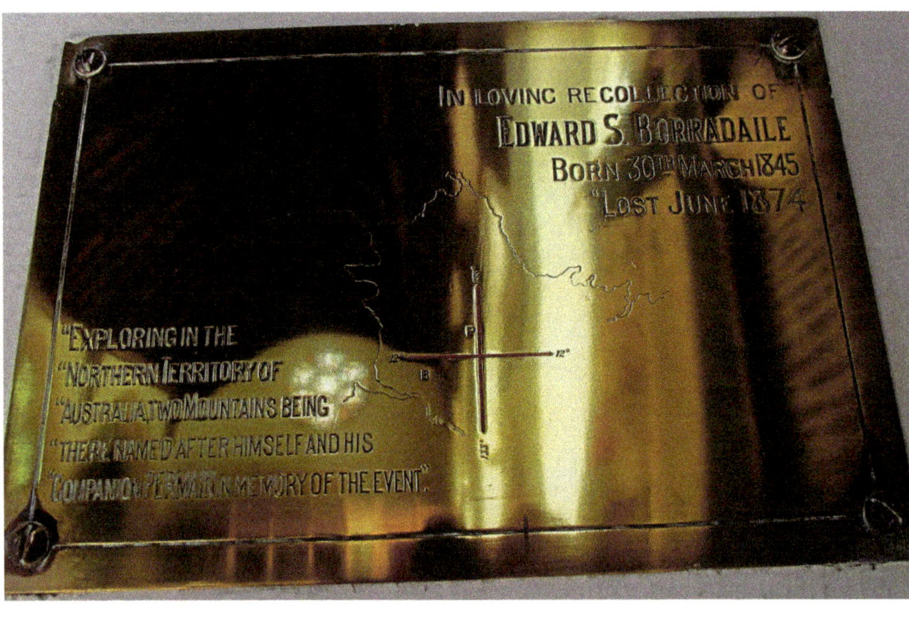

Lychgate, St Andrew's Church

The lychgate was built in 1908 as a memorial to Queen Victoria. In 1990, the gates were replaced with wood given by the superintendent of Richmond Park after the great storm of 1989. In 2005, the Victorian railings from the lychgate to the stable were replaced. The churchyard has some notable people buried in it: Hesba Stretton, novelist; Sarah Morffew, who resided at Toll Gate House in Ham; and Violet Hyacinth Bowes-Lyon, the eldest sister of HM Queen Elizabeth The Queen Mother, who died at the age of eleven from diphtheria. She was staying at Forbes House in Ham at the time of her death with her grandmother, Mrs Scott.

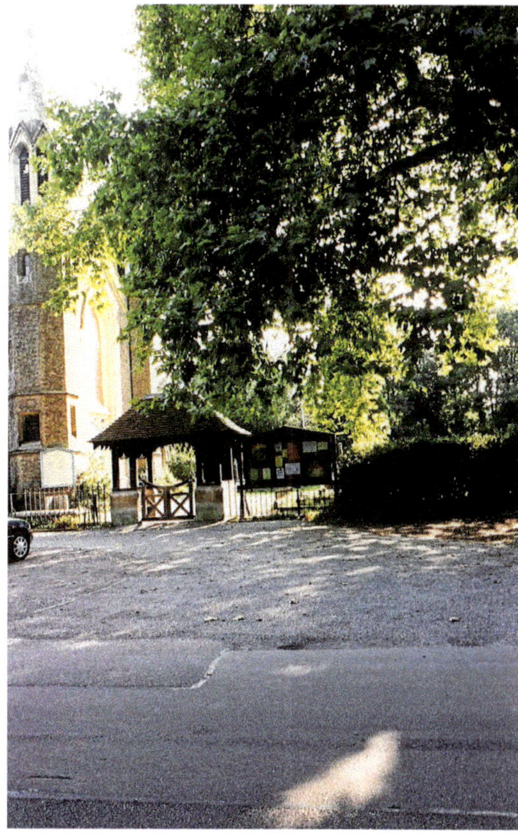

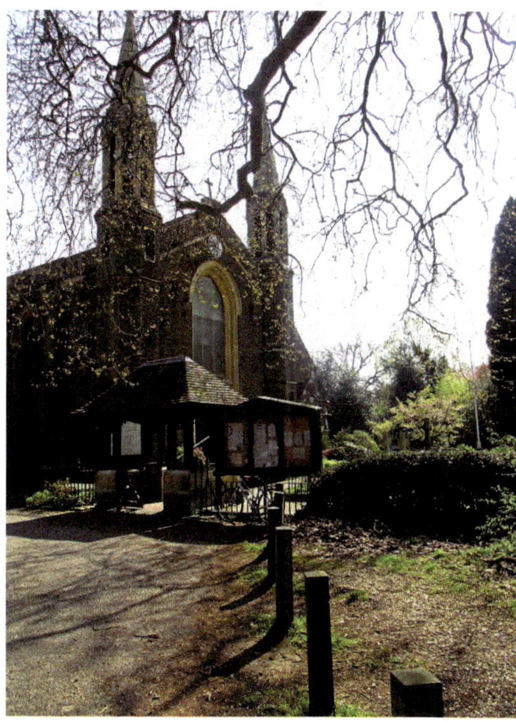

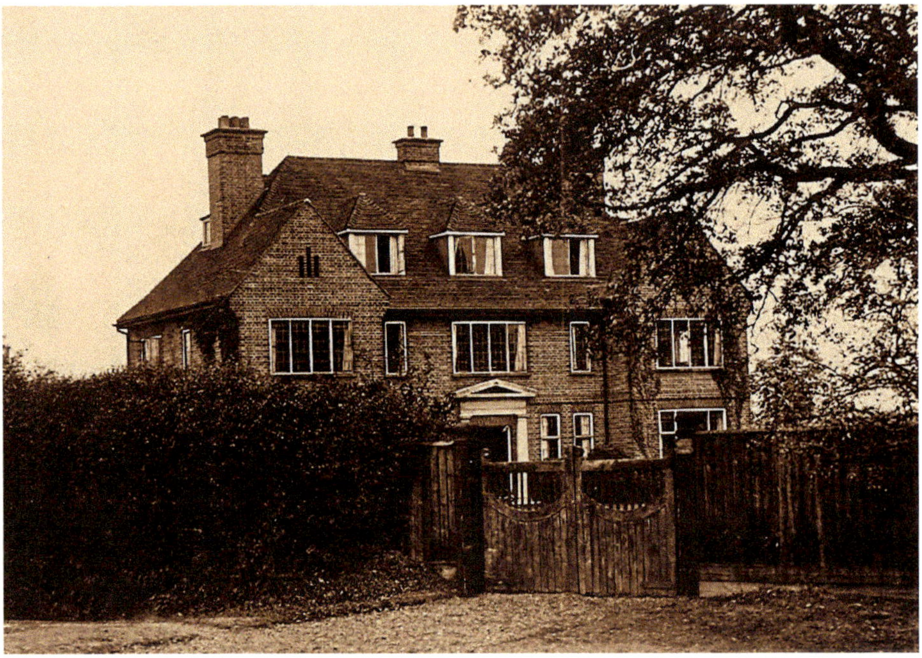

Hollybush House, Church Road

Originally called Hollybush Corner, the house was built in 1915 in a neo-Georgian style. Dr Arthur Shadwell was the first tenant; he remained in residence until 1933. The house was owned by the Earl of Dysart, who rented it to tenants until the Ham and Petersham Estate Sale of 1949 when it was bought by Mr Alexander McLeod Symington. He then sold it to Margaret Bramwell in 1953. It was at this time that the name was changed to Hollybush House. The property is situated in a quiet secluded road and has a sizeable garden of just over an acre.

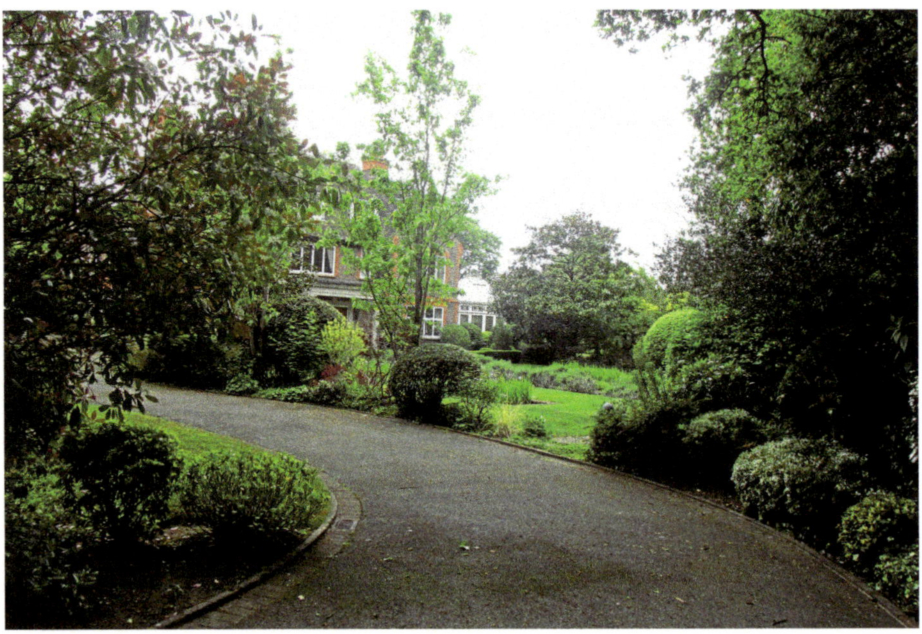

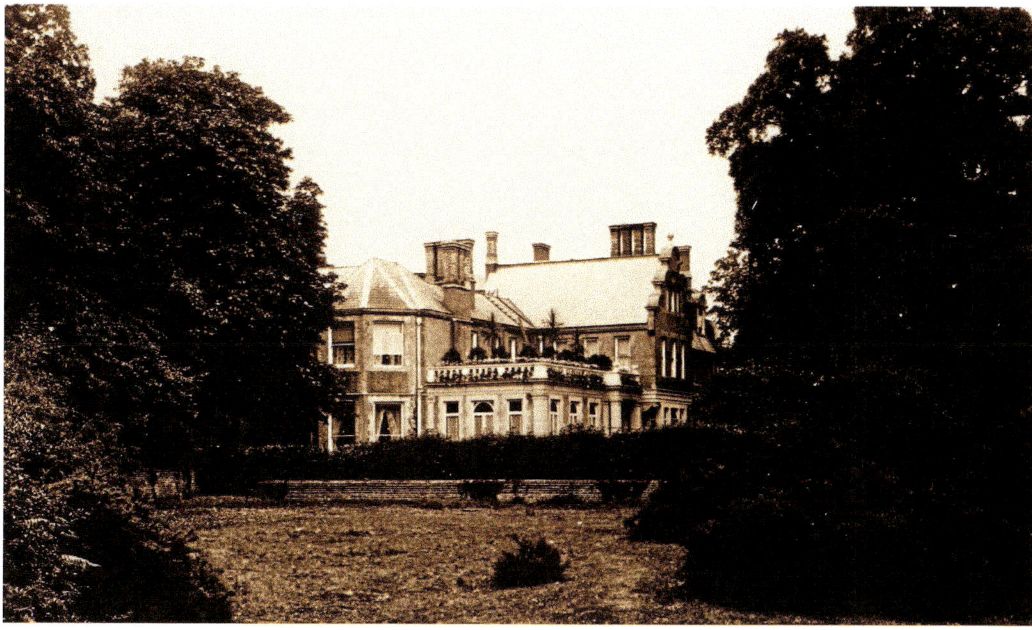

Latchmere House, Church Road

Originally a private residence, Latchmere House can be identified on a tithe map of 1842 when it was occupied by Mr George Shum Storey. In 1860, Captain William Barron lived here and, in 1867, James Spencer Pomeroy, 6th Viscount Harberton (1836–1912), a classical scholar. During the First World War it functioned as a hospital for officers suffering from shell shock. In the Second World War it became a detention and interrogation centre known as Camp 020. William Joyce (known as Lord Haw Haw) was detained here. In 1948, it became a young offender's institution, which closed in 2011. The site was sold to Berkeley Homes in 2013 and, as can be seen in the current photograph, has now been converted to luxury apartments.

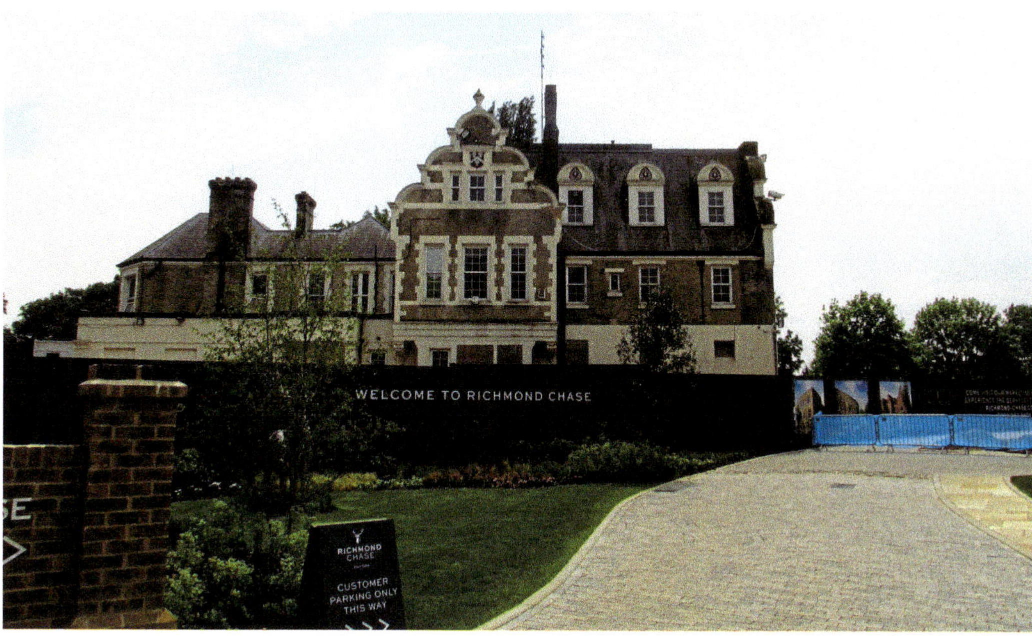

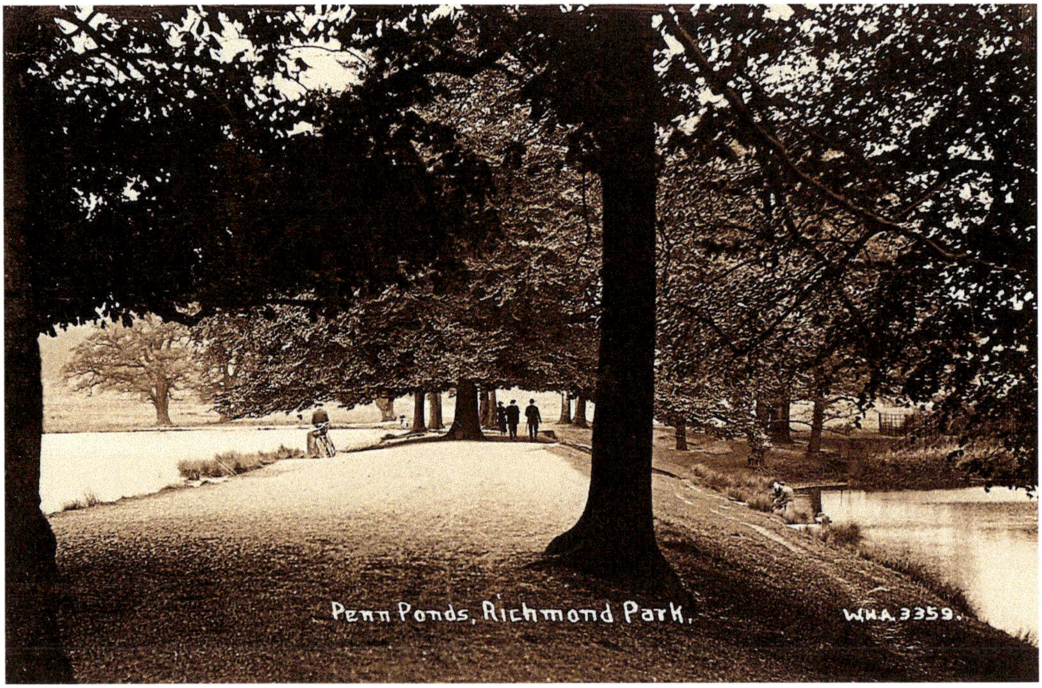

Pen Ponds

The Ham parish boundary used to run across the smaller of the two Pen Ponds, pictured here on the left-hand side. During the annual Beating of the Bounds ceremony, one of the stronger boys would be required to swim across the pond. The parish boundary extended as far as Robin Hood Gate and much of Richmond Park actually came under Ham at one time. The pond's original function was to keep elvers (young eels). They are thought to date back to the time of Princess Amelia, who was a daughter of George ll. The ponds are still a popular spot for visitors today.

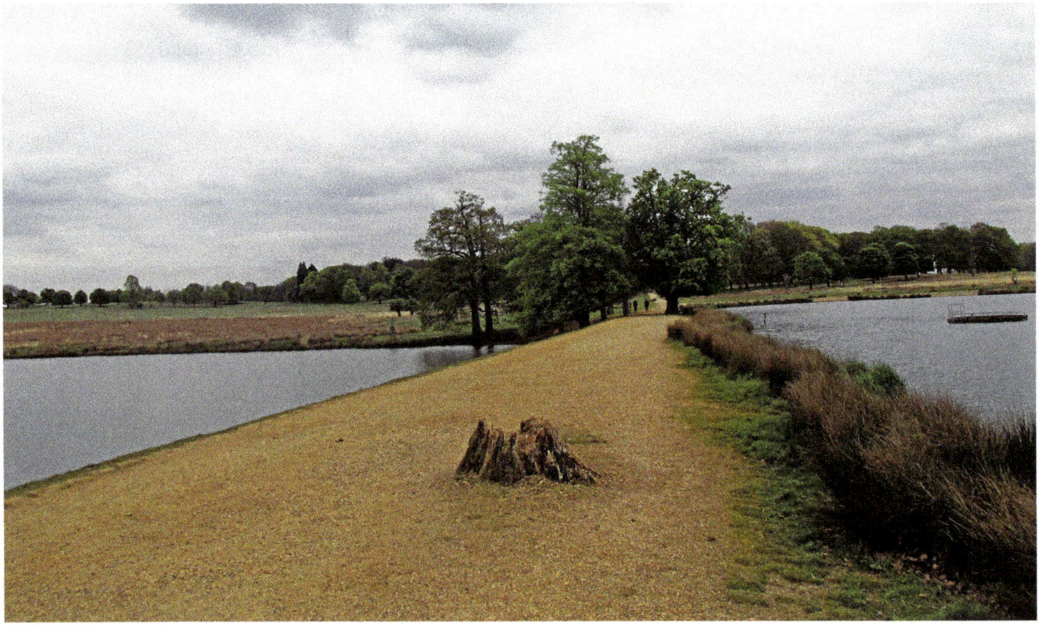

PETERSHAM

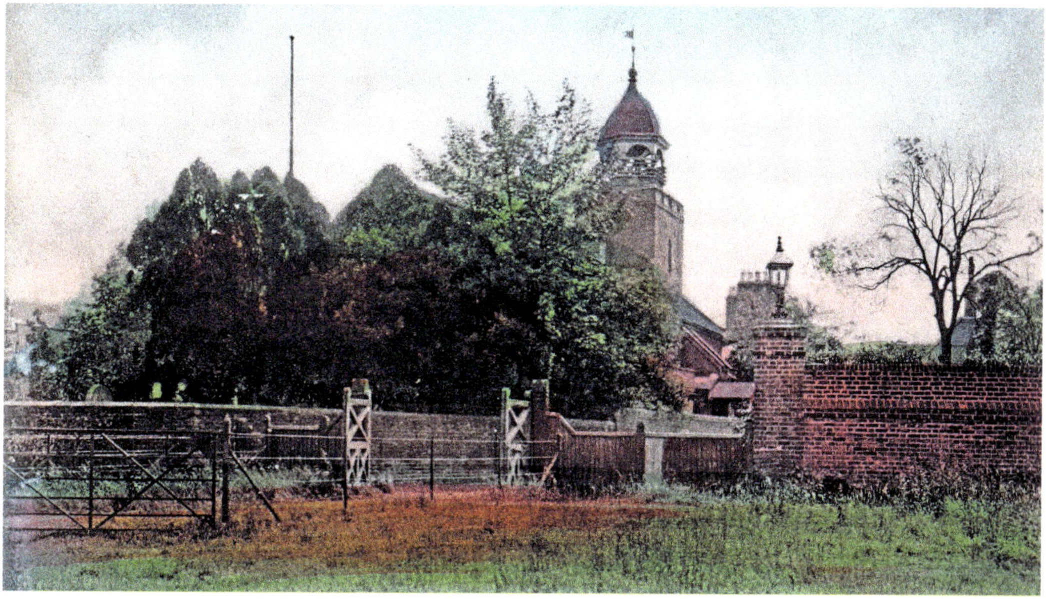

St Peter's Church, Petersham

'Ibi ecclesia', meaning 'there is a church', appears in the entry for this hamlet in the Domesday Survey of 1086, which indicates that this church probably dates back to the Saxon period. The oldest remaining part of the church survives from the thirteenth-century chancel. The church was rebuilt during the Georgian period and has some original box pews from this time. The curacies of Petersham were joined with Kew and were only separated in 1885. The vicar of St Peter's in 2017 is the Revd Canon Tim Marwood.

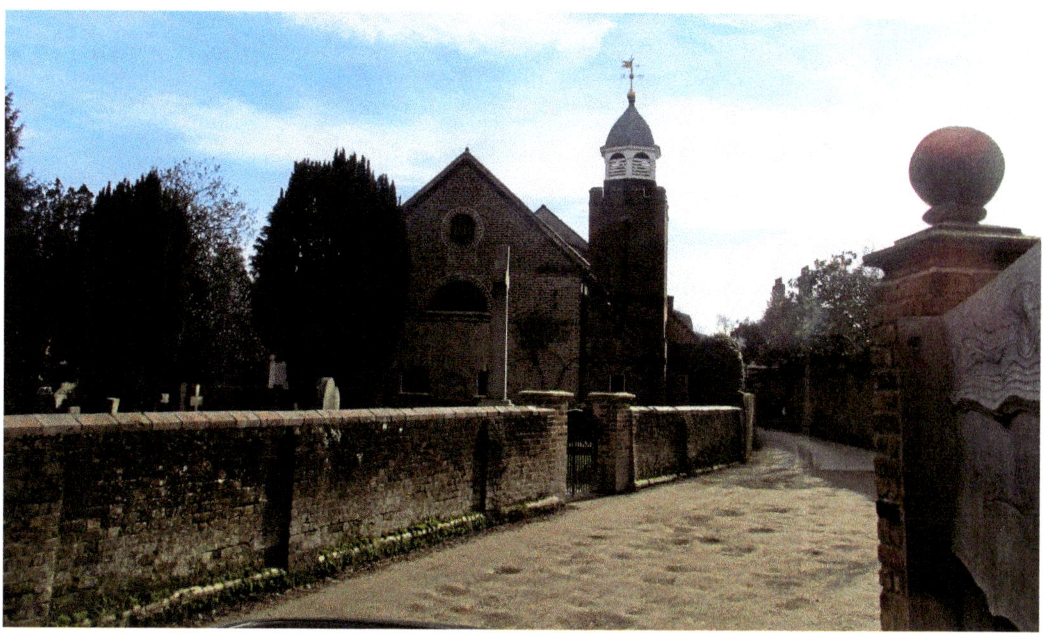

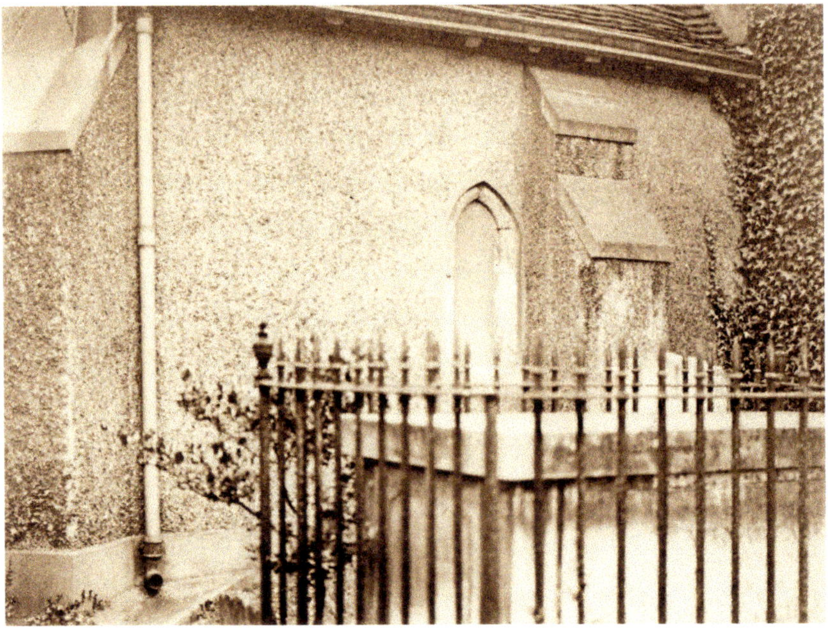

Chancel Window, St Peter's Church

The oldest surviving parts of the church, including this blocked-up thirteenth-century lancet window, are from the chancel that was built in 1266 and which remain as part of the fabric of the later chancel of 1505. The north-facing exterior of the chancel was re-rendered in 2016 with traditional lime render, replacing an earlier non-permeable material. The brickwork uncovered during the 2016 works is recorded on the Historic England website. Inside the chancel is the imposing Cole monument, which shows George Cole, the Tudor Lord of the Manor, and his wife in Elizabethan dress.

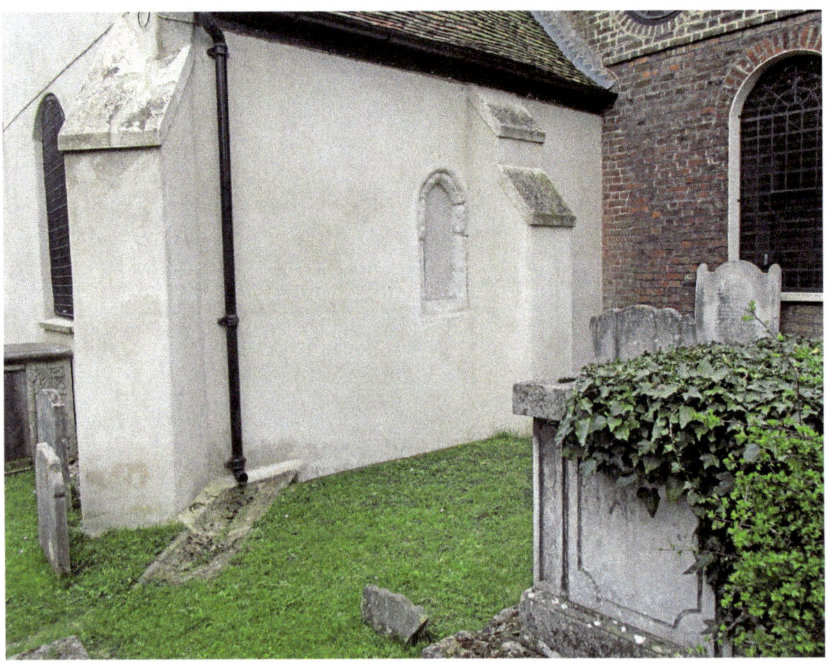

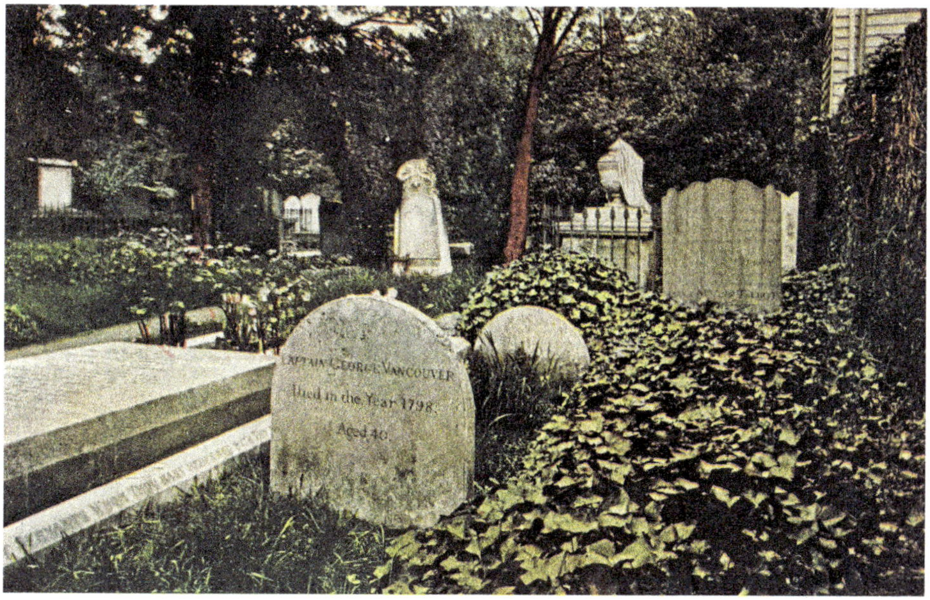

Vancouver's Grave, St Peter's Churchyard

Captain George Vancouver (1757–98), famous navigator, resided in Petersham at Glen Cottage in River Lane, near to the church where he is now buried. He died tragically young at the age of forty on the 10 May 1798 at the Star and Garter Hotel. Vancouver was well known for his explorations of Alaska and British Columbia. His headstone originally faced in the opposite direction. This is the most visited grave in the churchyard; there is even a sign by the main entrance to direct visitors. The latest restoration to his memorial was in 2013.

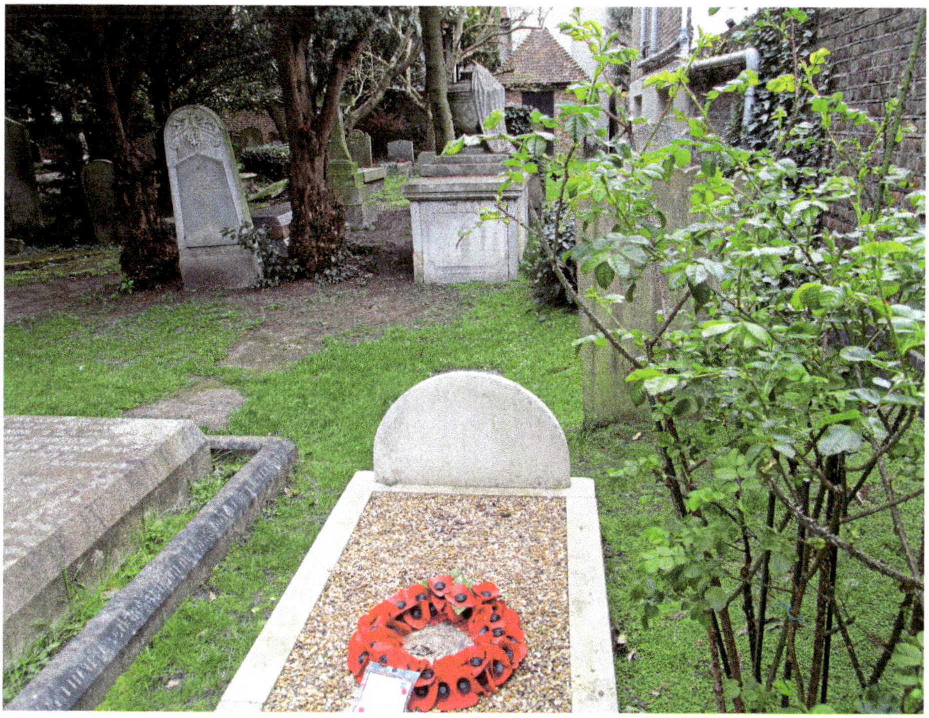

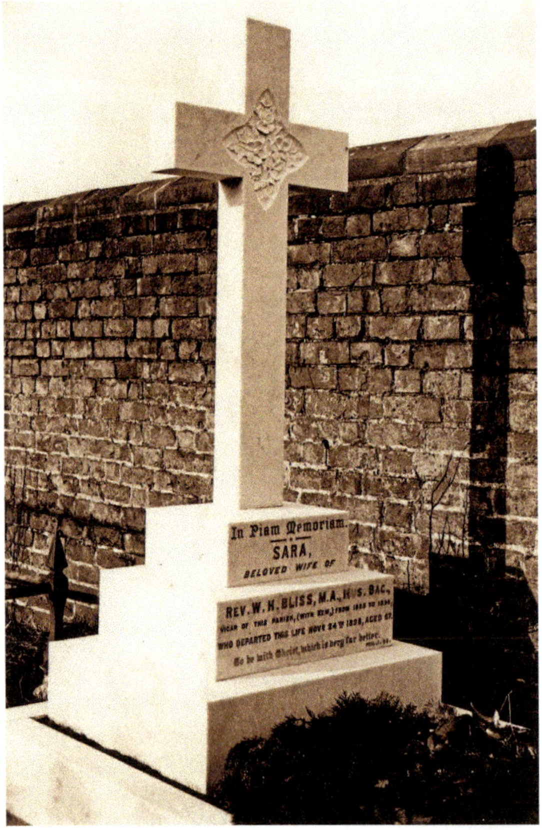

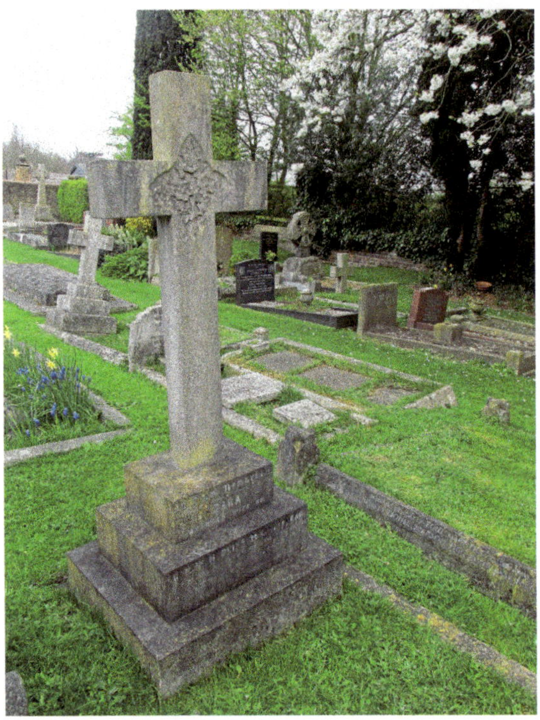

Memorial to Revd William Henry Bliss, St Peter's Churchyard

Under the Kew and Petersham Vicarage Act of 1890 William Henry Bliss ceased to be the vicar of Petersham; however, he continued as the vicar of Kew until 1915. He died in 1919 at Windsor. He had a distinguished career, being an honorary chaplain to Queen Victoria from 1874 to 1876 and chaplain in ordinary from 1876 until Victoria's death in 1901. He was then appointed honorary chaplain to King Edward VII. The current photograph shows that his gravestone has been moved from its original position and is quite weathered in comparison to the older image.

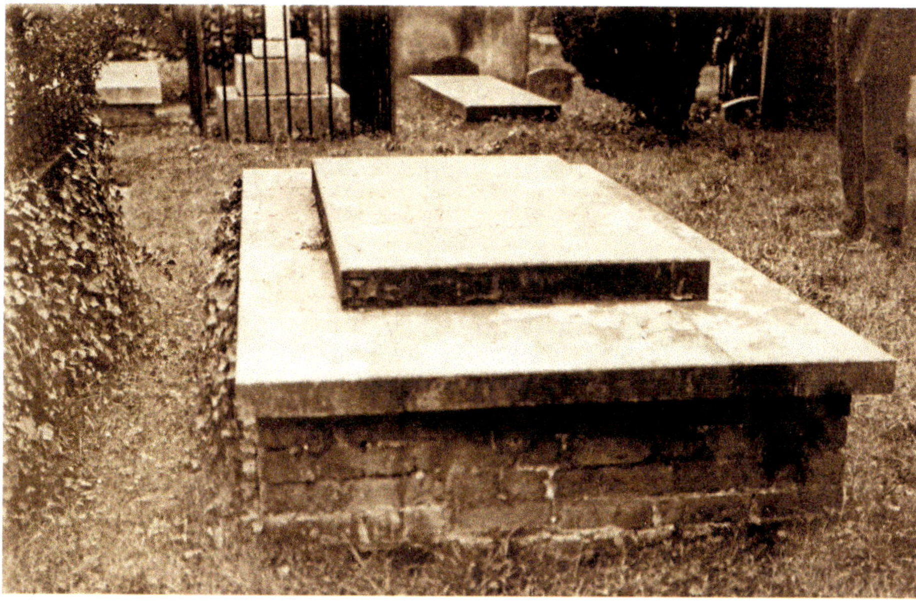

Richard Crisp's Tombstone, St Peter's Churchyard

The author of *Richmond and Its Inhabitants from the Olden Times* (1866), Richard Crisp (1813–73), was also the collector of the water rate for Richmond, a post he held following his retirement from business. He received only £50 from the publication of his book on Richmond – he used the money to buy a diamond ring for his wife, which was inherited by his granddaughter, Miss Marian Long. Crisp also contributed to Hiscoke's *Richmond Notes*. He assiduously collected the playbills of the old Richmond theatre, which eventually, after his death, passed into the possession of Mr Harry Crisp. It was reported that Mr Crisp's death in July 1873 cast quite a gloom over the town.

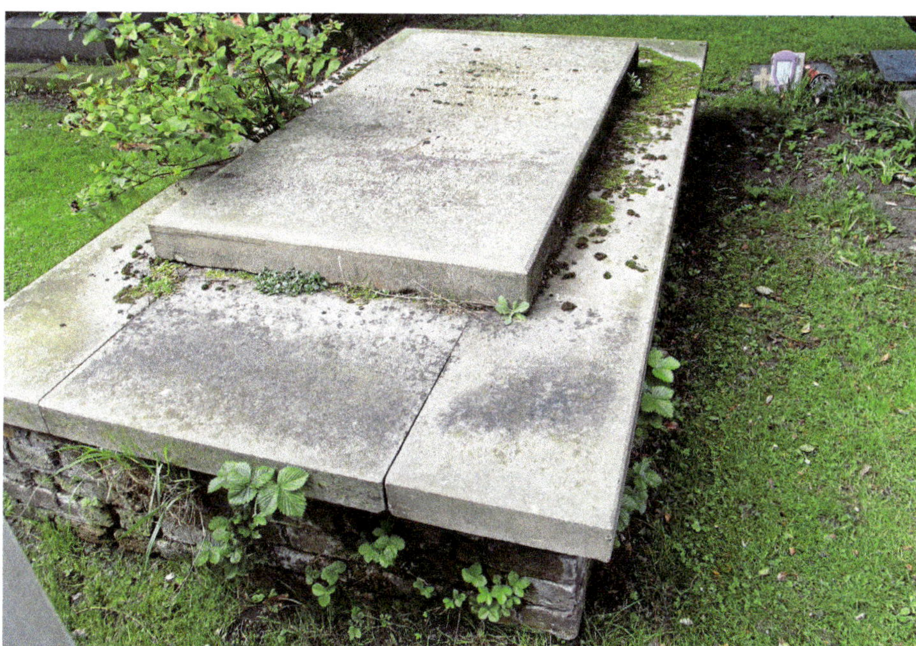

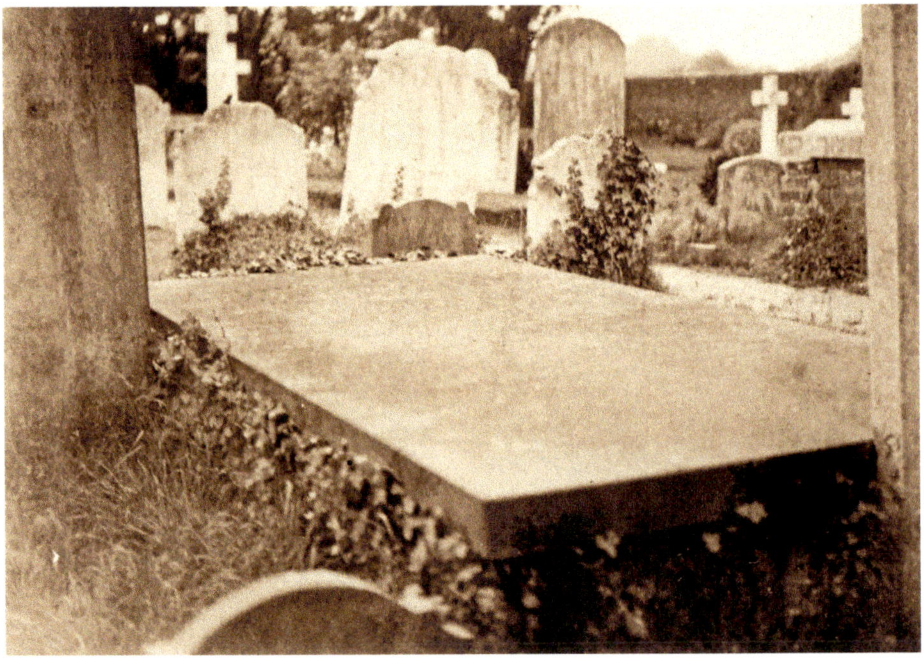

The Berry Sisters' Tombstone, St Peter's Churchyard

Horace Walpole, 4th Earl of Orford (1717–97), so valued the friendship of Mary and Agnes Berry that when he died he left them £4,000 each and Little Strawberry Hill House in Twickenham. After his death, Mary Berry published the *Works of Horace Walpole* in five volumes. The sisters were both extremely talented. The inscription on their tombstone in St Peter's churchyard, written by the Earl of Carlisle, reads 'Mary Berry, born March 1763, died Nov 1852. Agnes Berry, born May 1764, died Jan 1852. Beneath this stone are laid the remains of these two sisters amidst scenes which in life they had frequented and loved, followed by the tender regret of those who close the unbroken succession of friends devoted to them with fond affection during every step of their long career.'

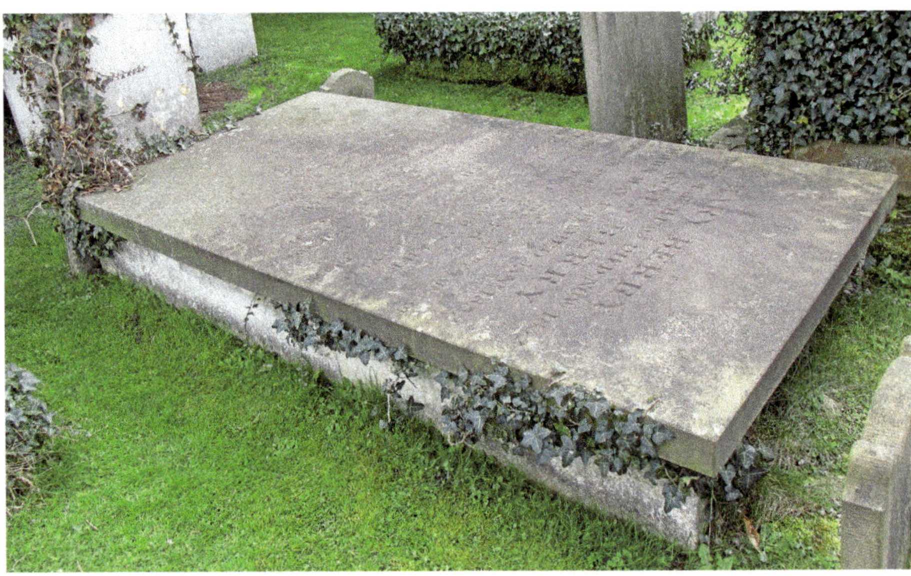

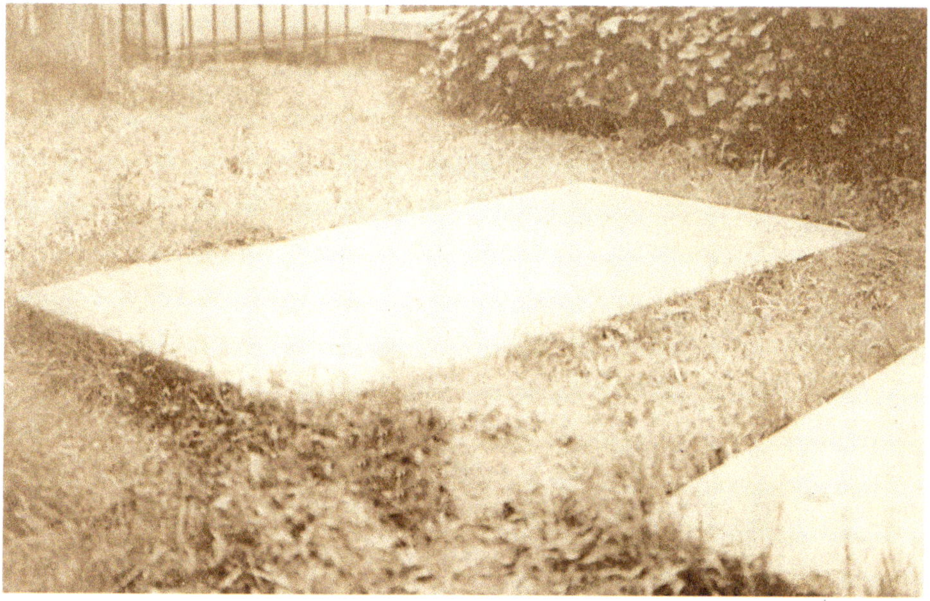

Theodora Jane Cowper's Tombstone, St Peter's Churchyard

Famous poet William Cowper (1731–1800) wrote personal and affectionate poems to Theodora Jane, addressing her as 'Delia'. They wanted to marry but, as they were cousins, Theodora's father absolutely refused permission. Their affection for one another can be seen not only in the poems and letters but in the objects given to William by Theodora, such as the seal ring with the head of Omphale, listed in the 1891 catalogue to the Exhibition of the Royal House of Guelph. Theodora was a resident of Richmond and died at the age of ninety on the 21 October 1824. The current photograph shows that only her name at the top of the grave slab is legible.

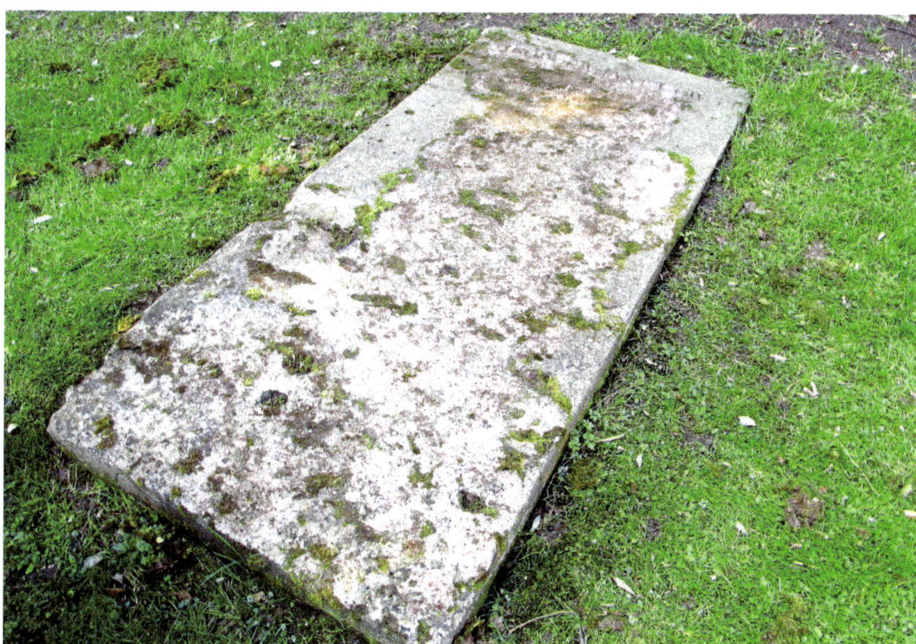

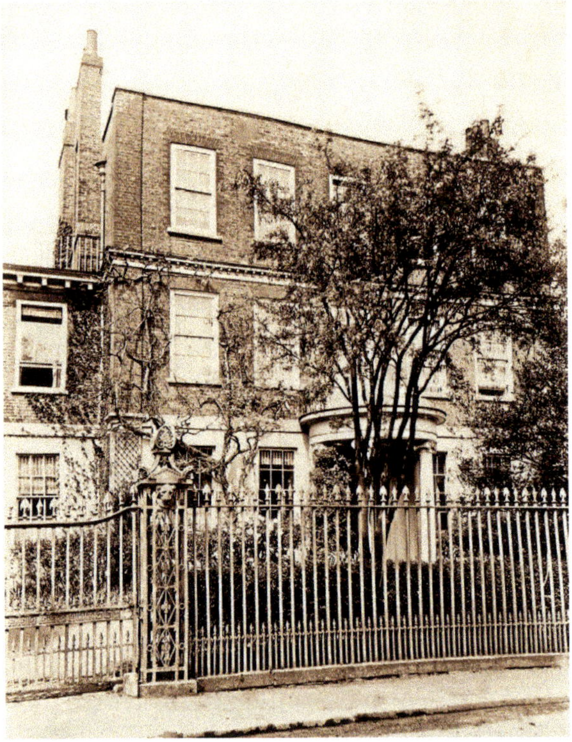

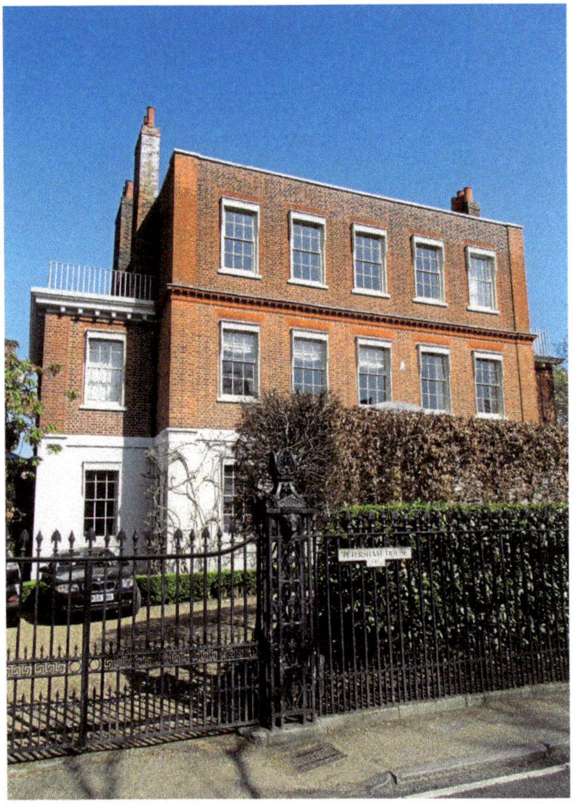

Petersham House, Petersham Road

The house dates to the late seventeenth century and is believed to have been built by Col Thomas Panton. His son, also called Thomas, sold it to Sir Henry Furnese, a member of the Drapers' Company. In 1750, Sir Robert Manners resided here and by 1770 the Duchess of Montrose had taken possession. By 1786 the ownership had passed to James Grieve. In 1898 Letitia Rachel Warde bought the property. The upper storey was a nineteenth-century addition, as was the semicircular porch, which adds a refined architectural touch to the building.

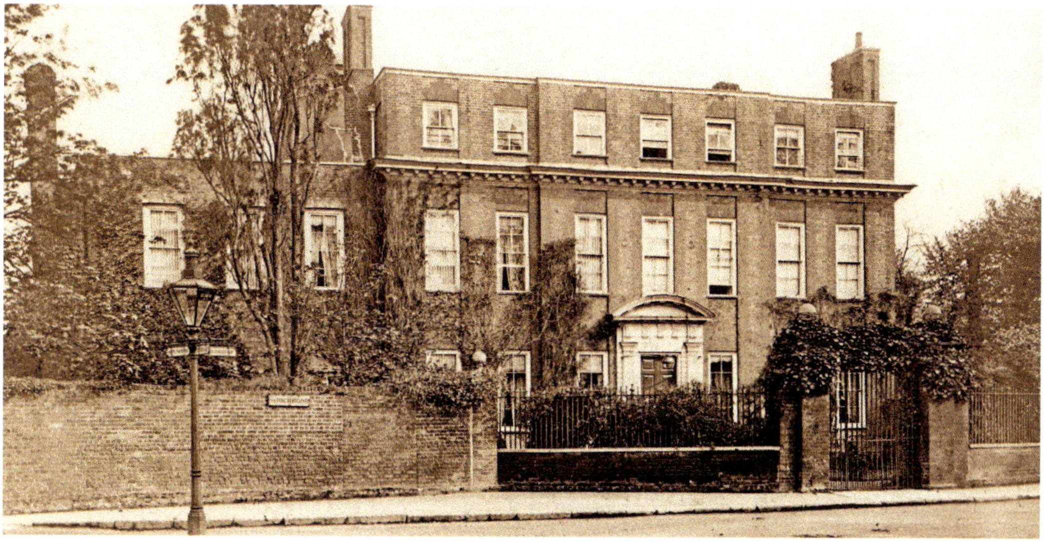

Rutland Lodge, Petersham Road

Sir William Bolton, a Lord Mayor of London, was responsible for having Rutland Lodge built in the seventeenth century. Other early residents were Sir John Darnell and his son, also named Sir John. The house was modified in 1720 when a wing and an upper storey were added. During this reconstruction a bell dated 1668 was found in the roof. After the Darnells' residency, the Duchess of Rutland lived here – hence the name was adopted for the house. Rutland Lodge is a real treasure chest of eighteenth-century craftsmanship, reflecting an age of elegance and style. Note the lamp post in the road shown in the original 1903 image. Petersham Road is so busy now that a closer view of the lodge had to be taken.

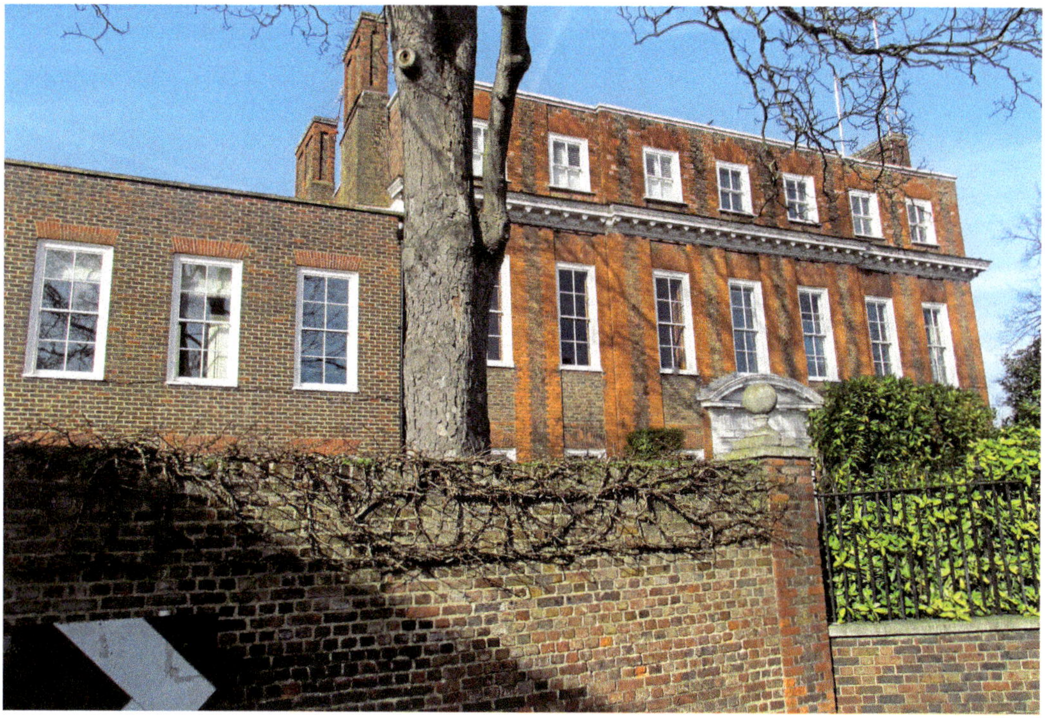

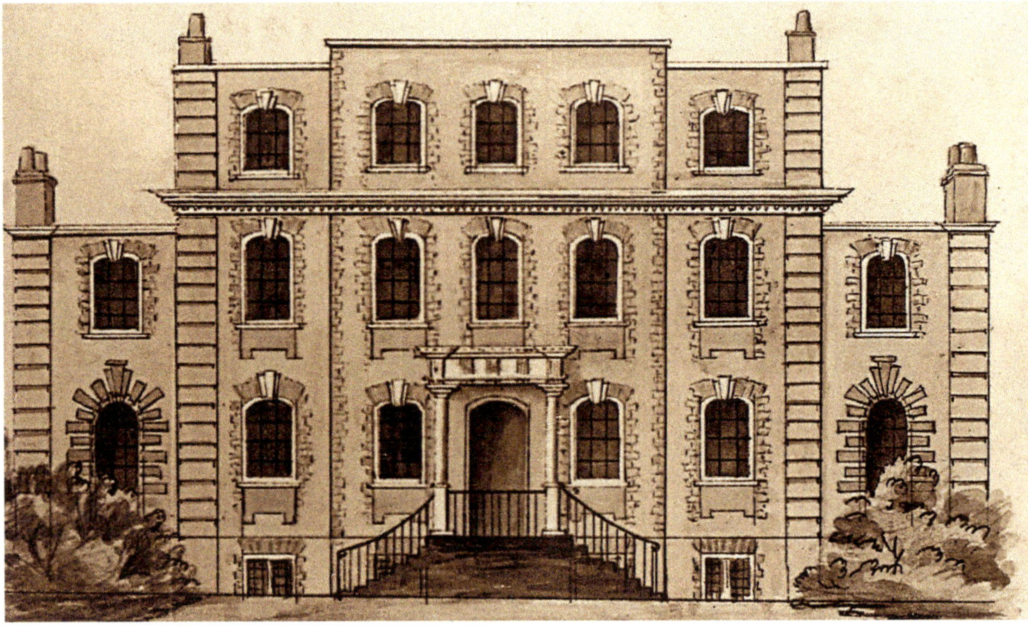

Montrose House, Petersham Road

Named after Caroline Maria, Dowager Duchess of Montrose who resided here from 1836 until her death in 1847, the property actually dates back to the late seventeenth century. The house was built for Sir Thomas Jenner who was a lawyer. When he died in 1707 the building was acquired by Bartholomew Burton, a deputy governor of the Bank of England. In more recent times, from 1919 to 1969, the property was owned by Sir Philip Carr, the Chairman of Peak Frean & Co. Ltd, the famous biscuit manufacturers. It was then bought by Tommy Steele, the pop star of the late 1950s and early 1960s, the owner who is perhaps most remembered by the public in connection with this house.

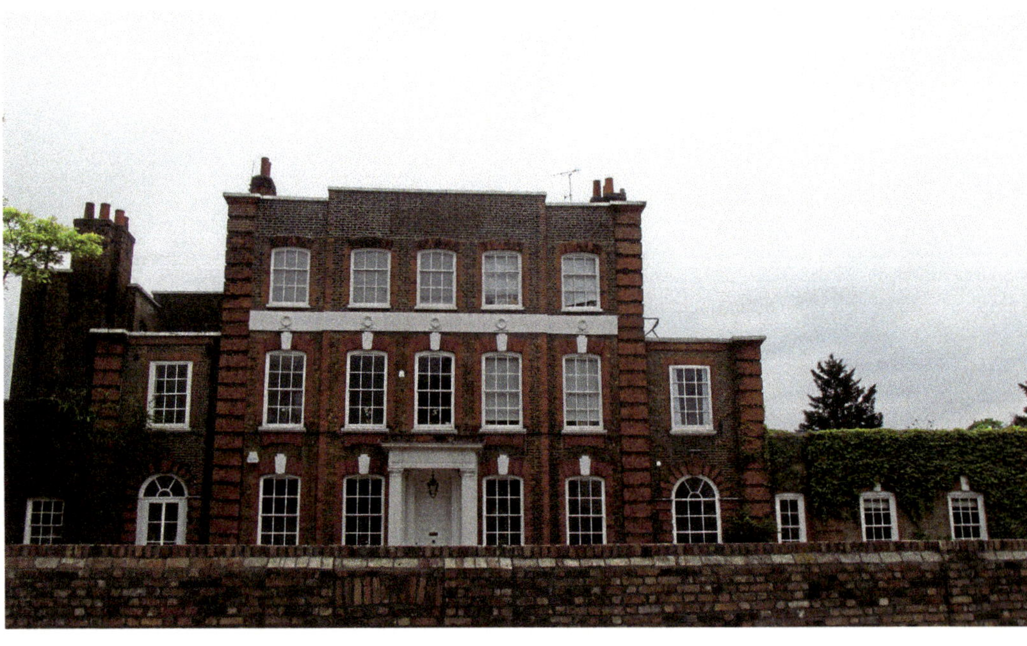

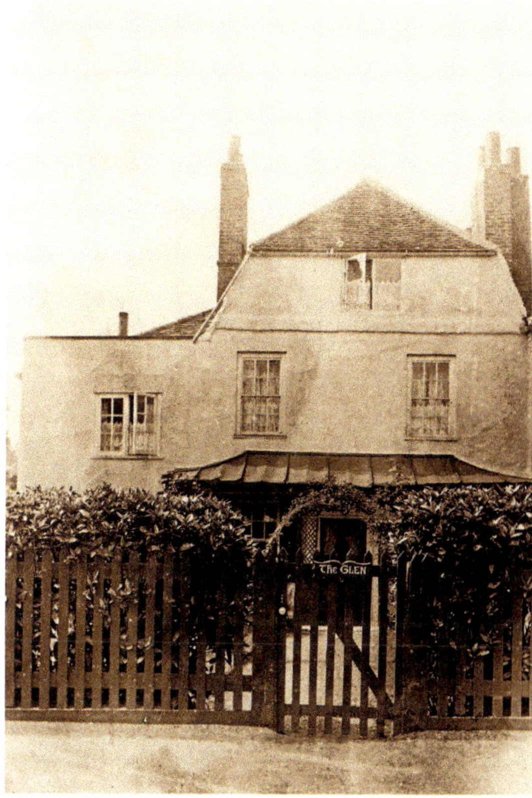

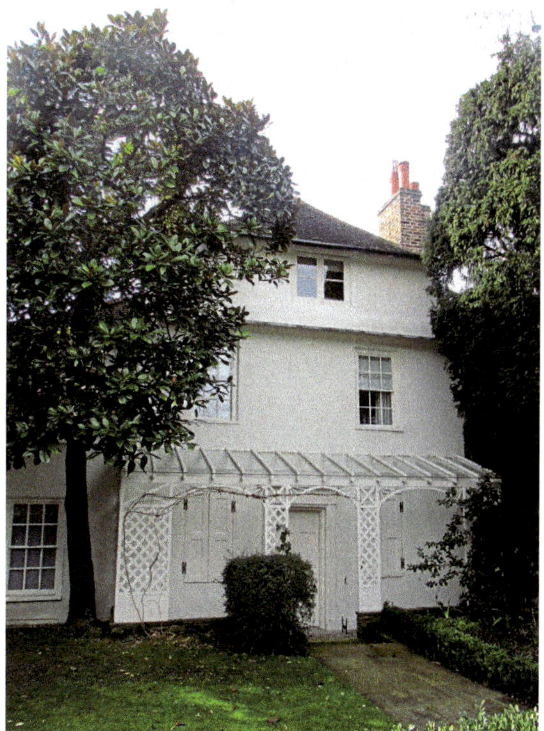

The Glen, River Lane

The Glen and the adjacent cottage, now called Navigator's House, formerly Craigmyle, date to the 1670s, so are much older than they appear. Captain George Vancouver lived in this cottage for the last years of his life. He wrote an account of his voyages called *Voyage of Discovery to the North Pacific and Round the World*, probably in this very building. The city of Vancouver in Canada is named after him, so he has left a lasting legacy. He died at the young age of forty in May 1798, and is buried not far away in Petersham churchyard. The cottage is now a private residence.

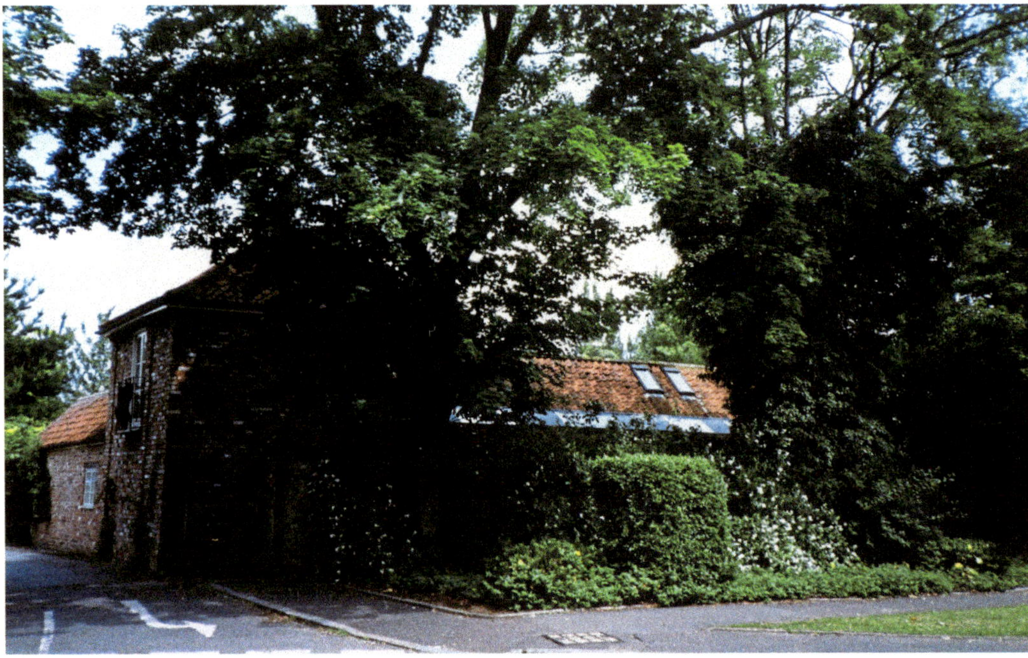

The Old Stables, River Lane

Originally the stable building served Petersham Lodge, directly opposite on the other side of River Lane. The gardener's cottage was also on this side of the lane. In the late 1960s, Richmond Parks Department owned the land, which included the Old Stables and which had formerly belonged to Carter seeds nursery. Now the Old Stables building is used for residential purposes. The original photo was taken in 1999 and clear differences can be seen when compared with the modern photo.

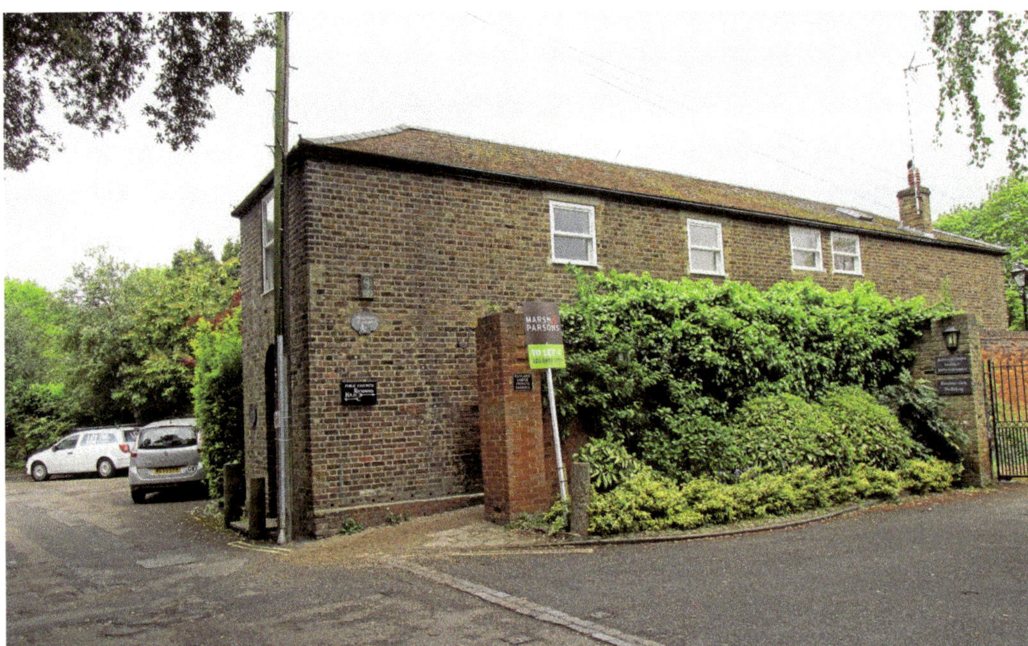

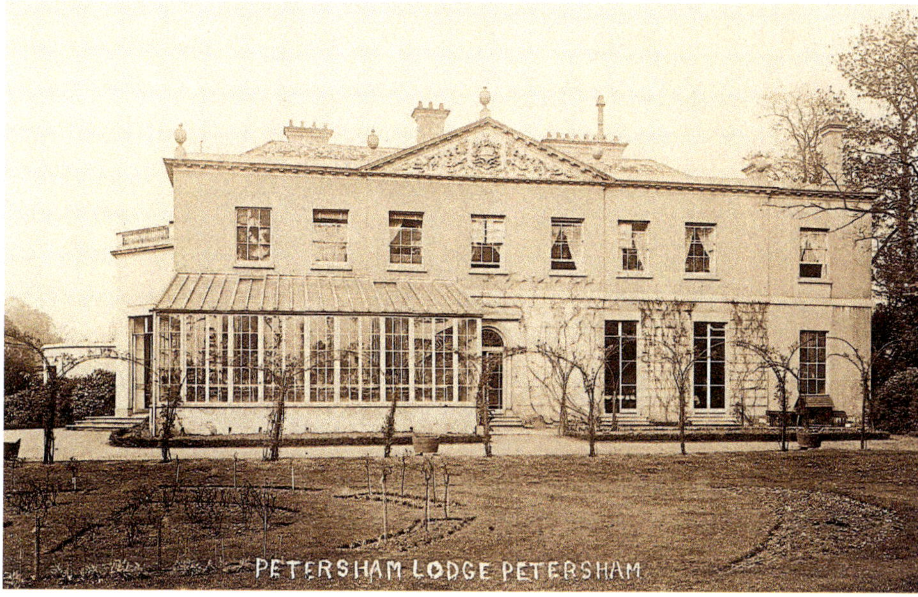

Petersham Lodge, River Lane

There have been previous houses called Petersham Lodge dating back to the sixteenth century. These stood in what was then called New Park (now Richmond Park) not far from the junction of the Petersham Road with Star and Garter. George Cole, the Lord of the Manor, resided here in the early phase of the building. The last Petersham Lodge in the park was demolished in 1833. However, in 1850, Richard Powney built the Petersham Lodge that we see today in River Lane. It was bought in 1902 by Sir Max Waechter, who wanted to preserve it from the threat of development; he turned it into a holiday home for governesses. The Princess of Wales Holiday Home for Governesses was in use right up until the Second World War.

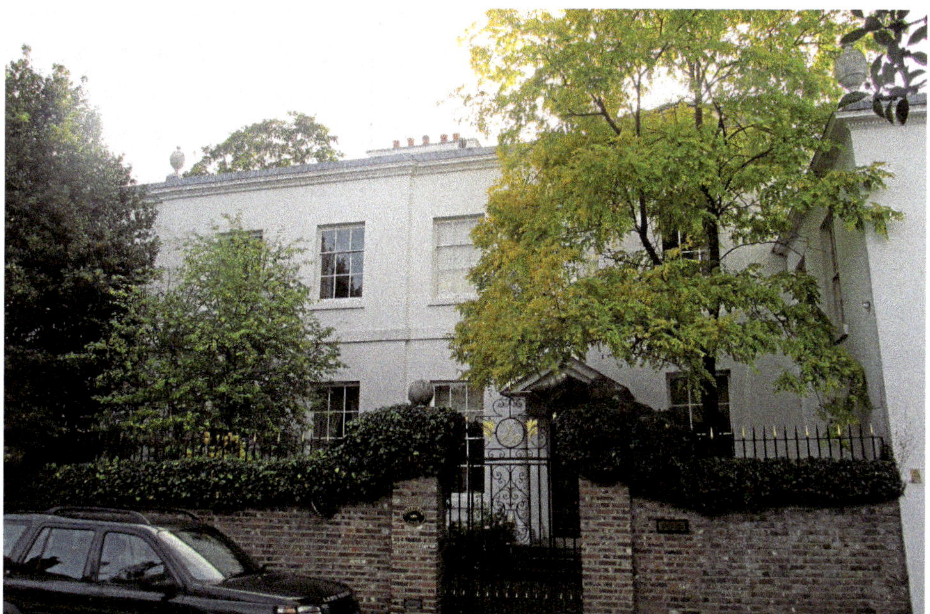

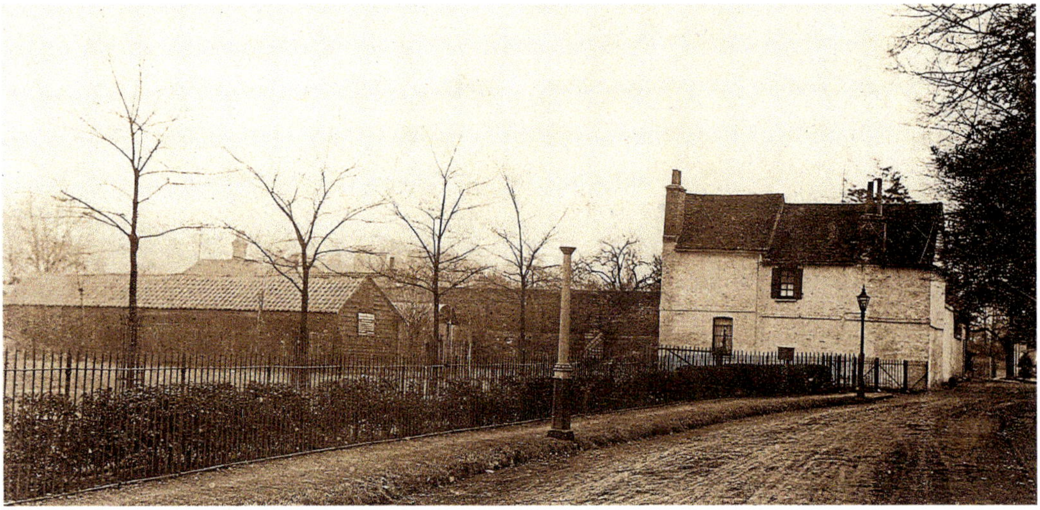

Gardener's Cottage to Petersham Lodge, River Lane

Gardeners were in great demand in the Edwardian period, helping to maintain the grounds of the large houses. Both Petersham and Ham had an exceptionally high concentration of notable estates, which together employed a considerable number of gardeners. The gardener's cottage pictured here is shown in February 1908 and was on the opposite side of the road to Petersham Lodge itself. William Cosham, gardener, lived here in 1911 with his wife Fanny; they had no children. The cottage itself contained six rooms. Also, note Hornby & Clarke's sheds to the left of the cottage. These belonged to the dairy farm that existed from 1870 up until 1935.

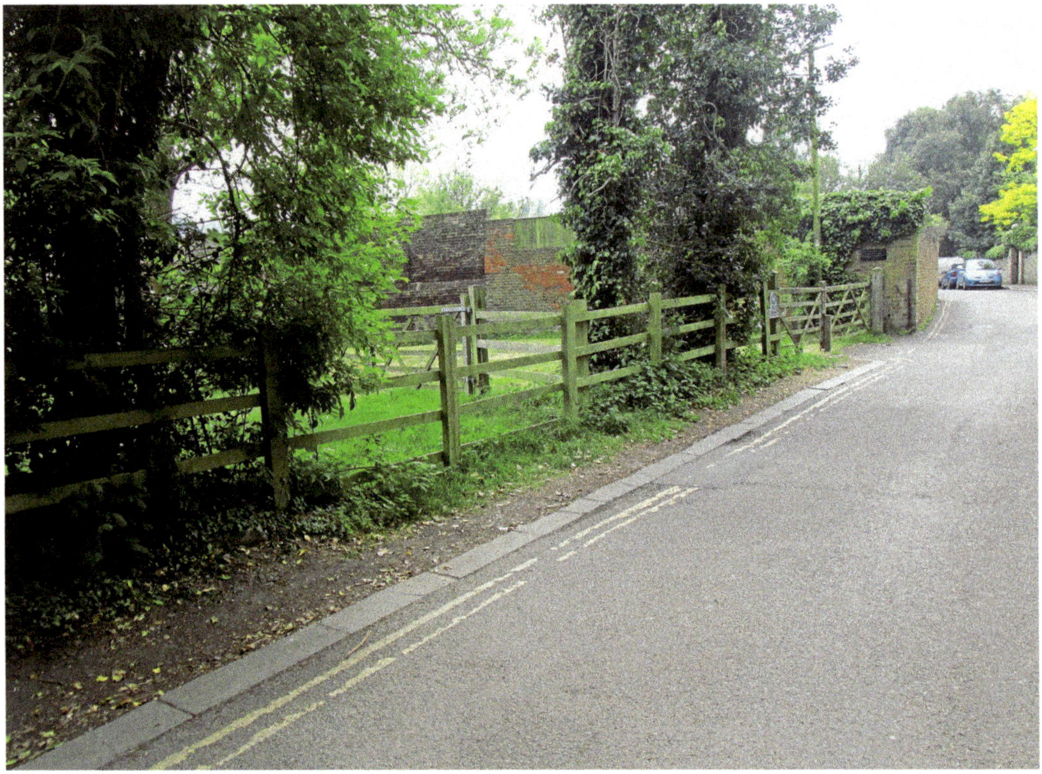

Hornby & Clarke's Milking Sheds, River Lane

An advertisement for this dairy states 'Returns for 1934 show that in the whole of England only 270 herds of cows were licensed by the Ministry of Health to supply "Certified Milk"'. One of these is Hornby & Clarke's Guernsey herd at Petersham Meadows Farm. This image shows the milking sheds along River Lane in Petersham. The company existed from 1870 right up until 1935 when the Express Dairy took over control. The current photograph shows that the former sheds have now been returned to meadowland.

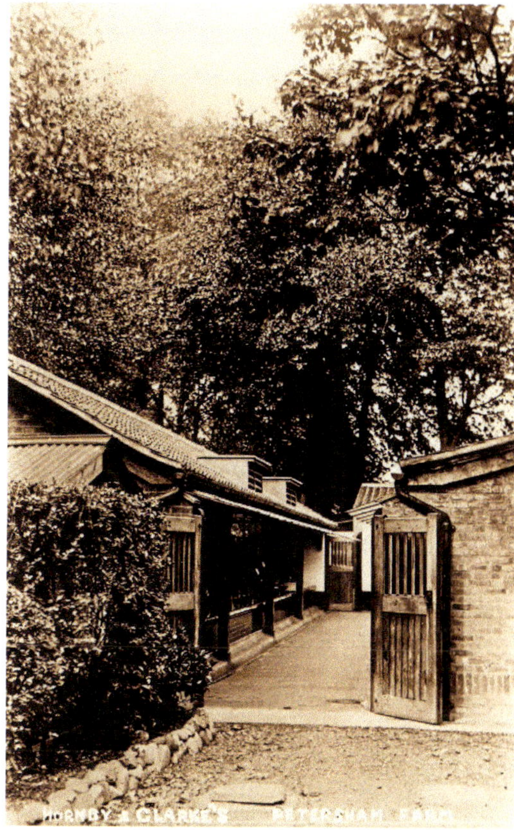

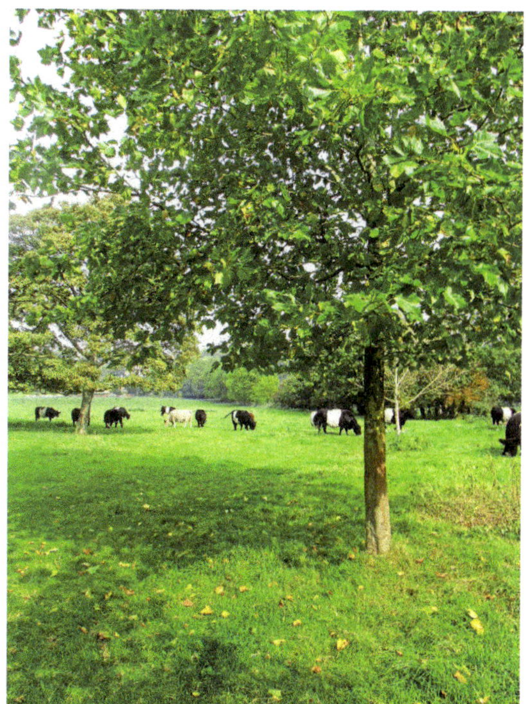

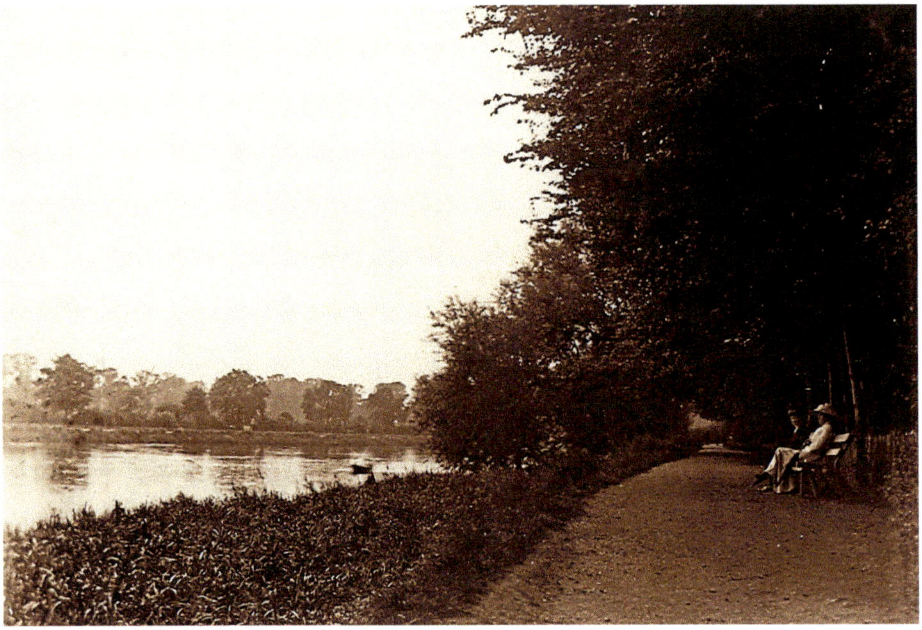

The Thames at Petersham

Trees of the Petersham Lodge Woods can be seen on the right-hand side of the photograph dating to *c.* 1910. This woodland area is a total contrast to the Petersham Meadows not far away, and a real haven for wildlife. Glover's Island is just out of view on the left-hand side. The river reminds us how popular this stretch of riverbank is and even today many people park along River Lane and go for long recreational walks along the towpath. This view demonstrates how unspoilt parts of Petersham have remained up to the present day.

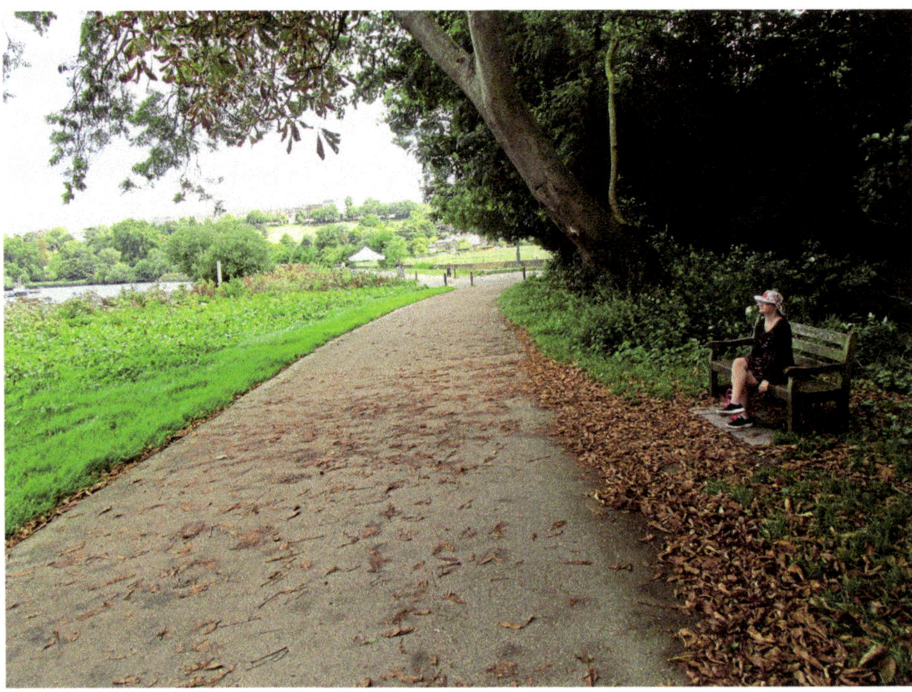

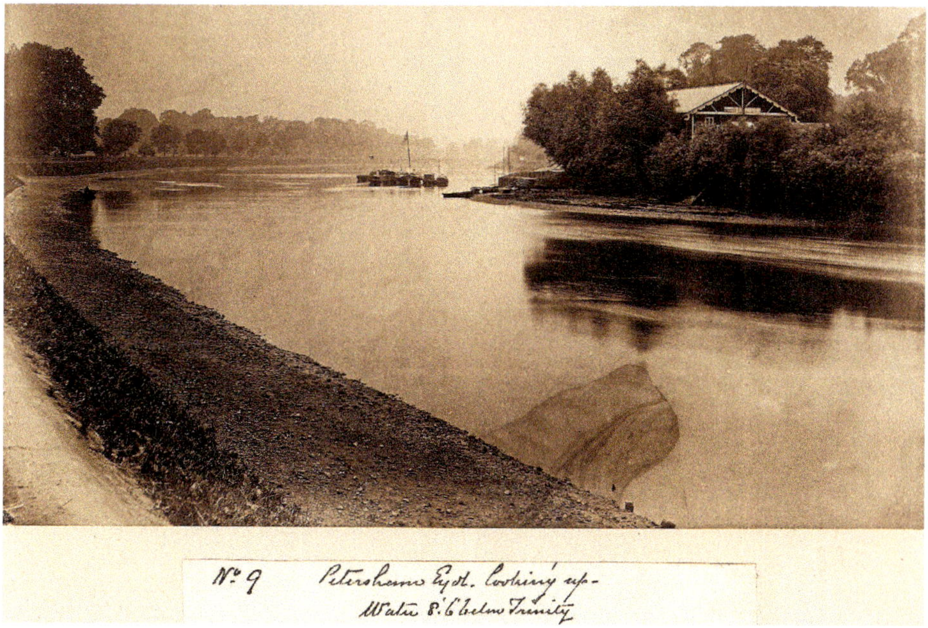

Petersham Ait

Mr Max Waechter purchased Petersham Ait, or Glover's Island as it was also called, from Mr Joseph Glover for the sum of £1,600 in 1900. There were rumours that the island was to be developed, which is why Mr Waechter stepped in to save it for the Corporation of Richmond. He stipulated two vital points in the conveyance of January 1901. Firstly that the island be maintained at its present limits and the banks kept secure from destruction and decay, and secondly that by the planting of trees when and where necessary the ornamental character of the island be preserved. As can be seen in the up-to-date photo, this beautiful island still remains unspoilt and looks especially stunning when viewed from the top of Richmond Hill.

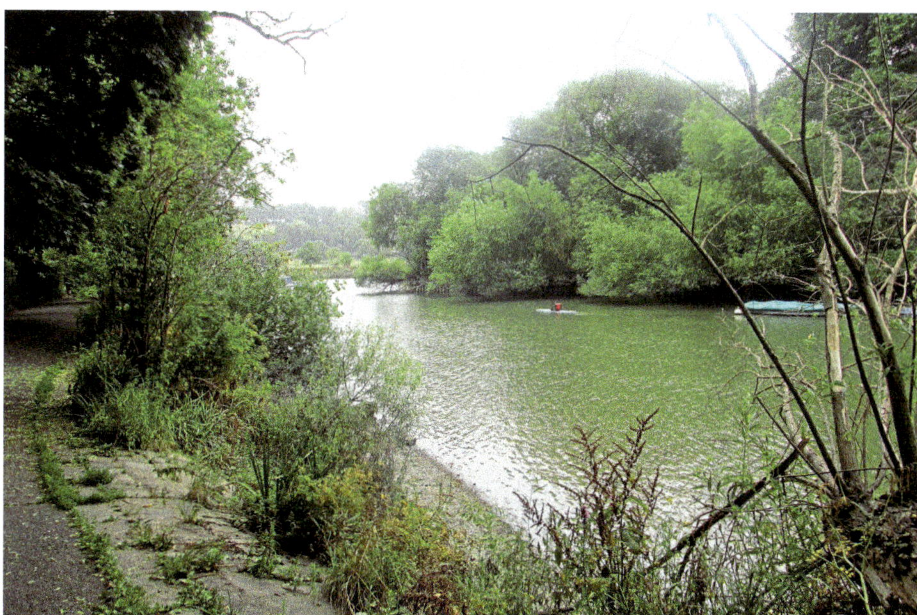

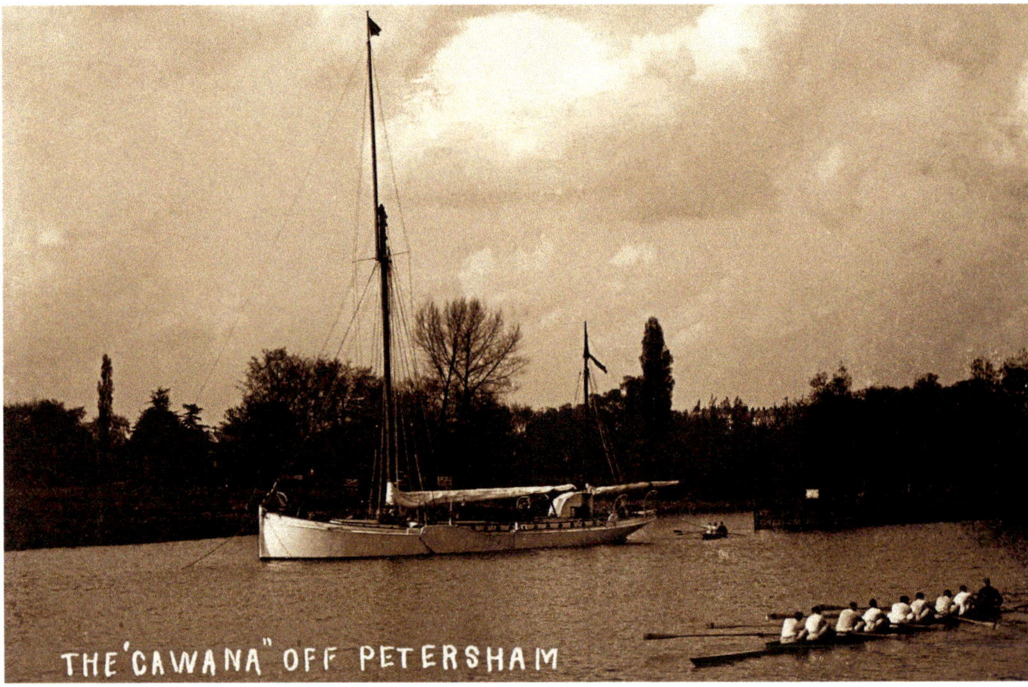

The *Cawana*, off Petersham

This rare view of the yacht *Cawana* anchored in the Thames off Petersham must have been taken after 1904, as the boat was built in that year. Glover's Island can be seen on the right-hand side and the scene also shows how very popular rowing was in the Edwardian period. The *Cawana* was a wooden barge yacht 85 feet in length that could carry 89 tons of cargo. She was owned by Dawe & Hill of Westminster and was designed by Gill & Sons of Rochester. The modern photo shows that rowing is still popular in this stretch of water.

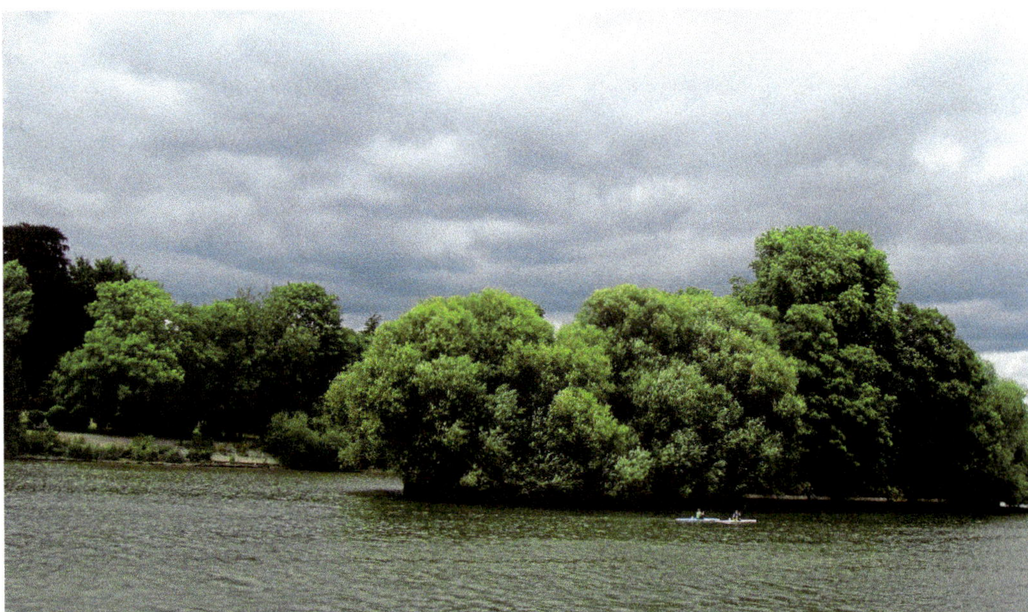

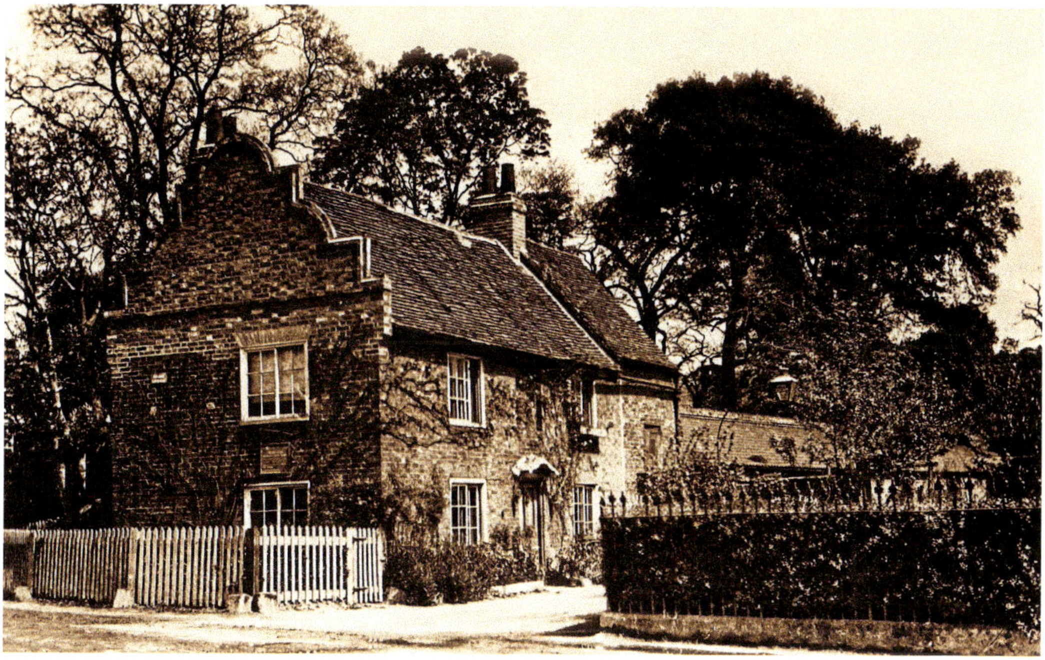

Farm Lodge, Petersham Road

This striking Jacobean-style gabled building was possibly originally connected with Montrose House. Farm Lodge exemplifies the elegance and quality that was lavished on such relatively simple vernacular buildings in the eighteenth century. The lodge was leased by the Earl of Dysart to Robert Walter and the twin building, Avenue Lodge, to John Veal. In the 1860s the occupier of Farm Lodge was Arthur Colborne, a carpenter by trade. More surprisingly, Mr Colborne's widow Rachel ran a branch library from this building, which continued until 1908. In 1911 Alfred Tuckwell, who worked for the borough council, lived here with his wife and children. The companion Avenue Lodge later became a smithy and, later still, a motor garage.

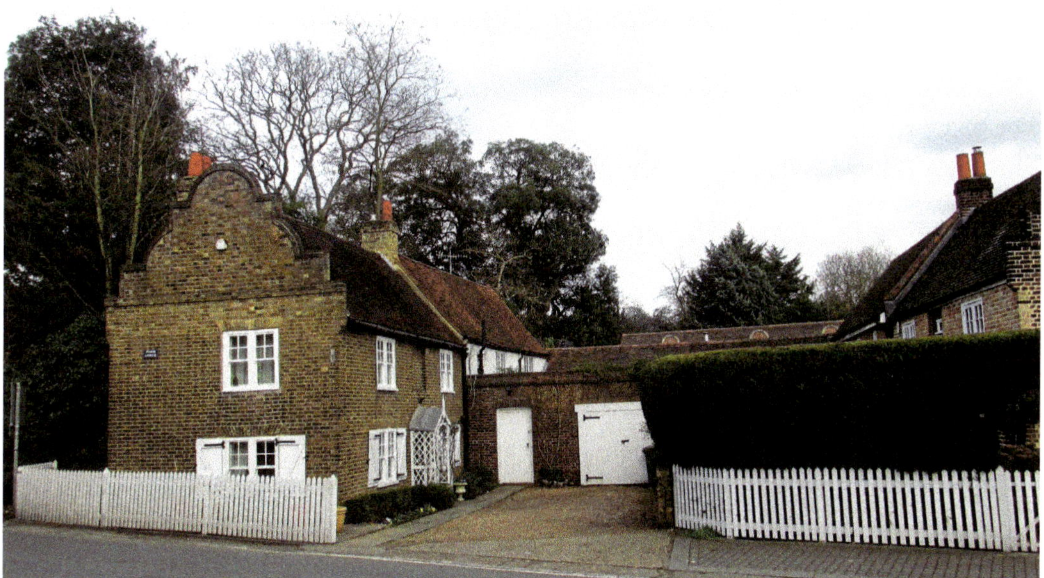

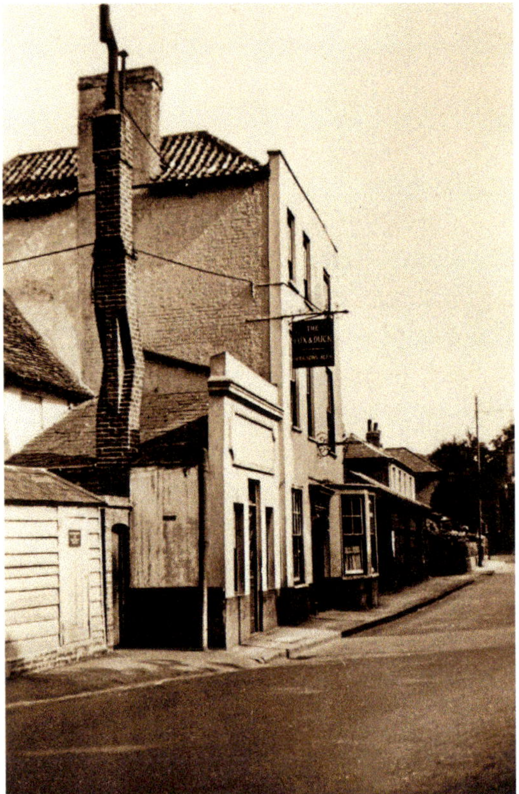

Fox & Duck Hotel. 7.

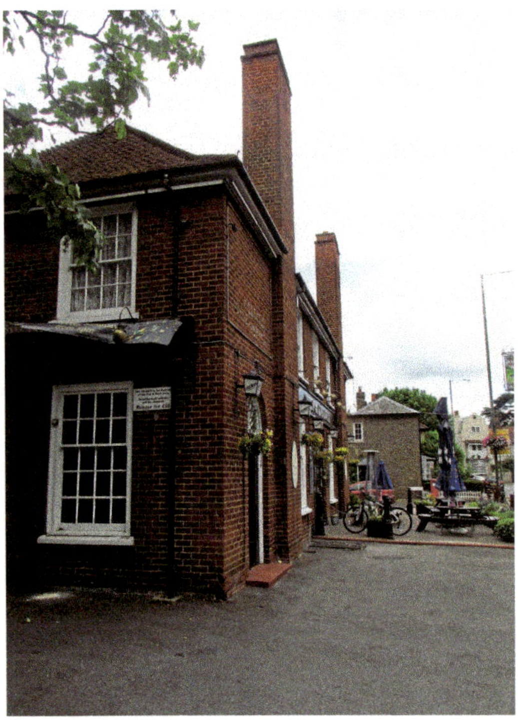

Fox & Duck Public House, Petersham Road

Originally an old posting inn, the Fox & Duck dates to the 1770s. An old inn sign inscribed 'Fox & Duck, Petersham, Surry' was found in a house in Ladbroke Grove, of all places. The sign is oval in shape, painted in the style of George Morland, dates to the 1770s and is now displayed in the museum at Richmond. The original photo shows that the old timber-framed building had a very distinctive crooked chimney, which gave it real charm and character. The building was demolished in 1940, unusually not because of war damage but because it had leaked for many years. The lock-up stood adjacent to the pub, as did the village pound for stray animals. In the up-to-date photo we see that the new building is more functional in its design.

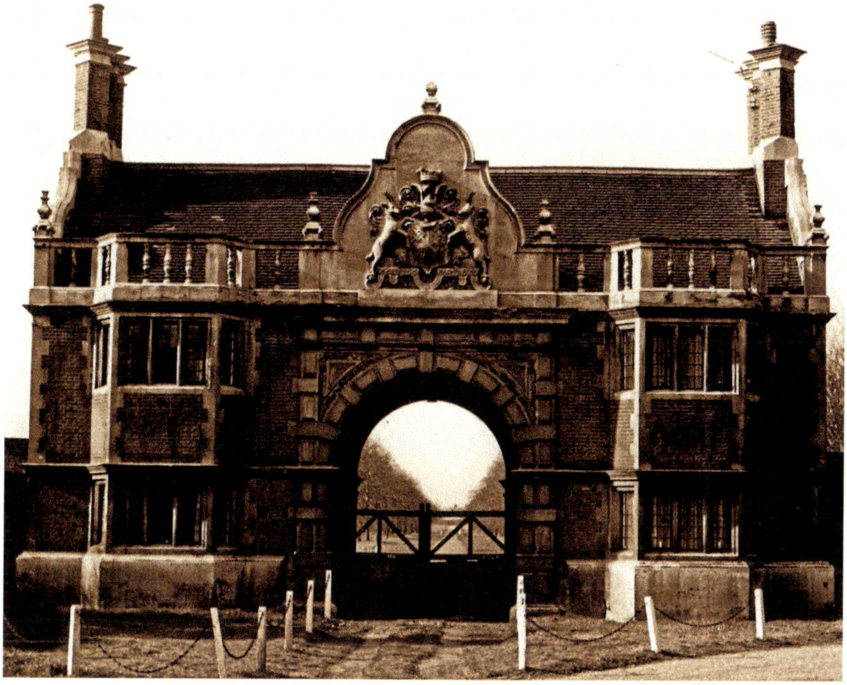

The Lodge, Petersham Road

William John Manners Tollemache, 9th Earl of Dysart (1859–1935), was responsible for the erection of this quasi-Jacobean entrance lodge in 1900. The building was designed by the architect and Royal Academy artist Robert Dudley Oliver (1856–1923). The lodge is a striking building with a very impressive coat of arms of the Earls of Dysart. The building acts as a good focal point with the path behind (Petersham Avenue) leading to Ham House.

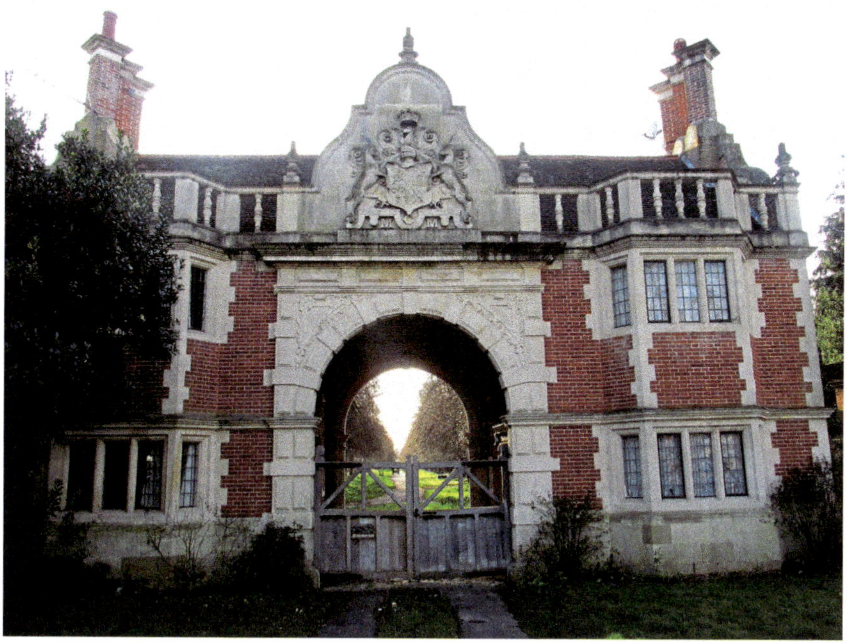

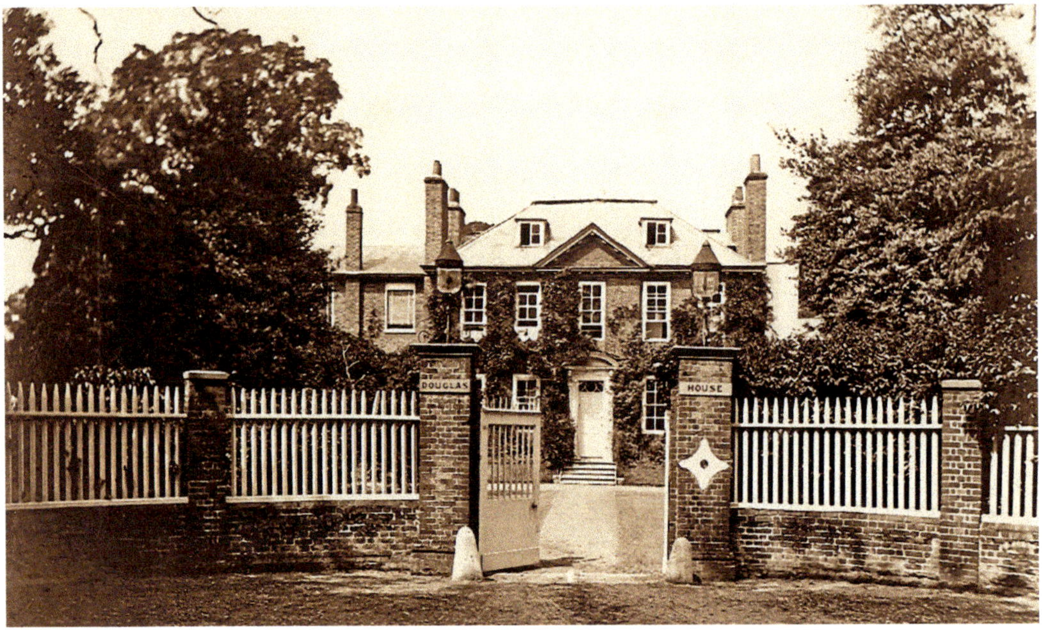

Douglas House

Originally known as Petersham Place, the house later became known as Douglas House and dates to the 1700s. The house was owned by Charles Douglas, 3rd Duke of Queensbury, who married Catherine Hyde, known as 'Kitty'. She was the daughter of Henry, Earl of Clarendon, and was famed for her beauty. They lived at this house in the 1720s, but also had another residence in Buckinghamshire. The property was bought for use as a German school in 1970 and more up-to-date buildings were added around the nucleus of the house. The 'Deutsche Schule' was officially opened in 1981.

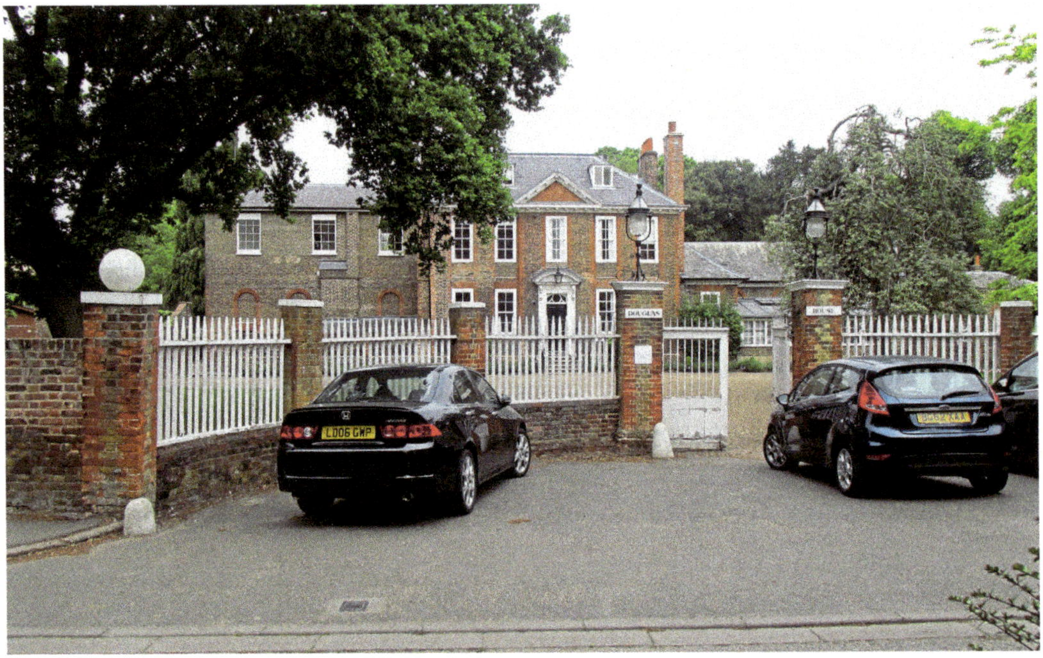

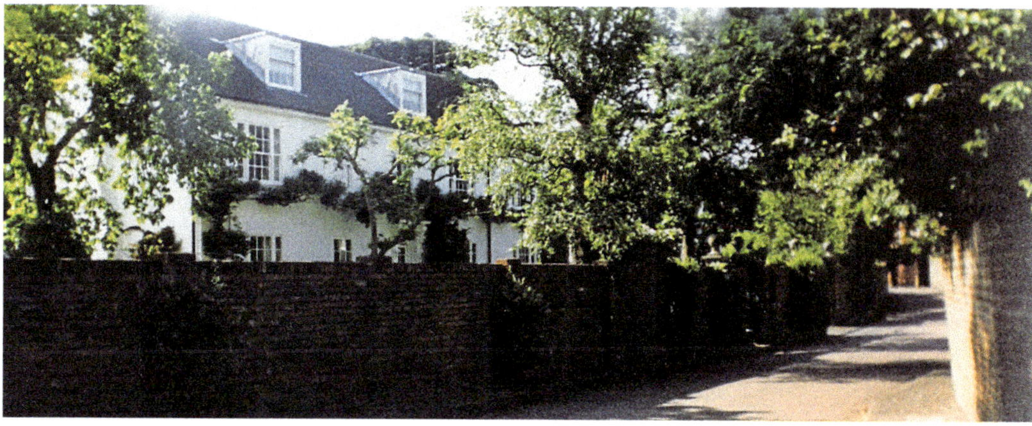

Sudbrook Lane

The original main road that ran from Richmond to Kingston went down Sudbrook Lane, across Sudbrook Park to Ham Common and then to Latchmere Lane. The 2nd Duke of Argyll was unhappy with the course of this road; he was eventually granted permission to construct a new road that followed the route of today's main road. Although Sudbrook is known to be an ancient hamlet of Petersham, very little is known about its history. We do know that in 1637 a map was produced of Richmond Park which marks this area as 'Rex Sudbrook', so it was Crown property. It will be seen from the photograph that some very distinguished houses now line this lane.

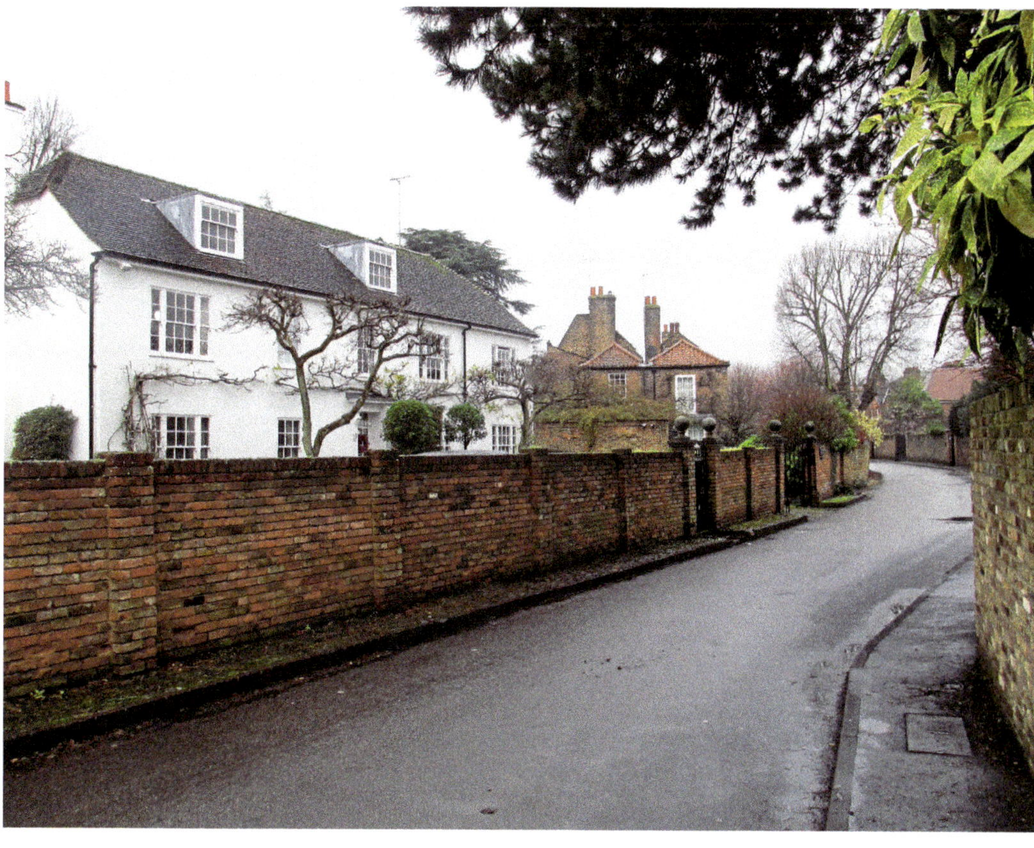

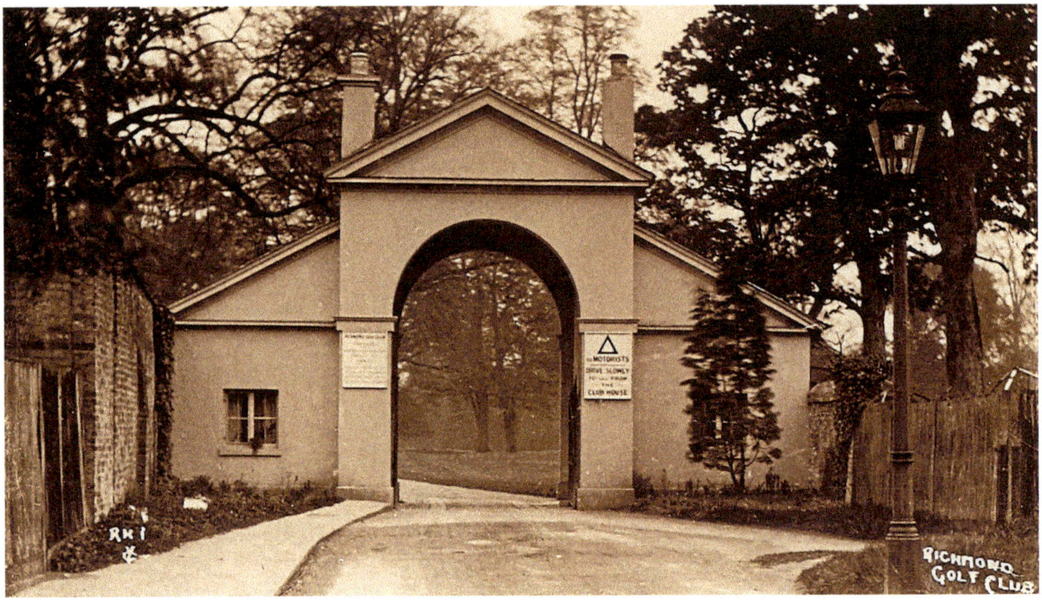

Entrance to Golf Course, Sudbrook Lane

One of the oldest buildings in Petersham, apart from the parish church, is Sudbrook House, built around 1726 by John Campbell, 2nd Duke of Argyll, Ist Duke of Greenwich (1680–1743). He was the victor of the Battle of Sheriffmuir in 1715.The house was designed by the distinguished architect James Gibbs (1682–1754). The duke extended his grounds by taking in several acres of Richmond Park. When the duke died in 1743, the Duchess of Greenwich succeeded to the property. It was then owned by the Duke of Buccleuch and, in 1824, it was sold to Sir Robert Wilmot Horton. In more recent times the house and grounds have been used by the Richmond Golf Club, who lease the property from the Crown.

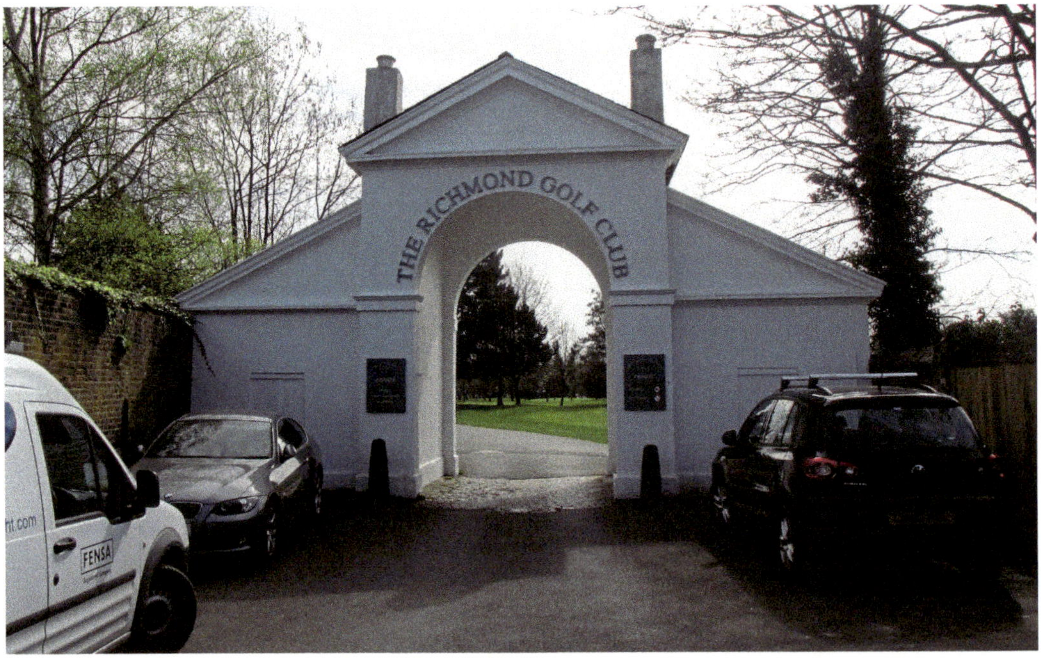

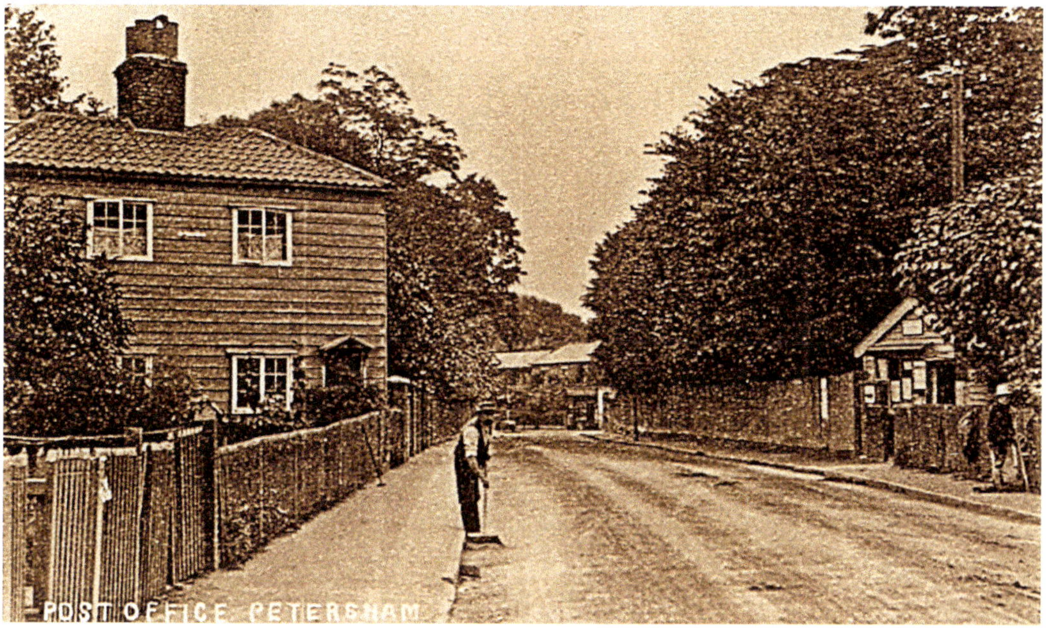

Old Post Office, Petersham Road

John Keay & Son owned this small post office in the Petersham Road, pictured here in 1905. It lost its licence in the 1920s. The manager of this establishment was Mr Harold Gent. The shop was very small, being around 10 feet square with a back storeroom of a similar size and an outside toilet that was later shared with Columbine Cottage. When it closed as a post office it became a cobblers and then a greengrocers, which was rented by Mrs Smeadon. The building was destroyed by a bomb in 1941 which exploded in the road directly in front of the shop – apparently some bottles of vinegar in the back storeroom were entirely untouched by the explosion. The new post office moved to premises nearer to the junction with Sudbrook Lane, but is now a private residence.

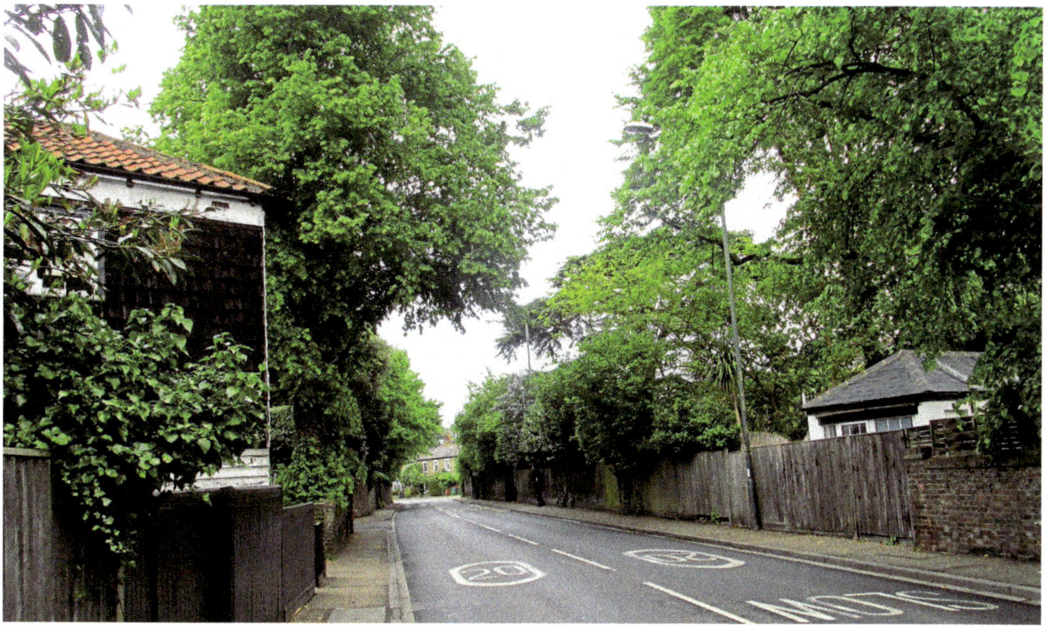

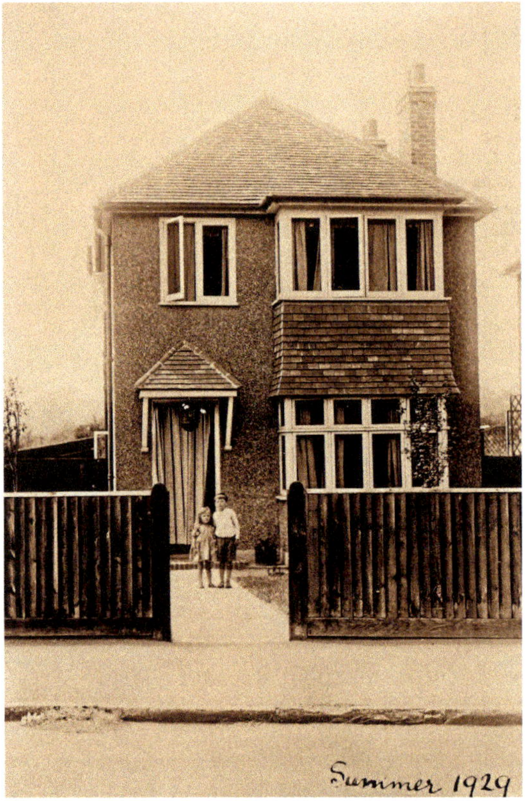

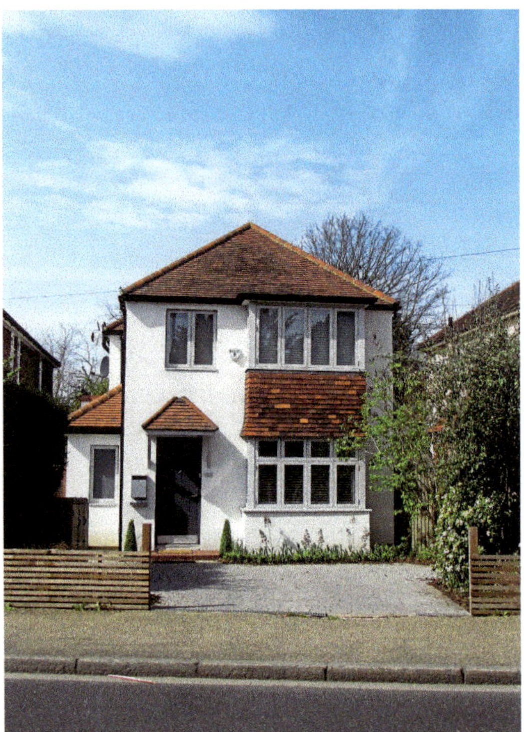

No. 201 Petersham Road, Petersham
The Right Honourable Sir William John Manners Tollemache, Earl of Dysart (the 9th Earl) sold the land along the Petersham Road from River Lane up to Sandy Lane in the 1920s. The house shown was originally called 'Stowe', the number 201 coming later. The land was purchased by Mr Samuel Henry Eaton, my wife's grandfather, in March 1928. The current photograph shows that the house has recently been modernised.

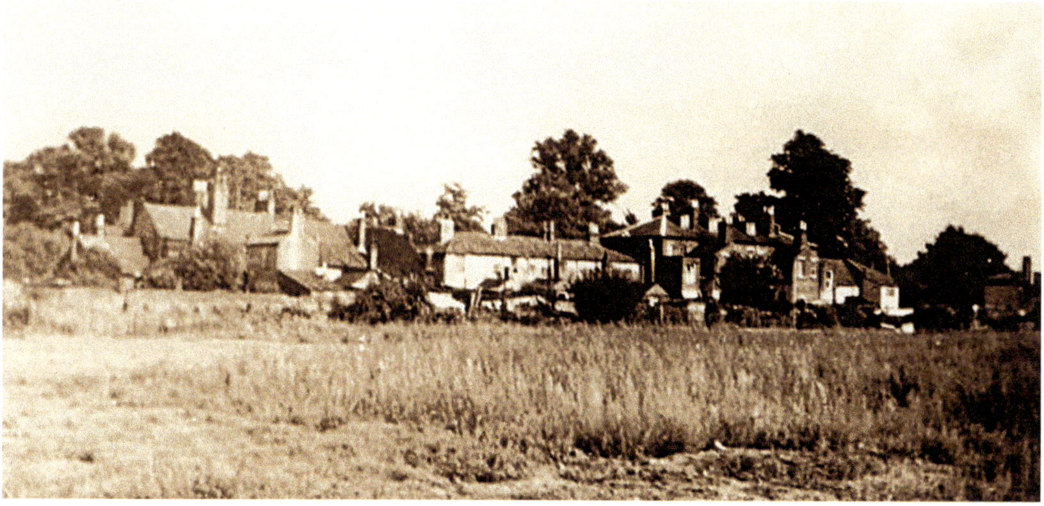

Back of Cottages, Petersham Road

A rare photograph taken by Mr Samuel Henry Eaton, one of my wife's relatives, around 1950. The photograph shows a panoramic view of the back of the houses along the west side of the Petersham Road. The scene is believed to be taken just past No. 201 looking south. The land in front of the buildings was still part of Mr Steven's farm at this time. However, shortly afterwards houses were erected on what is now the Clifford Estate. The nearest approximation to this view had to be taken along the alleyway that runs behind the current houses of this part of the Petersham Road.

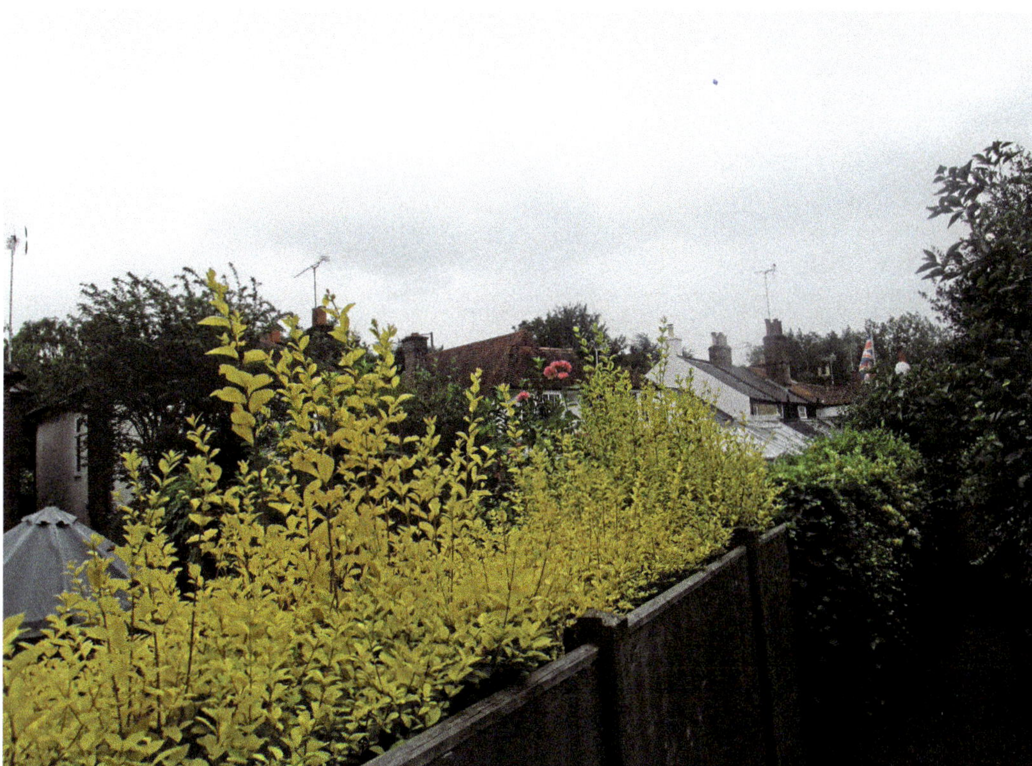

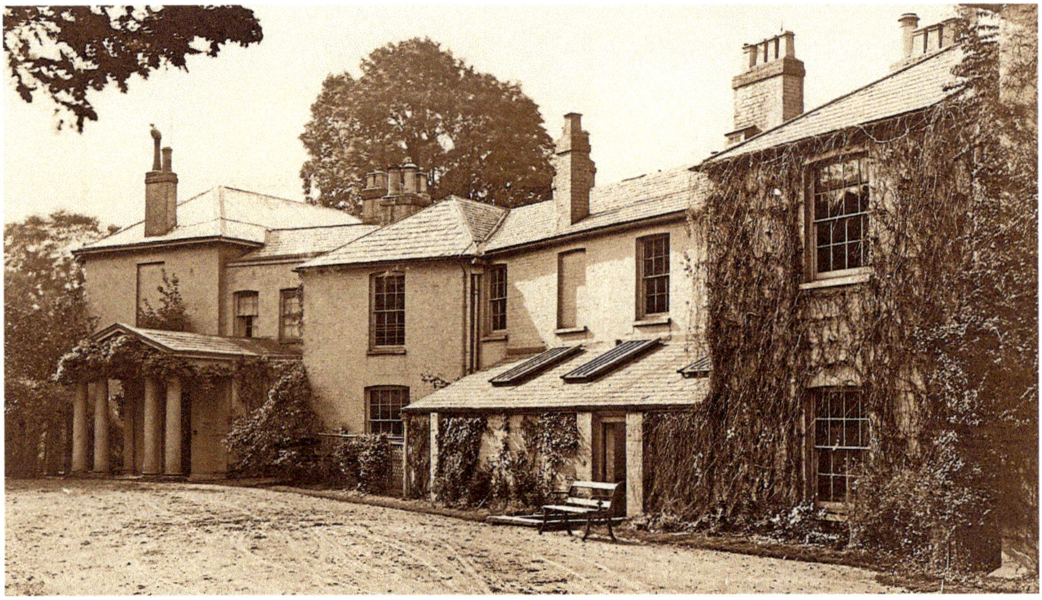

Pembroke Lodge, Richmond Park

Elizabeth Herbert, Countess of Pembroke, the wife of the 10th Earl of Pembroke, was responsible for building Hill Lodge, which was later renamed in memory of the countess. Prior to this its original genesis was as a much more humble mole-catcher's cottage. Queen Victoria granted the lodge to Lord John Russell in 1847, who enlarged the building and greatly improved it. Many details of the Russell's family life and the many visitors to the lodge are to be found in *The Recollections of Lady Georgiana Peel: Compiled by Her Daughter Ethel Peel.* Lord Russell was Prime Minister from 1846–52 and from 1865–66. He died at Pembroke Lodge on 28 May 1878. The view shows the main entrance to the lodge looking down the drive, and showing the side of the house facing the park. The lodge commands spectacular views across the countryside and is much visited today.

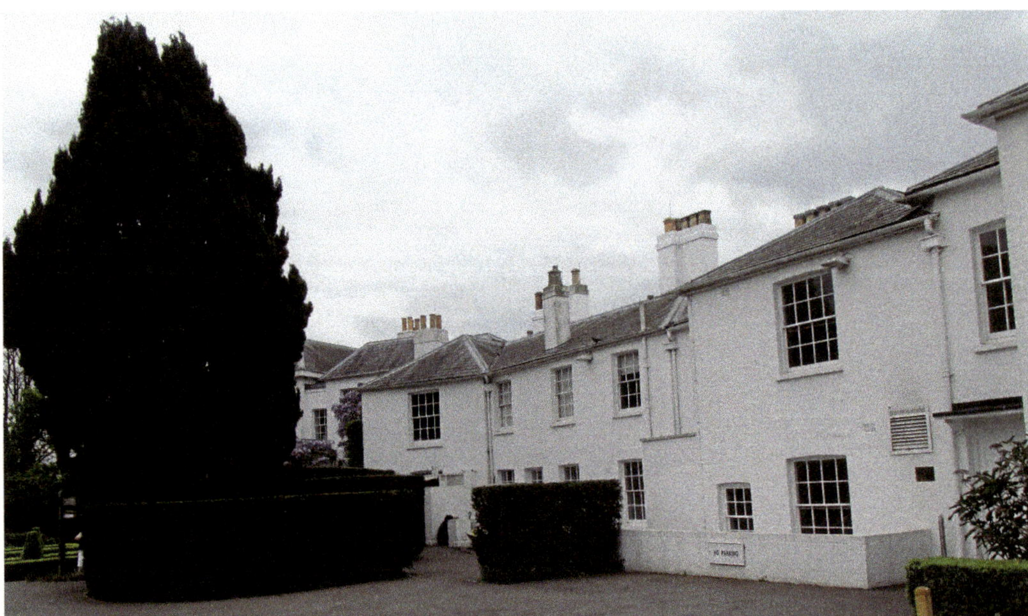

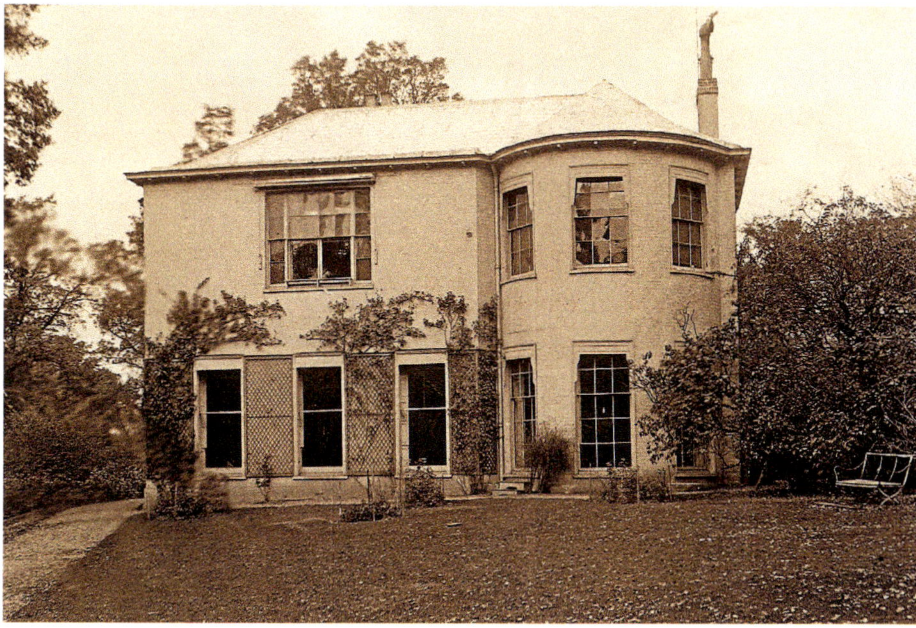

Pembroke Lodge, Side View

This side view of Pembroke Lodge facing south was taken in October 1902. From left to right the ground-floor windows are the drawing room and Lord John Russell's sitting room. On the first floor they are the sitting room and bedroom of the Dowager Countess Russell. The modern photo shows that the ground floor is now occupied by the restaurant, but the view overall remains little changed.

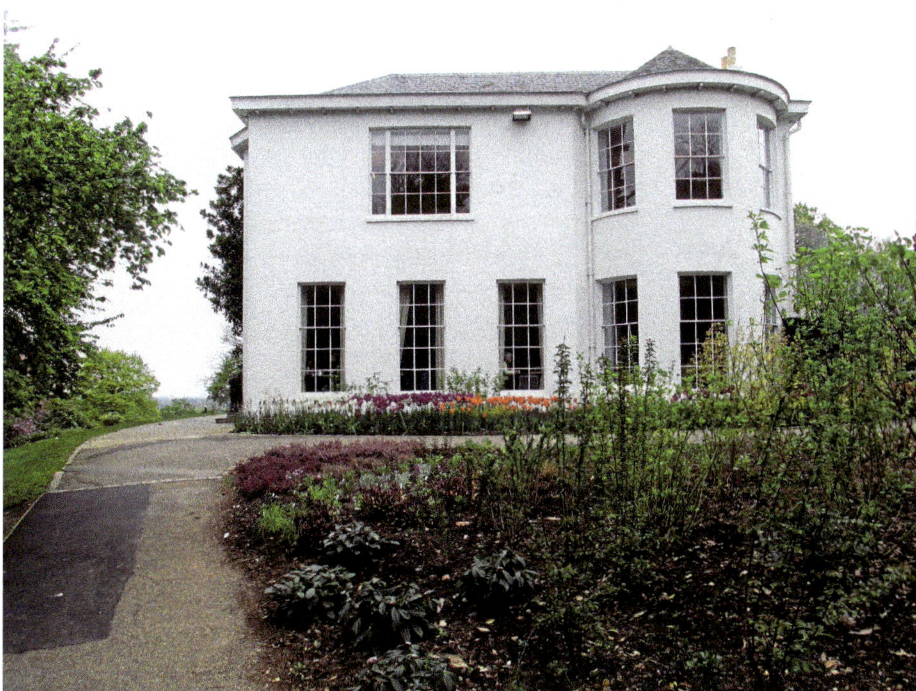

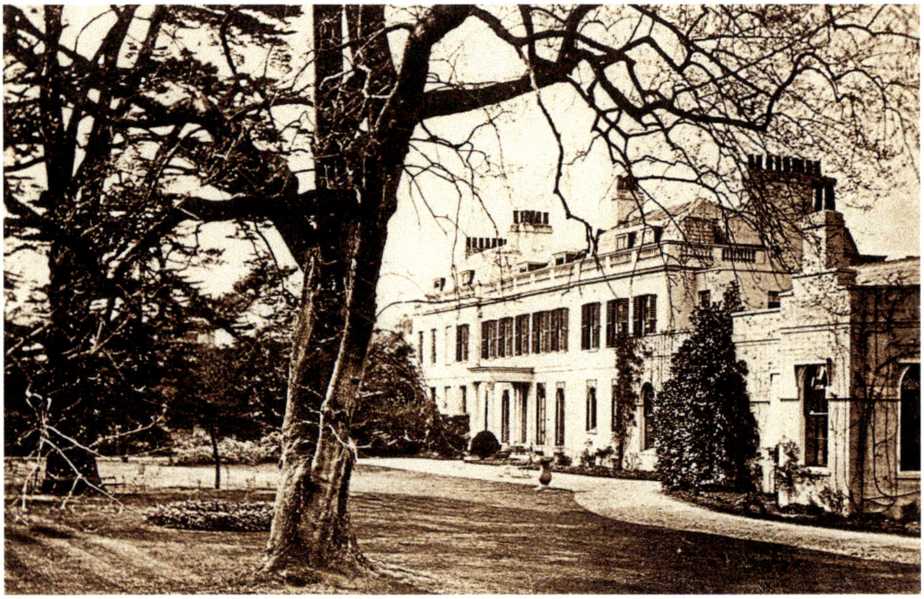

Bute House, Petersham Road

Robert Mylne (1733–1811), the famous architect who designed 'The Wick' in Richmond, was also responsible for Bute House in 1805. The Bute family resided here from the late eighteenth century until 1870. It was then used by Revd Charles Vincent Godby as an 'Academy for the sons of Gentlemen', until this moved to Queen's Road in Richmond in 1894. Sir John Whittaker Ellis bought the house in 1894 and it was demolished shortly after. The Petersham Highway Trustees minutes for 20 May 1805 records that the Marquess of Bute was given permission to make a subterranean passage from his house under the road to premises opposite, next to the churchyard. The houses in Cedar Heights now cover the area where Bute House once stood.

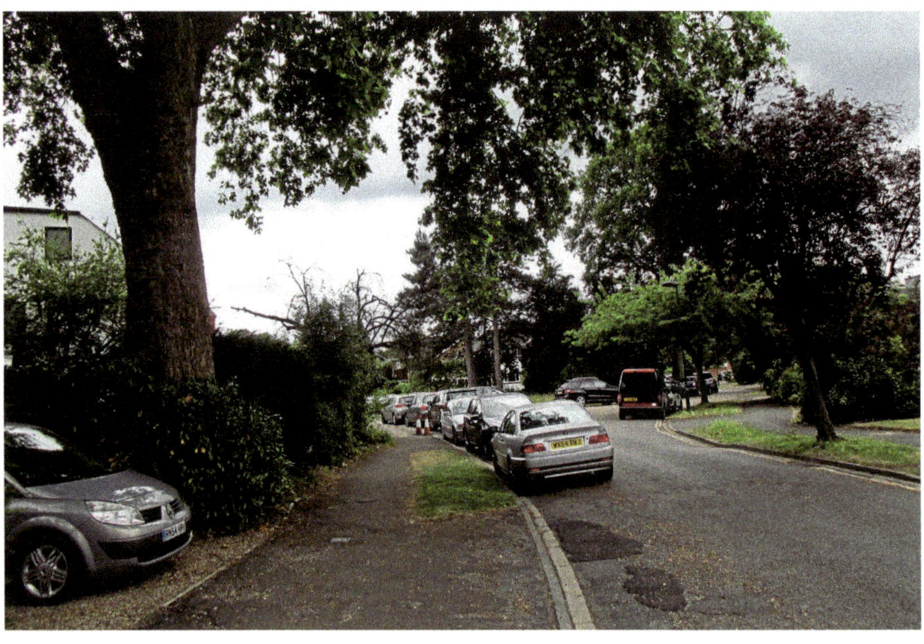

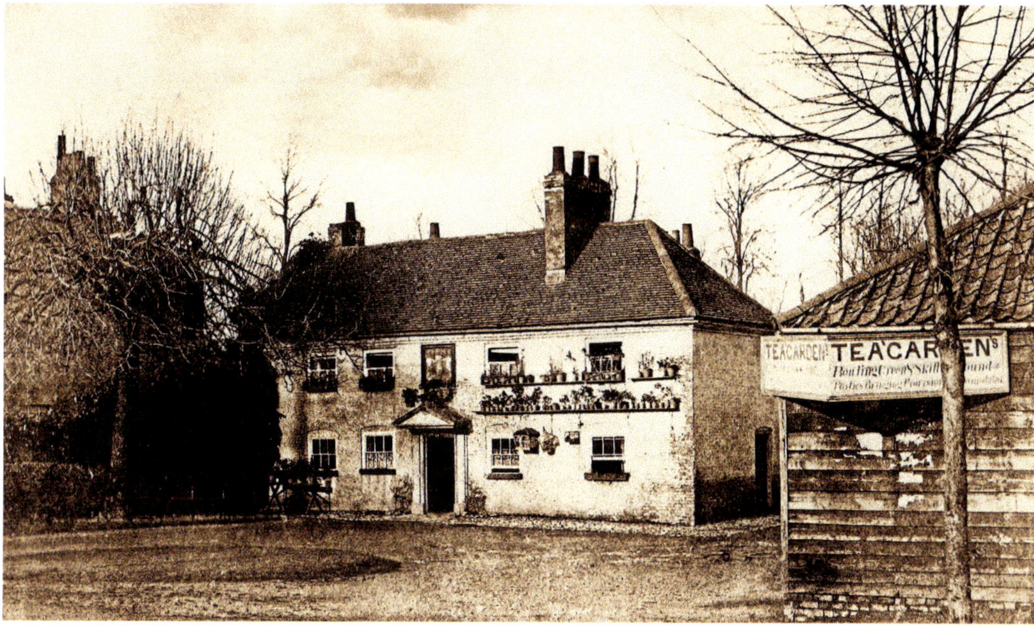

The Dysart Arms, Petersham Road

Originally known as the Plough and Harrow, the inn can be traced back to the late eighteenth century, although the original farmhouse dates back to the century before. The Countess of Dysart is said to have paid to have the name changed to The Dysart Arms early in the nineteenth century. The picture we see here dates to *c.* 1850 and has a naïve charm about it, with the row of flower pots arranged along the front. It was rebuilt in a Tudor style in 1902 and looks startlingly different from its original appearance.

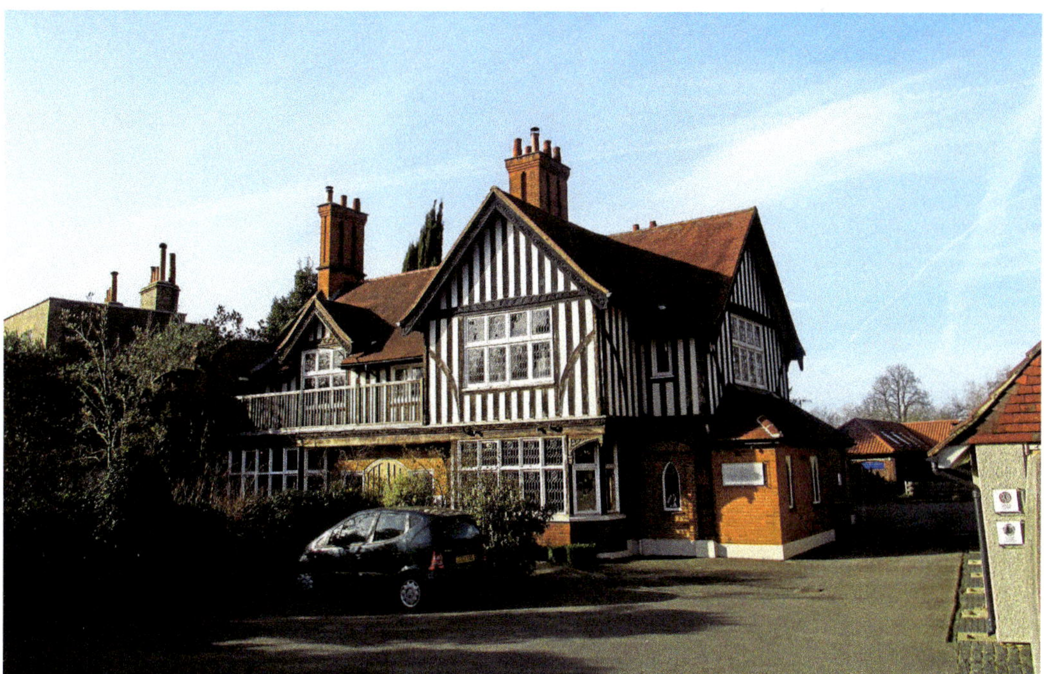

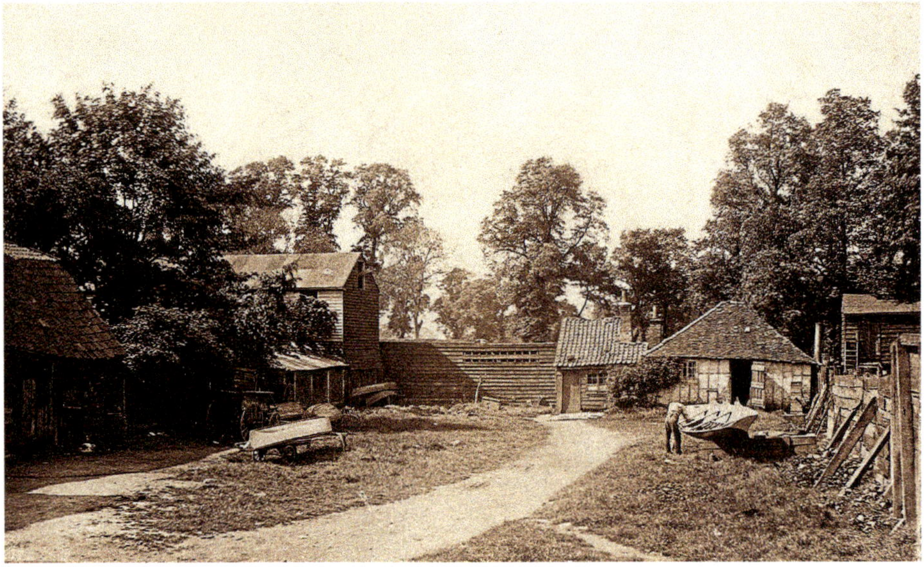

Boats at Petersham Vale

This rare photograph must have been taken prior to 1896 as these rather dilapidated wooden buildings were demolished in that year. The buildings were situated along the Petersham Road opposite to the Russell British School and backed on to the Star and Garter Farm. Presumably the boats were a seasonal means of making money between more agricultural pursuits, particularly as River Lane is relatively close by, giving access to the Thames. The current photograph shows that residential houses now occupy the site of the former, rather ramshackle, buildings.

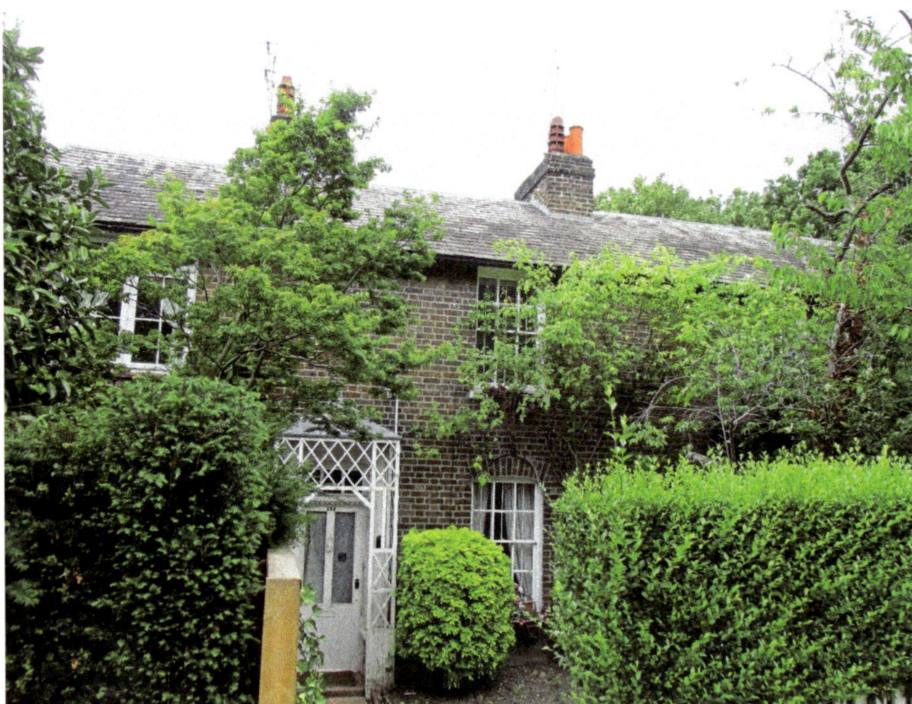

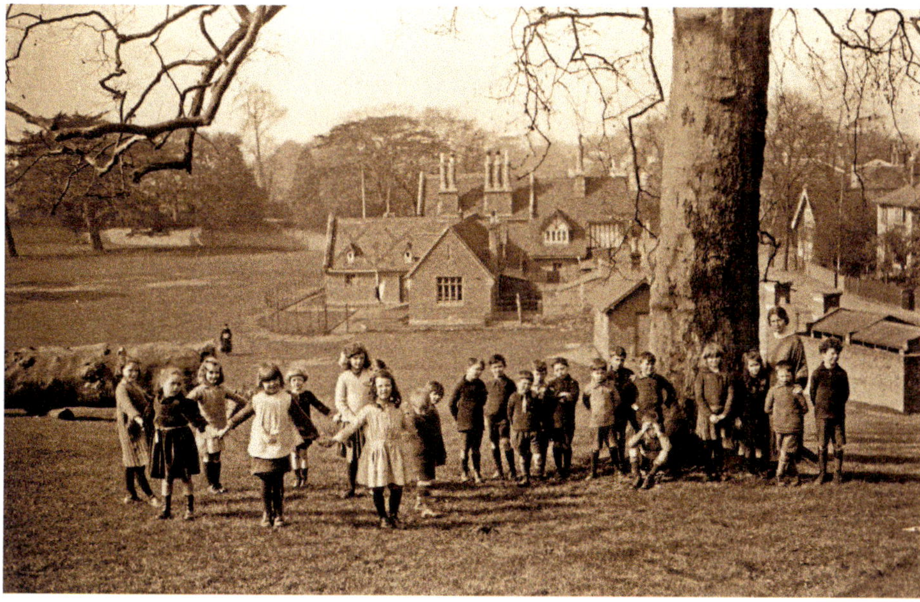

Russell British School, Petersham Park

Miss Kathleen Haynes can be seen on the extreme left of the photograph taken in 1922. The children are from the Petersham Village School founded by Lord Russell in 1849. In 1852 a purpose-built school was erected in Petersham Park on the opposite side of the road to the Dysart Arms public house, but further up the hill. The British & Foreign School Society adopted the school in 1891, its name changing to the Russell British School. Sadly, the school was destroyed by enemy action in November 1943. The replacement school now stands opposite to the Fox & Duck public house. The current photograph shows the position of the former school.

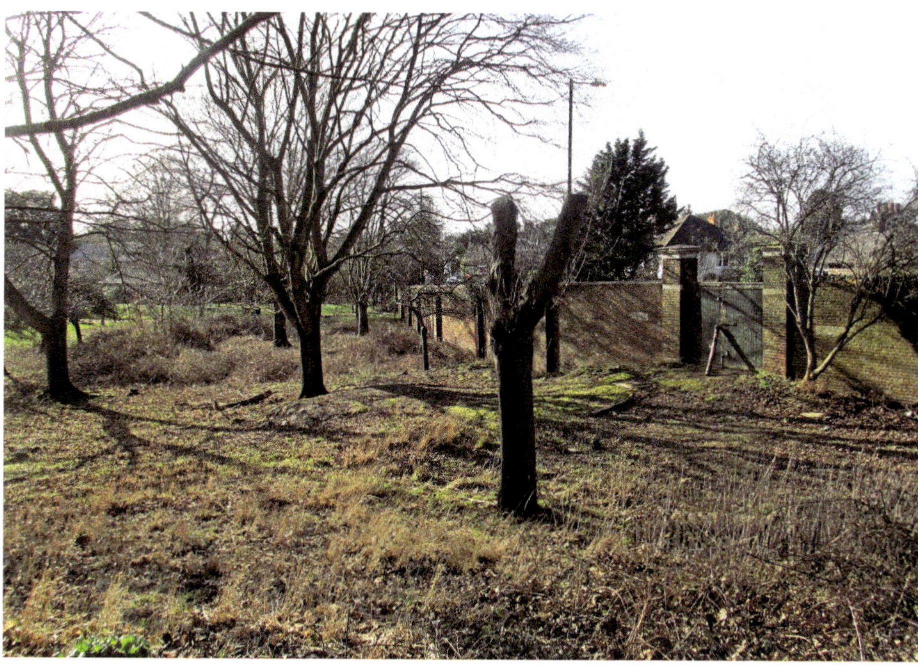

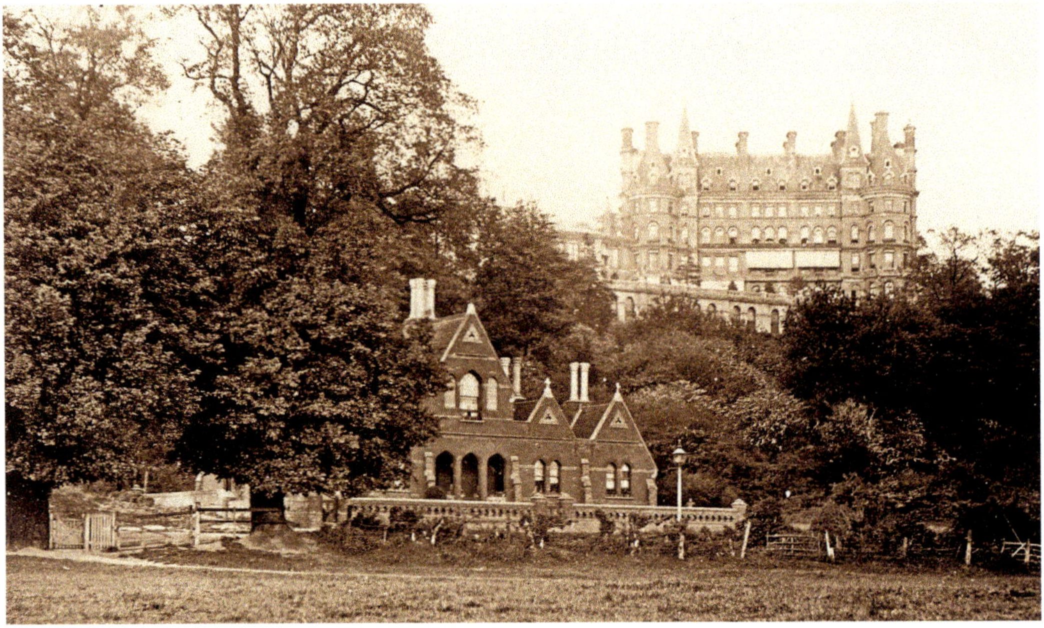

Petersham Almshouses, Petersham Road

Madame Tildesley de Bosset is thought to have been the benefactress who gave funds for the rebuilding of the Petersham Almshouses in 1855, with a further endowment in 1861 amounting to £3,500. The almshouses facing the main road on Petersham Common were very old, but their exact origin is unknown. A subscription was raised in 1909 to rebuild them, but they gradually fell into disrepair. They catered for six inmates, each tenant having a sitting room with a small bedroom. By 1952 the premises were in a dangerous condition, and they were finally demolished in 1953.

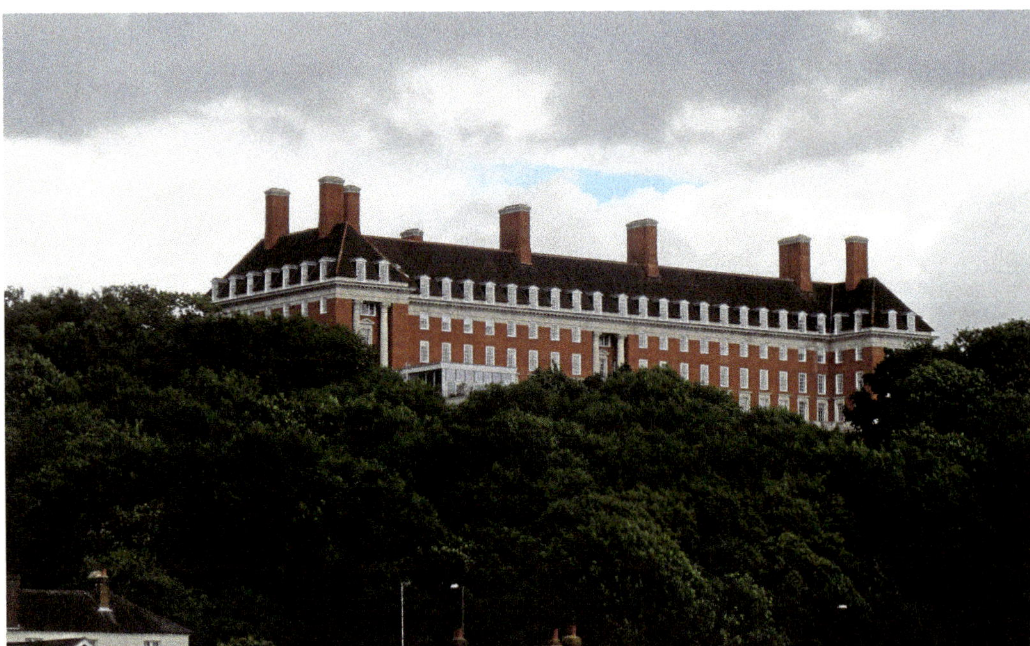

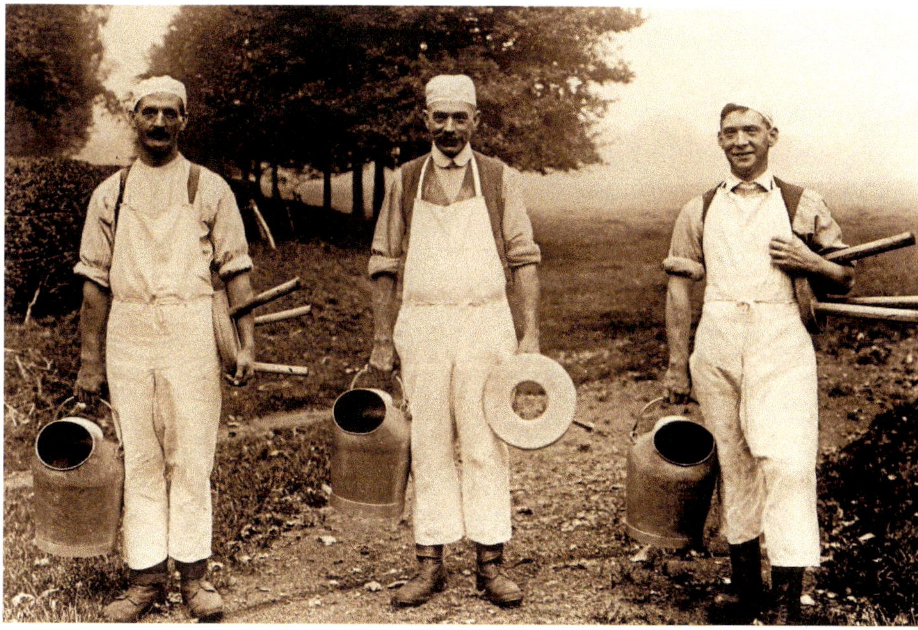

Hornby & Clarke's Dairy Farm, Petersham Road

Foreman Mr Kidd can be seen in the centre of the picture with Mr Badcock to the left and Mr Wheeler on the right. The photograph was taken in 1924. Hornby & Clarke grazed their herd of cows on Petersham Meadows and were in business from 1870 until 1935, when the Star and Garter Farm was taken over by Express Dairies. Although the farm was in Petersham, Hornby & Clarke's head office was in the Quadrant, Richmond, and their branch dairies extended from Putney in the east to Ealing in the north. The photograph is taken from the position, just off the Petersham Road, where the original photo was taken.

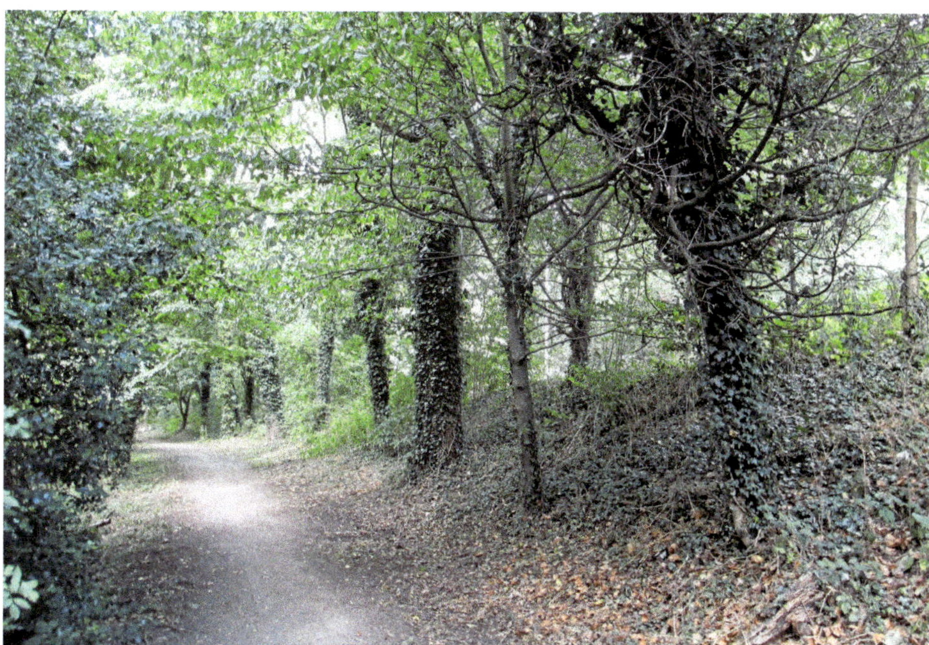

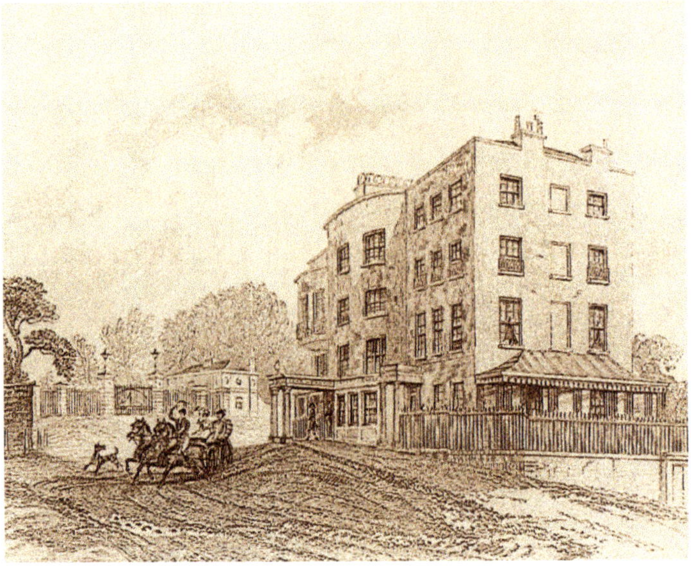

Star & Garter Hotel

The Star & Garter building, formerly a hotel, stands at the north-east extremity of Petersham, on the boundary with Richmond. An inn of this name has stood on this site since 1738. However, it was in the nineteenth century that the Star & Garter Hotel achieved its greatest notoriety. It was to this establishment that Charles Dickens, who lived for a time in Petersham, brought his friends for various celebrations. The charming engraving pictured here dates to 1850. Architect E. M. Barry rebuilt the hotel in a French chateau style in 1864. In 1924, Sir Edwin Cooper completely redesigned the building as a home for ex-servicemen following the First World War. It recently underwent a major restoration as private luxury apartments.

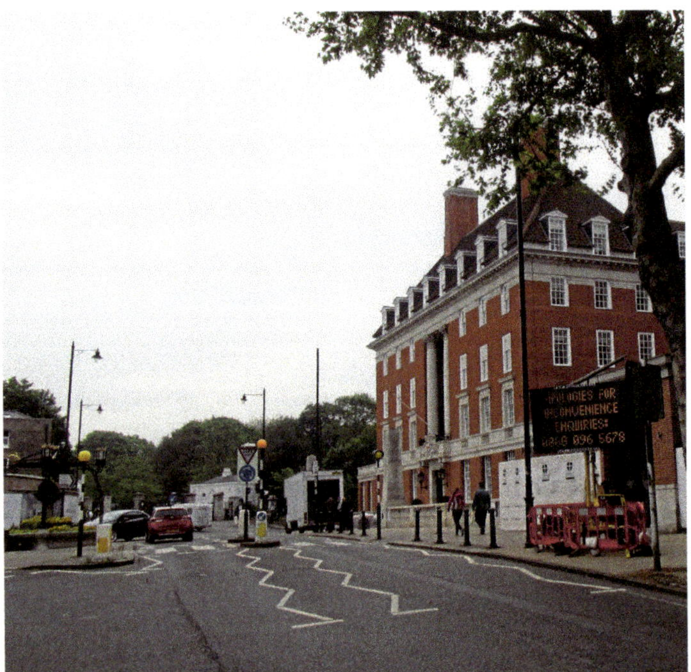

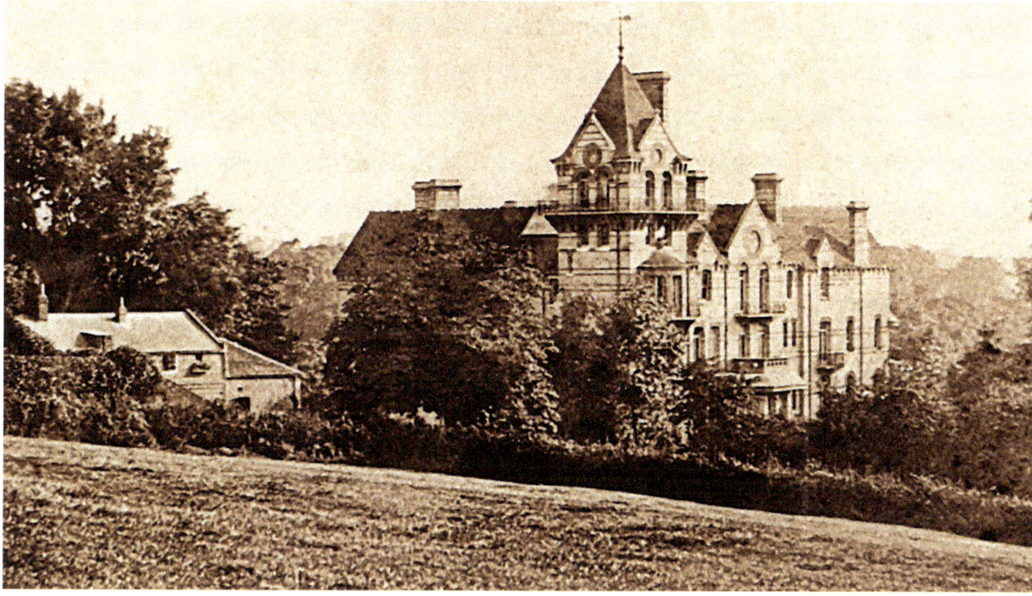

The Petersham Hotel

Commanding breathtaking views of the river and surrounding countryside, Petersham Hotel stands in Nightingale Lane. (Richmond Hill was renowned for the song of the nightingales in days gone by.) In fact, the building was originally called Nightingale Hall when first opened in 1864. A year later it was renamed the Richmond Hill Hotel. It then became 'The Mansion' in 1878, then the 'Mansion Hotel' in 1889. In 1924 it was renamed The Star & Garter as the old Star & Garter Hotel at the top of the hill had fallen into dereliction, and was later turned into a home for disabled servicemen. It finally became the 'Petersham Hotel' in 1978. An old boundary marker between Petersham and Richmond was unearthed in the grounds of the hotel.

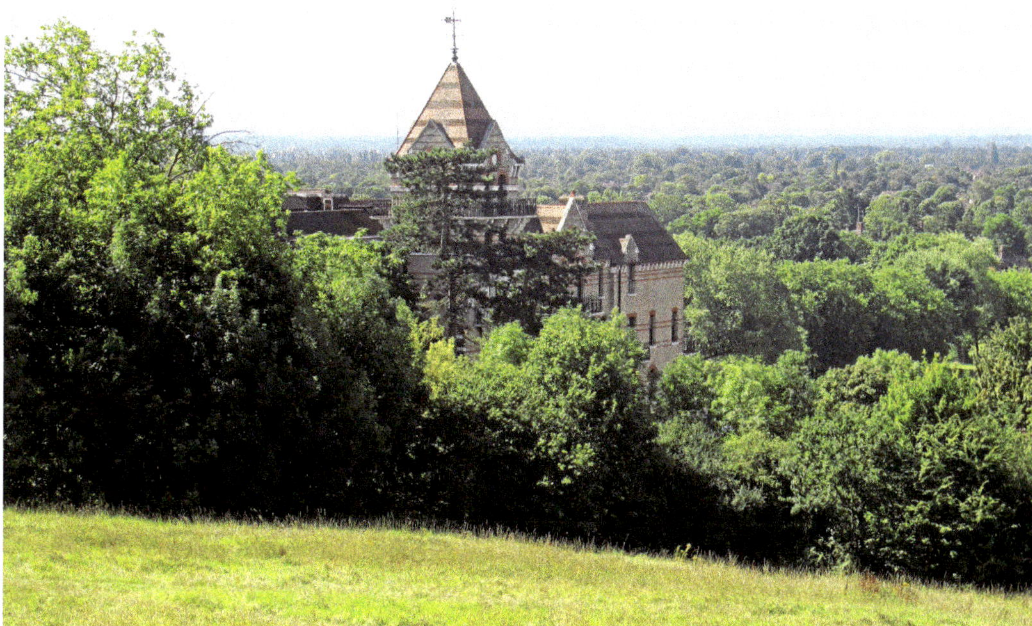

Acknowledgements

Firstly I wish to thank all the staff at the Richmond Local Studies and particularly Jane Baxter, Janine Stanford and Patricia Maloney for the use and help with the early photographs. I also wish to thank Ann Dewar for the photograph of the School House in Ham Street, and information. I would also like to thank the Revd Canon Tim Marwood, vicar and the churchwardens of St Peter's Church, Petersham, for information and permission to reproduce the images of the church and churchyard. Also many thanks to Sister Susan of St Michael's Convent and the trustees of this establishment. Debbie Low, Development Manager of Beechcroft Ltd, Christine Zahner of St Andrew's Church, and Sarah Dickinson, Ham Parish Administrator. Mr Richard Hughes who supplied information on the Old Post Office in Petersham. Eleanor Casson, Royal Borough of Kingston Local History Centre. Dr Jonathan Oates for proofreading. Also thanks to Colin Harris, Philip Edney and Stephen Hardy. Mr Charles Jobson and Tasmin Lang for accompanying me on my photographic sojourns around Ham and Petersham. Postcards and photographs from my personal collection are to be found on pages 1, 4, 5, 9, 13, 23, 36, 48, 52, 54, 68, 71, 73, 79, 80 and 87.

I dedicate this book to the twins Jill Whiteside and Sarah Edney, who loved this area.